Bound

Bound

Essays on Free Will and Responsibility

Shaun Nichols

OXFORD
UNIVERSITY PRESS

88299253

OXFORD
UNIVERSITY PRESS

Great Clarendon Street, Oxford, OX2 6DP,
United Kingdom

Oxford University Press is a department of the University of Oxford.
It furthers the University's objective of excellence in research, scholarship,
and education by publishing worldwide. Oxford is a registered trade mark of
Oxford University Press in the UK and in certain other countries

Published in the United States of America by Oxford University Press
198 Madison Avenue, New York, NY 10016, United States of America

British Library Cataloguing in Publication Data
Data available

Library of Congress Control Number: 2014941106

ISBN 978-0-19-929184-7

Printed in Great Britain by
CPI Group (UK) Ltd, Croydon, CR0 4YY

To Heather

Acknowledgments

This book has been in progress for over a decade, and I've accumulated a lot of intellectual debt over the years. For helpful comments on various chapters, I'd like to thank Matt Bedke, James Beebee, Mike Bishop, Gunnar Bjornsson, Bruce Bowers, Pascal Boyer, David Brink, Susan Brower-Toland, Sarah Buss, Joe Campbell, Gregg Caruso, Randy Clarke, Juan Comesaña, Jonathan Dancy, Colin Dawson, Oisin Deery, Alison Denham, Steve Downes, Julia Driver, Ian Evans, Brian Fiala, Trisha Folds-Bennett, Jerry Gaus, Michael Gill, Todd Grantham, John Greco, Josh Greene, John Heil, Ted Honderich, Rachana Kamtekar, Josh Knobe, Benji Kozuch, Larry Krasnoff, Uriah Kriegel, Victor Kumar, Trevor Kvaran, Heidi Maibom, Bertram Malle, Ron Mallon, Eric Mandelbaum, Kelby Mason, Michael McKenna, Al Mele, John Mikhail, Thomas Nadelhoffer, Eddy Nahmias, Dana Nelkin, Lex Newman, Tim O'Connor, Ángel Pinillos, Jesse Prinz, Peter Railton, Henry Richardson, Philip Robbins, David Rose, Adina Roskies, Eric Schwitzgebel, Oliver Sensen, David Shoemaker, Paulo Sousa, Dan Sperber, Steve Stich, Folke Tersman, Hannah Tierney, Mike Valdman, Jonathan Weinberg, and David Yokum.

A few more specific acknowledgments are due. I'm indebted to Michael McKenna for several discussions on the contemporary literature on free will. I'm positive that I've failed to respect the subtleties of that complex literature, but thanks to Michael, there are fewer egregious oversights and errors. Josh Knobe has been a wonderful conversant and occasional co-conspirator on these topics for nearly a decade. Josh has been willing to discuss every idea I've concocted—no matter how outlandish—and provided excellent philosophical advice on each occasion. Terry Horgan, Neil Levy, Dominic Murphy, Carolina Sartorio, and Mark Timmons all kindly read the entire manuscript and provided valuable comments.

I'm grateful to Peter Momtchiloff both for his patience with the book and for his selection of referees—Derk Pereboom and Tamler Sommers. I couldn't have asked for a better pair of referees. Tamler's relentless focus on big philosophical questions and his attention to writerly issues led to a number of changes. And Derk's *Living without Free Will* is one of my favorite books on free will, so I was delighted to get his advice on the manuscript.

My greatest debts are to John Doris and Manuel Vargas. Manuel read multiple drafts of the manuscript and provided copious helpful comments each time. My own view on free will is close to Manuel's view, so it was enormously helpful to get this feedback. John also read and commented on multiple drafts of the manuscript. In addition, John endured hours on the phone discussing everything from the naturalistic fallacy to hierarchical theories of agency. These invigorating discussions led to numerous improvements in the book.

Some portions of the book are drawn from previously published work. I am grateful to the publishers for permission to use material from the following articles:

"Folk Intuitions about Free Will," *Journal of Cognition and Culture*, 6 (2006), 57–86.

"After Incompatibilism: A Naturalistic Defense of the Reactive Attitudes," *Philosophical Perspectives*, 21 (2007), 405–28.

"How Can Psychology Contribute to the Free Will Debate?" In J. Baer, J. Kaufman, and R. Baumeister (eds), *Are We Free?* New York: Oxford University Press, 2008.

"The Indeterminist Intuition: Source and Status," *The Monist*, 95 (2012), 290–307.

"Brute Retributivism." In T. Nadelhoffer (ed.), *The Future of Punishment*. New York: Oxford University Press, 2013.

"Free Will and Error." In G. Caruso (ed.), *Exploring the Illusion of Free Will and Moral Responsibility*. Lanham, MD: Lexington Books, 2013.

"Process Debunking and Ethics," *Ethics*, 124 (2014), 727–49.

Contents

Contents

Introduction

The problem of free will, like many great philosophical problems, reaches deep into our conception of ourselves and the world. It is not some esoteric problem that crystallizes only for those who have studied philosophy for years. The problem of free will is immediately gripping, and like many vexing philosophical problems, it can induce a wave of philosophical nausea. Determinism provides the most familiar entry point. There is something disorienting about the thought that everything I do is inevitable given the past: what I will say in this sentence, my deliberations themselves, how they unfold—all inevitable. Whether or not I *initiate* a process of deliberation—inevitable. My *thought* that the initiation of the process is inevitable—that too was inevitable. In contemporary discussions of free will, such vertiginous episodes are not much discussed. But they are, I think, at the heart of what makes free will such a disturbing problem even to otherwise disaffected students.

The fact that the problem of free will is immediately gripping distinguishes it from many philosophical problems. If you tell people that some philosophers, the Logicists, think that mathematics can be derived from logic, the common reaction will be profound indifference. Most people simply don't have intuitions about the logical foundations of mathematics. This is not what happens when people are told that some philosophers maintain that every decision a person makes is an inevitable consequence of what happened prior to the decision. That is a disturbing suggestion even to students whose only interest in Logicism is whether it will be on the final exam. The problem of determinism and free will strikes a deep worry in us. The fact that the problem of free will resonates with people is a *psychological* fact. This book begins with that psychological fact.

The core of the book attempts to discern the psychological underpinnings of the problem of free will and to explore the implications of the resulting account. This is not a repudiation of traditional philosophical work on the topic. On the contrary, traditional philosophical work on the problem of free will informs almost every aspect of this book. But my hope is that by exploring these issues with different tools, we might gain additional insights into the nature of the problem of free will and the prospects for a solution.

Two axes and three dimensions

Traditionally, the problem of free will has two axes. Both axes pivot on the notion of determinism. Determinism has been characterized in different ways, but much work on free will focuses on *causal* determinism, and that will be my focus as well. Philosophers have offered precise technical definitions of the thesis of causal determinism.[1] But a useful short characterization is provided by Galen Strawson: "Briefly, determinism is the view that everything that happens is necessitated by what has already gone before, in such a way that nothing can happen otherwise than it does" (Strawson 2005, 286). This notion that every event is causally necessitated by prior events is naturally expressed in common language in terms of *inevitability* (see also Kane 1996, 8). According to causal determinism, every event is an inevitable outcome of the past conditions and the laws of nature.[2]

"Free will" also gets defined in different ways. One important proposal characterizes free will in terms of the ability to do otherwise. Here is Clarke: "Following many other writers . . . , I shall say that when an agent

---

[1] For instance, here is Randy Clarke's characterization of causal determinism: "On a widespread understanding, determinism is the thesis that our world is such that any possible world that has exactly the same laws of nature and that is exactly like our world at any one point in time is exactly like it at every point in time . . . I shall take determinism to conjoin this claim with the thesis that for every event E (except those beginning at the very first time, if there is a first time), at every time t prior to the occurrence of E there is some event (or some plurality of events) that occurs at t that deterministically causes E. One event is taken to deterministically cause another just in case, in every possible world in which the actual laws of nature obtain and in which the first event occurs, it causes the second" (Clarke 2003, 4).

[2] Throughout the book, where I speak of causation, I have in mind deterministic causation, not the kinds of non-deterministic causal processes sometimes endorsed by libertarian accounts (see, e.g., Clarke and Capes 2013). There are interesting questions about how non-determinist notions of causation bear on the debates, but I won't be able to take up those questions here.

acts freely (or with free will), she is able to do other than she does then" (Clarke 2003, 3). Another important proposal characterizes free will in terms of the source of intentions. Kane writes: "Free will, in the traditional sense I want to retrieve... is the power of agents to be the ultimate creators (or originators) and sustainers of their own ends or purposes... to will freely, in this traditional sense, is to be the ultimate creator (prime mover, so to speak) of your own purposes" (Kane 1996, 4). Yet another approach characterizes free will in terms of the ability to act freely (e.g., Mele 2006, 17). For the purposes of this volume, I will adopt a functional definition of "free will": free will is the (alleged) aspect(s) of action, decision, or choice that is disputed in the traditional debates from Hobbes to Pereboom. As a consequence of adopting this functional definition, I will generally refrain from talking about what non-philosophers think about "free will."[3] Rather, when describing lay views about issues surrounding the free will debate, I will use terms like "decision," "choice," "act," and "moral responsibility."[4] The term "free will" will occur frequently, however, in discussing philosophical positions.

One axis of the free will problem is metaphysical—it concerns the character of human agency. Some maintain that human decisions are determined by the past (e.g., Hume, Leibniz, Hobbes, Spinoza). Others maintain that human decisions[5] are outside the sphere of deterministic causation; for instance, some philosophers maintain that agents enjoy a special kind of causation, *agent causation*, that is not a mere function of deterministic forces (e.g., Reid, Campbell). The other axis of the problem concerns the conditions for moral responsibility.[6]

Although the issues of agency and responsibility are at the heart of the matter, the philosophical geography is rather complicated. The broad

---

[3] The one major exception will be in Chapter 3, where I will discuss arguments for eliminativism about free will.

[4] The empirical literature on folk uses of "free will" is mixed. Monroe and Malle (2010) found that when participants were asked to explain what the term meant, very few said anything that invoked indeterminism. By contrast, Rose and Nichols (2013) presented participants with a description of a deterministic universe and asked whether people in that universe had free will. In that study, participants denied that people had free will. One explanation for the disparity is that in free response tasks (like that of Monroe and Malle), people aren't really thinking about all the ways free will might be defeated.

[5] I will use "decision" and "choice" interchangeably, unless otherwise noted.

[6] The relevant notion of moral responsibility itself is contentious in the free will debates. For present purposes, I intend "moral responsibility" to pick out the notion of responsibility that is tied to praise, blame, and retributive punishment.

inquiry into free will and responsibility can be divided into three quite different projects: a descriptive project, a substantive project, and a prescriptive project.

The descriptive project strives to capture lay attitudes surrounding the problem of free will—what is it that we think about choice and responsibility? Where do our views about the nature of choice come from? By uncovering the folk intuitions, one hopes to be able to sketch out the folk theory that underlies these intuitions.[7] However, if it turns out that there is no unified folk theory for the domain, then the researcher engaged in the descriptive project will mark this fact. For the aim is to give the best account of the folk intuitions and their psychological underpinnings, even if this means allowing that the folk have blatantly inconsistent intuitions. Of particular interest for the free will debate is whether folk notions of choice and moral responsibility are consistent with determinism. *Incompatibilists* maintain that our conceptions of choice and moral responsibility are at odds with determinism. If our notions of choice and moral responsibility are consistent with determinism, *compatibilism* is right.[8]

The goal of the substantive project is then to determine whether the folk views are correct. Does choice have the nature people think it does? Given the folk concepts and the way the world is, does free choice exist? Are people morally responsible?

The prescriptive project is different from both the descriptive and substantive projects. For here the question is whether, given what we know about our concepts and the world, we should revise or preserve our practices that presuppose moral responsibility, like practices of blame, praise, and retributive punishment.

We can summarize with a tree diagram the philosophical positions that emerge from these questions (see Figure 1).

This diagram oversimplifies a number of issues,[9] but it is intended only to illustrate the distinctions between descriptive, substantive, and

---

[7] "Theory" is intended in a weak sense here. Roughly, any internally represented body of information will count as a theory in the intended sense.

[8] "Semi-compatibilists" maintain that moral responsibility is compatible with determinism, but demur from making the same claim about free will (see Fischer 1999).

[9] For instance, the tree omits the fact that free will eliminativism depends not just on how people think about choice but also on issues about concepts and reference. In addition, the tree fails to allow for different branches for free will and moral responsibility. Some contemporary theorists want to leave open the possibility that we are morally responsible even if we don't have free will.

Descriptive question:
Is determinism consistent with the way people think about choice?

Yes   No
Compatibilism   Incompatibilism

                   Substantive question:
                   Does the way people think about choice reflect the nature of choice?

               Yes   No
          Libertarianism   Free will eliminativism

                                    Prescriptive question:
                                    Should we change our practices?

                                   Yes   No
                             Revolutionism   Conservativism

Figure 1 A taxonomy of positions organized by descriptive, substantive, and prescriptive questions

prescriptive projects. Let's start at the top with the central descriptive question, "Is the folk concept of choice compatible with determinism?" If the answer is "yes," then *compatibilism* is the right view, and at that point, as far as the free will/determinism issue goes, we need not bother with the substantive and prescriptive matters. If our concept of choice is happily consistent with determinism, then determinism poses neither a substantive nor a moral threat to our current views and practices (Hume 1955 [1743]). However, if the answer at this juncture is "no," then *incompatibilism* becomes an important position (Holbach 1889 [1770]; Kant 1956 [1788]; Reid 1969 [1788]), and we face a pressing substantive question: "Does the folk concept of choice reflect the nature of choice?" In particular, it becomes a major concern whether determinism is true. According to *libertarianism*, determinism is false. Libertarians typically hold that on the folk view, choices are not determined, and also that the folk view of choice matches the way the world is. If libertarianism is right, then the prescriptive question is not pressing. For our normal practices of regarding people as free are perfectly appropriate— people *are* free and responsible. Thus the free will problem exerts no pressure for changing our practices. According to *free will eliminativists*, however, the answer to the substantive question is that we lack the kind of free will we think we have. On their view, the facts about the world are at odds with the way we think of ourselves. If this distressing view is correct, then the prescriptive question takes on great significance. If there is no free will, what is the appropriate response? Should we stop treating each other as free and morally responsible agents? *Revolutionism* is the view that we should overhaul our practices that presuppose free will and moral responsibility. *Conservatism* is the view that we should leave practices more or less untouched.[10]

The descriptive project

Let's now consider the three projects in just a bit more detail. The goal of the descriptive project is to determine the character of folk intuitions surrounding agency and responsibility. This project has important similarities to more traditional philosophical endeavors in conceptual analysis. Indeed, the descriptive project that I'll promote has significant debts to methods used in conceptual analysis. But the project also diverges in significant ways from the traditional armchair approaches. Most obviously, unlike traditional approaches, I will draw extensively on experimental work on commonsense conceptions. While traditional armchair approaches have been extremely productive, they have obvious limitations when it comes to characterizing folk conceptions. Armchair approaches are unlikely to reveal cultural or individual differences in conceptions (but cf. Nichols and Ulatowski 2007; Feltz and Cokely 2008). Such approaches will be poorly positioned to pick up on how the order in which examples are presented affect intuitions (but cf. Swain et al. 2008; Wright 2010). And of course, consulting one's own intuitions will not reveal the effects of indoctrination. The core concern that underlies all of these worries is that intuitions might vary in ways that will be missed by philosophers working only from the armchair.

Although I share these concerns about the limitations of the traditional project, for present purposes, a more important problem with prominent approaches to characterizing folk conceptions is that they

---

[10] One can, of course, regard revolutionism and conservatism as on a continuum with lots of room for moderately revolutionary positions in the middle.

fail to sustain the descriptive project as purely descriptive. Rather, philosophers taking an armchair approach often fuse revision into the project of conceptual analysis, providing "reforming analyses." Jackson is quite explicit in building extra-descriptive considerations into the project of conceptual analysis, saying "conceptual analysis has a prescriptive dimension" (2001a, 618). Similarly Allan Gibbard writes:

An analysis can be offered not as a bald statement of fact about what people mean, but as a proposal. Where a term is problematical, a new and clearer sense may serve its purposes—or some of them. No unique analysis need be correct; rather, we can expect some analyses to work better than others (1990, 32).

Indeed, Gibbard goes on to write "Any philosophical analysis strains its concept" (1990, 32). Fortuitously, Jackson uses the concept of free will as an example in reforming analysis. He maintains that the ordinary notion of free will is incompatibilist and perhaps "embodies some kind of confusion" (2001a, 618), but he claims that compatibilists nonetheless provide a successful analysis of the concept of free will. So, even though compatibilist accounts conflict with some folk intuitions, a compatibilist can give a proper analysis of the notion of free will (e.g., 2001b, 661). This form of conceptual analysis delivers proposals that are effectively of the form, "T is the folk theory, suitably revised to eliminate various mistakes." Thus, on this approach to conceptual analysis, we provide analyses that will partly reform the folk concept.[11]

The idea that we should not rest content with folk notions is perfectly sensible, but fusing reformation with analysis is a dangerous path to take if the goal is to understand folk concepts. When we try to determine the nature of philosophically important concepts used by the folk, we are basically doing a kind of cognitive anthropology. Elsewhere in cognitive anthropology, we wouldn't brook reforming analyses. Imagine that an anthropologist returned from an isolated isle and provided the following executive summary of his research: "The indigenous people have a concept that is identical to our concept of anger, once their concept is revised to eliminate various errors." The problem with this isn't so much

---

[11] In the previous section, I charted three projects in the broad inquiry: a descriptive project, a substantive project, and a prescriptive project. Gibbard and Jackson maintain that conceptual analysis isn't purely descriptive, but they do not explicitly address whether both substantive and prescriptive considerations might come into play in generating a reforming analysis.

that it would patronize the indigenous people. The problem is it would take all the wonderment out of anthropology and sap it of much of its interest. We *want* to know when a culture's emotion concepts differ from ours. A similar lesson applies to the project of characterizing philosophically important folk concepts. If substantive and prescriptive considerations are fused into the project of conceptual analysis, we will be quick to eliminate inconsistencies in folk intuitions about a domain. But if folk intuitions concerning philosophically important issues are wrong or inconsistent, that's a richly interesting anthropological fact that we should acknowledge, contemplate, and investigate, not sweep away in a blur of revision.

There are, of course, other disadvantages with giving a reforming analysis without first doing the purely descriptive project. Arriving at the best view about how to reform folk concepts presumably depends on having a clear-eyed view of what the folk concepts *are*. Furthermore, since people inevitably disagree about *how* to reform the folk concepts, those disputes can be made much sharper if the descriptive project is done independently.

The empirical approach adopted here, as in the social sciences generally, is quite explicitly a purely descriptive enterprise. We are trying to discern exactly what the folk think about the cases. Attempts at revision are inappropriate for this part of the inquiry. This empirical approach carries a further advantage. Traditional conceptual analysis doesn't allow us to plumb the psychological underpinnings of the folk intuitions that underlie philosophical problems. Some of the most interesting questions about the psychology of philosophy simply won't be available to traditional conceptual analysts. From the armchair we can't discern which psychological mechanisms subserve the intuitions. Nor can we determine whether conflicting intuitions have their origins in different psychological mechanisms. Empirical methods do allow us to investigate these matters. For instance, we can vary experimental conditions to determine which factors will influence people's intuitions. We can also use such methods to glean which psychological mechanisms are implicated in generating the intuitions. The empirical approach allows us to investigate matters that are entirely closed off to the armchair theorist.

The substantive project

The goal of the descriptive project is to determine the character and origin of folk views surrounding philosophical problems. Once we have the characterization of folk conceptions in place, we can turn to the substantive project of determining whether the folk views are correct. In light of the descriptive characterization of free will, does free will exist? Are people morally responsible? Here a number of considerations come into play. Facts about psychology, neuroscience, and physics might all have bearing on whether we are free and responsible. So, for instance, hard determinists effectively maintain (i) the folk concepts of *choice* and *moral responsibility* are indeterminist and incompatibilist, and (ii) determinism is globally true. From this hard determinists draw the conclusion that free will doesn't exist and no one is morally responsible. Hard determinists are thus error theorists about free will and moral responsibility. This error-theoretic conclusion seems to depend, however, on one's view concerning the basic criteria for what determines the reference of a concept. On some approaches (e.g., Lewis 1972; Jackson 1998), if a concept is implicated in a significant set of false beliefs, this can mean that the concept fails to refer. On other approaches (e.g., Lycan 1988; Fodor 1998), on the other hand, even if a concept is implicated in numerous false beliefs, the concept still might refer. Thus, even if the hard determinist is right that our concept of *choice* is enmeshed in false beliefs, it doesn't immediately follow that there is no such thing as choice. It will depend also on how the reference of a concept is determined (see Vargas 2005).[12]

A rather different strand of the substantive project attempts to determine not whether free will exists, but whether we are justified in believing in it. If we have a psychological explanation for why we believe in free will, we might be able to draw on that characterization to assess the justificatory status of the belief, even if we are not in a position to say whether free will exists. The debunking strategy here is akin to Freud's critique of religion. Freud maintains that the reason we believe in God is because of wishful thinking. Freud goes on to say that he won't presume to say whether God exists, he will only presume to say that our reasons for believing in God are bogus. A similar kind of substantive argument

---

[12] This issue will be taken up in Chapter 3.

might be marshaled in the case of free will. Given limitations of our understanding of the mind, it might be premature to proclaim that there is no free will; but that needn't stop us from investigating whether our *belief* in free will is well grounded.

The prescriptive project

The prescriptive project concerns whether we should revise or preserve our practices that presuppose moral responsibility, like practices of blame, praise, and retributive punishment. Interestingly, simply knowing the answer to the substantive question, "are people really morally responsible?" might not tell us whether we should preserve our practices. For, as noted earlier, on some accounts of concept-reference, it's not all that easy for a concept to be in error. So it might turn out that our false beliefs about responsibility do not suffice to make it the case that no one is morally responsible and yet at the same time recognizing our false beliefs might well give us reason to change our practice. After all, rectifying false beliefs about a domain is often sufficient to warrant changing our practices even in the absence of any invocation of error theory. When the Western medical profession came to reject the old view that infants don't feel pain, this should have had (and did have) a significant impact on the treatment of infants. But the medical professionals probably never even contemplated error theory about *infants*, *pain*, or *morality*. Similarly, then, if we discovered that people's beliefs about *responsibility* are mistaken in some respects, even if we avoid the error-theoretic conclusion that nobody is responsible, it might be that our revised beliefs about responsibility give us reasons to alter dramatically our practices towards people. Now consider the other side. On some accounts of concept-reference, it's fairly easy for a concept to be in error. As a result, on these accounts, it might well turn out that, because of various mistaken beliefs, the folk concept of *the flu* fails to refer.[13] Nonetheless, it might also be the case that our practices shouldn't significantly change. The same individuals who were said to have the flu should still be kept home from school and work, should still get plenty of rest, and should be given extra consideration around the house.

---

[13] Thanks to Steve Downes for this example.

Similarly, then, it might turn out that because of various false presuppositions, the folk concept of *responsibility* fails to refer, and yet it's still appropriate to treat people in much the same way.

This book advances views on each of these dimensions. On the descriptive dimension, I argue that the problem of free will arises because of two naturally emerging ways of thinking about ourselves. The conflict is real, not the result of a shallow confusion. On the substantive dimension, I argue that while people believe in indeterminism, that belief is grounded in faulty inference and should be regarded as unjustified. However, even if determinism is true, it's a further substantive question whether that means that free will doesn't exist. I argue that, because of the flexibility of reference, there is no single answer to this question. In some contexts, it will be true to say "free will exists"; in other contexts, it will be false to say that. With this substantive background in place, I argue for a pragmatic approach to prescriptive issues. In some contexts, the prevailing practical considerations suggest that we should deny the existence of free will and moral responsibility; in other contexts the practical considerations suggest that we should affirm free will and moral responsibility.

The plan

The primary issues about agency that I'll consider are metaphysical, and the issues concerning moral responsibility are largely ethical. As a result, the book will treat agency and responsibility independently. The first three chapters will focus on agency.

In the first chapter, I'll argue that the problem of free will derives from fundamental conflicting intuitions about the nature of agency. It is a deep fact about us that we are compulsive seekers of causal explanation. The explanatory compulsion shows up already in very young children, and it applies indiscriminately. People expect there to be causal explanations for any particular events, including decisions. At the same time, people find it jarring and counterintuitive to think that their own choices are determined. These two tendencies are at the root of the problem of free will.

Under certain contexts, people think decisions aren't determined. But why do people think this? Chapter 2 takes up this question. I will argue that the belief in indeterminism depends on what is effectively a default presumption that if our decisions were determined, we would know it. That presumption might have been reasonable at earlier points in intellectual history. But in light of work in cognitive science, we are no longer justified in sustaining the confidence about our ability to introspect the factors influencing our decisions. As a result, to the extent that we believe in indeterminist choice because of this faulty presupposition, our belief in indeterminist choice is unjustified.

The conclusion of Chapter 2 is that the belief that choice isn't determined is unjustified. Many philosophers think that the belief in libertarian free will is false, not just unjustified. This is the basis for one familiar strand of eliminativist argument. According to free will eliminativists, people have seriously mistaken beliefs about free will and hence free will doesn't exist. However, an alternative reaction is that free will does exist, we just have some mistaken beliefs about it. This dispute, like other eliminativist debates in philosophy, seems to depend on substantive assumptions about reference. In Chapter 3, I draw on the idea that reference is systematically ambiguous. In some contexts, it is appropriate to take a restrictive view about whether a term embedded in a false theory refers; in other contexts, it's appropriate to take a liberal view about whether a token of the very same term refers. This affords the possibility of saying that the sentence "free will exists" is false in some contexts and true in others. This in turn affords a flexibility in whether we embrace the eliminativist claim. I argue that in the case of free will, there are practical considerations for and against eliminativism, and that the right conclusion might be a *discretionary* (in)compatibilism.

Chapter 4 begins the discussion of moral responsibility. First, I'll argue that, as hard determinists have long held, incompatibilism is intuitive. That is, people tend to think that if determinism were true, this would threaten the idea that people are morally responsible. However, this is just one aspect of people's views about responsibility. I'll argue that the commitment to incompatibilism is isolated from the rest of our commonsense views about responsibility, including the view that manipulation undermines responsibility.

In Chapter 5, we turn to examine a general question about how descriptive results might affect normative issues. Understanding the nature and origin of our beliefs can often help us determine the extent to which those beliefs are justified. That is the key idea behind the recent wave of debunking arguments in naturalistic philosophy. I'll distinguish two different forms of debunking arguments. On the type of debunking argument that I will promote, the key question concerns the extent to which the belief was a product of epistemically defective psychological processes. I argue that there is a promising application of such a process debunking argument in metaethics. In normative ethics, however, process debunking arguments face greater obstacles.

In the next chapter, I focus on one particular ethical belief that is linked to responsibility—the belief that wrongdoers should be punished because and only because they did wrong. This retributive norm has historically resisted justification. Following on arguments from Chapter 5, I maintain that, given certain plausible views about ethics, the retributive norm forms part of a set of norms that do not need justification.

The previous chapter offers a partial defense of the propriety of punishing the guilty. But there remains the central challenge posed by incompatibilism. Given that incompatibilism is intuitive, the propriety of punishment and blame seems to be at risk of being completely undercut if determinism is true. In the final chapter I argue that often there are ethical reasons to abandon the incompatibilist commitment rather than give up the attitudes and practices surrounding moral responsibility.

PART I
Agency

1

The Folk Psychology of Agency

Mommy, I always ask why. Why do I always ask why?

(Child, aged 3;1; Callanan and Oakes 1992, 222)

Many of the oldest, most persistent problems in philosophy have their roots in commonsense. The problems of skepticism, consciousness, and free will all issue from our basic, untutored ways of thinking about the world. This is reflected in the fact that a decent instructor can get students to see the core issue in about five minutes. These are problems that are laying in wait, ready to be sprung with minimal prompting. It is a tantalizing speculation that we might diagnose these philosophical problems by identifying the underlying psychological processes that generate the problems. One result of such an analysis would be to illuminate why the problems are so persistent—what is it about our minds that makes us perpetually run up against the same philosophical perplexities? Another potential result of such an analysis would be to advance new lines of treatment. If we discover that one of the commonsense commitments at the base of the philosophical problem comes from a defective reasoning process, that might be a reason to suspend that commonsense commitment. But these are all very airy reflections. To make good, one must take each problem on a case-by-case basis. In this chapter and the next, I try to provide an analysis of the psychological underpinnings of one problem—the problem of free will. I will argue that the reason the problem of free will is so vexing, is because we are drawn to both sides of the conflict. Determinism is alluring when we think about explaining the world, but indeterminism is compelling when we contemplate our own actions. That, of course, is the thinnest of stories. It will thicken as we proceed.

1.1 The lure of determinism

One of the more striking suggestions in developmental psychology is that children are causal determinists (see, e.g., Gelman 2003, 118; Schulz and Sommerville 2006, 440).[1] Are preschoolers really causal determinists? This seems preposterous. Causal determinism is a grand, ambitious theory of the universe. Consider a few standard definitions of determinism:

> Briefly, determinism is the view that the history of the universe is fixed: everything that happens is necessitated by what has already gone before, in such a way that nothing can happen otherwise than it does (Strawson 2005, 286).

> ... determinism is the view that given the complete state of the world at a particular point in time, for any given future point in time, only one state is possible (Millstein 2006, 683).

> Determinism ... is the thesis that there is at any instant exactly one physically possible future (Van Inwagen 1983, 3).

> By determinism I ... mean ... this: the prevailing laws of nature are such that there do not exist any two possible worlds which are exactly alike up to some time, which differ thereafter, and in which those laws are never violated (Lewis 1973, 559).

There are important differences between these characterizations, but they all make a pronouncement about every event in the universe. Given the sophistication and universal ambition of the notion of determinism, why would anyone think that children might be causal determinists?

1.1.1 Causal inference in children

Part of the answer comes from recent evidence that children are remarkably adept with causal inference. The suggestion that children are determinists largely stems from this evidence, so it's worth reviewing some of the experimental details. In an influential paradigm developed by Alison Gopnik and colleagues, children are shown a "blicket machine" and told that "blickets" make the machine go (Gopnik et al. 2001, 623). Wooden blocks are put on the machine, which sometimes lights up and plays music. If children see that the machine lights up when block A is put on it, but not when B is put on it, children say that A is a blicket but B isn't (623). In another experiment, 3–4-year-old children were shown the

---

[1] Schulz and Sommerville are actually guarded about embracing the claim that children are determinists (440).

device and told, "Some blocks make this machine go, and some blocks don't." The experimenter placed object B on the device, with no activation. Object B was removed and object A was placed on the device, which lit up and played music. Then object B was placed alongside object A on the device, which continued to play. Children were asked, "Can you make it stop?" The child's options were to remove A, B, or both. Most children removed only object A.

The results from the blicket experiments indicate that young children are rather good at causal inference. The blicket experiments suggest that even 3-year-old children are sensitive to the distinction between causation and mere correlation. This interpretation is reinforced by a later study (Sobel et al. 2004) in which children were again shown the blicket detector. A and B were put on the device at the same time, and the device was activated. Both objects were removed, and then B was placed back on the device, but the device was not activated. Children were asked of each object whether it was a blicket. Children tended to say that A was a blicket but B wasn't. This despite the fact that they had never seen the device activated without B being on it. They use the fact that B, by itself, didn't activate the device as evidence that B didn't activate the device previously when it was conjoined with A.

The experiments bring out a number of striking features of the young child's capacity for causal inference. First, children make causal inferences that are independent of any perceptual cues in the objects themselves. Whether a given object will be regarded as a blicket depends on patterns of effects and not on perceptual features of the object. Second, the child only gets contingency information about objects and outcomes, but this is enough for the child to categorize appropriately and to intervene effectively. Finally, no training is required to get children to do this appropriately. An entire task takes only a few minutes. The whole process seems quite effortless. Causal inference is a natural talent.

Schulz and Sommerville use a blicket-style experiment to investigate deterministic reasoning. In all conditions, the children were shown a toy box with a ring on top of it, as well as a remote-control switch. The experimenter said, "See this switch? This switch makes my toy light up," and proceeded to demonstrate this several times. Then the experimenter said, "The toy only works if this ring is on top of the toy. If I remove the ring, the switch won't work and the toy won't light up" (430). The experimenter then removed the ring and flipped the switch, with no concomitant lighting up. After this initial orientation, children were exposed either to a "determinist" or an "unexplained stochastic" condition. In the *determinist* condition, a confederate flipped the switch several times, and each time the box lit up. In the *unexplained stochastic* condition, when the confederate flipped the switch, the box only lit up a fraction of the time. In both conditions, the experimenter then opened her right hand and called attention to an unfamiliar object (a keychain flashlight) that had been concealed there. The experimenter told the child that she was going to flip the switch and asked the child, "Can you make it so the switch won't work and the toy won't turn on?" (431). In the determinist condition, almost 90 percent of the children removed the ring from the box. By contrast, in the stochastic condition, the children overwhelmingly reached for the unfamiliar object rather than the ring on top of the box. It's interesting that they didn't simply reach for the ring, because they knew that removing the ring would definitely achieve their goal of inhibiting the box lighting. But what is most important here is that the children in the stochastic condition seem to infer that there must be some other factor at work that explains why the box didn't light up. When they witness an apparently random pattern of events, children look for a hidden cause that would explain the pattern. Schulz and Sommerville suggest that one explanation for this pattern is that children believe in causal determinism: "a belief in causal determinism gives children a powerful and systematic basis for inferring the existence of unobserved causes" (440).

The experimental results don't really provide much reason to think that children are determinists. Determinism is a global theory, after all. The experiment involves a very small set of cases from which to infer the child's theory of the universe. Moreover, there is a perfectly sensible account of their performance that is neutral about determinism—when observing the apparently stochastic process, the children might be thinking that *most* events have causal explanations, so this one probably does. That is consistent with allowing that *some* events don't have causal explanations.

1.1.2 Determinism and the explanatory compulsion

Although the experiments provide scant evidence for childhood determinism, they do indicate that children naturally seek out causal explanations.[2] Even when events seem to be random, children expect there to be a causal explanation. That, I think, is the critical lesson to be drawn from the experiments recounted here. Children have a kind of *explanatory compulsion*. When presented with events, children naturally expect the events to be causally explicable. It is this compulsion to explain that drives their responses in the stochastic experiments.[3]

It's plausible that this explanatory compulsion is indiscriminate—it will apply to any event that is presented to the child. This suggests a kind of enumerative induction such that all possible cases should be amenable to causal explanation. *This*, it might be urged, yields a commitment to universal determinism. Even if we grant that enumerative induction would yield a commitment to determinism, it's not like that enumerative induction is typically performed, by children or adults. That's just not the way most people spend their time. At most, determinism might be an implicit or a dispositional belief, like the belief that Lincoln never played Donkey Kong.[4] But even if children have an implicit belief in determinism, a merely implicit belief can't do any *causal* work in explaining their responses in the experiments. That is, the child's responses are not driven

---

[2] The most instructive work here (e.g., Schulz and Sommerville 2006) has not been explored in a cross-cultural context. So it will be important to explore whether this tendency to seek causal explanation is culturally specific.

[3] The postulation of an explanatory compulsion is closely related to other ideas in the developmental literature. Berlyne invoked a "curiosity drive" (Berlyne 1950; Mittman and Terrell 1964). Bruner postulated a "will to learn" (Bruner 1966). Even closer to home, Alison Gopnik posits a "theory drive," which she characterizes as "a motivational system that impels us to interpret new evidence in terms of existing theories and change our theories in the light of new evidence" (1998, 101). While I agree with much in Gopnik's work, her view has stronger commitments than are needed here. For instance, she maintains that there is a distinctive phenomenology of explanation (*hmm* and *aha*), but it is far from clear that this kind of phenomenology is distinctive of causal explanation—we might get similar phenomenology when faced with visual puzzles like autostereograms. Gopnik also maintains that this distinctive phenomenology is what motivates us to build theories, but one needn't assume that the motivation is primarily phenomenological. Finally, Gopnik maintains that the theory drive compels children to conduct experiments, e.g., by testing their parents during the terrible twos (107). The explanatory compulsion that I am invoking carries none of these commitments. Rather, the compulsion is just that, when presented with events, children will expect there to be a causal explanation for these events.

[4] Fodor offers a standard characterization of implicit or dispositional beliefs: "one's dispositional beliefs could reasonably be identified with the closure of one's occurrent beliefs under principles of inference that one explicitly accepts" (1987, 22; see also Lycan 1988). On that characterization, whether children (or adults) have an implicit belief in determinism depends on whether they explicitly accept that a principle of enumerative induction applies to cases of explanation. Which they don't.

by an actual representation of determinism. Rather, the responses are driven by a compulsive explanatory drive that seeks to apply itself to everything.

Of course it's not just children who have a compulsion to explain. Adults also expect causal explanations. If adults were presented with the Schulz and Sommerville experiment, they too would surely look for the hidden cause. The force of the explanatory compulsion is perhaps best illustrated by the uncanny pull of the cosmological argument for the existence of God. In its crudest version, the cosmological argument holds that there must be some explanation for why the universe exists, and God is the only explanation. The pull of the argument comes from the fact that it seems like there must be *some* explanation for why the universe exists. Interestingly, the obvious retort to this argument—but how do we explain the existence of God?—is another illustration of the explanatory compulsion. Telling me that the universe exists because God made it only postpones the problem. The quintessentially unanswerable question—why is there something rather than nothing?—doesn't lose its hold over us simply because we can't answer it. The reason these cosmological questions have such power for us is because of our compulsion for explanation.

In philosophy, we can see the explanatory compulsion reflected in the Principle of Sufficient Reason, characterized most famously by Leibniz: "there can be no fact real or existing, no statement true, unless there be a sufficient reason, why it should be so and not otherwise" (1714/1898, #32). Leibniz suggests that this principle "must be considered one of the greatest and most fruitful of all human knowledge, for upon it is built a great part of metaphysics, physics, and moral science" (Leibniz 1976, 227). Despite the importance accorded to the Principle of Sufficient Reason, it's hard to find an *argument* for the principle that doesn't presuppose it. Instead, what makes the Principle of Sufficient Reason seem plausible in the first place, I suggest, is the explanatory compulsion. And it is unlikely that working scientists have relied on an explicitly represented Principle of Sufficient Reason rather than their natural compulsion for explanation.

Although it's dubious that children (or adults) have any explicit representation of determinism, there is a plausible connection between the explanatory compulsion and determinism. To see this, let's turn away from *folk* views, for a moment, and consider the explicit commitment to determinism in philosophy and science. Why has determinism been so widely adopted at various points in the history of philosophy and science? It is a striking fact that even though determinism is largely presupposed in the modern era, *arguments* for determinism are hard to find. It is often assumed that Newtonian mechanics is deterministic, and so a commitment to Newtonian mechanics would entail a commitment to determinism. But there are reasons to think that this is false and that Newton's laws are neutral on determinism (e.g., Earman 1986; Norton 2003). Neither does the historical endorsement of determinism plausibly follow from empirical demonstrations. It's not like eighteenth-century philosophers and physicists accumulated a lot of data and said, "See, given the quality of our data set, we can infer that every single event is an inevitable consequence of what happened before it." This is especially apparent if we consider the deeper history of the idea. One of the oldest surviving scraps of Western philosophy is Leucippus' apparent proclamation of determinism: "Nothing happens at random, but everything for a reason and by necessity" (Irwin 1999, 230). This was an important strand of thought in pre-Socratic philosophy. But they had astonishingly little evidence about *anything*. What on earth could have led them to believe in a principle as audaciously ambitious as determinism? The real force of determinism for these philosophers was presumably not the evidence; rather their confidence in determinism was the result of embracing the explanatory compulsion and taking it to apply without exception.[5]

1.1.3 The explanatory compulsion and folk psychology

I have suggested that this explanatory compulsion is indiscriminate in that it can be activated for any event. The compulsion is also indiscriminate, I suggest, about domains. That is, the compulsion to explain is *domain general*. Of special significance is that the compulsion is not suspended for the domain of the mind. The drive to explain can be triggered just as easily by the surprising behavior of one's roommate as by the surprising behavior of one's air conditioner.

---

[5] We might thus construct an epidemiological account (Sperber 1996) of the success of determinism as a theoretical view. Determinism is a doctrine that resonates with the explanatory compulsion, and this would confer a cultural advantage for the view. The explanatory compulsion makes determinism intuitively attractive, which would enhance its cultural cachet.

The experimental work on child's theory of mind reveals children's disposition to look for explanations in the domain of action. In their classic paper on children's understanding of false belief, Wimmer and Perner (1983) presented children with a playground story in which Nancy is told by Thomas' mother that he can stay longer on the playground. However, the story continues, "Thomas never gets off the swing, but Nancy wants to use it immediately." Nancy proceeds to tell Thomas, "You've got to go home, your mom needs you." The children in the experiment were asked, "Why did Nancy say to Thomas that he has to go home?" (121). The older children were quite proficient at explaining this: 94 percent of them gave an explanation for Nancy's statement that appealed to the fact that she wanted to use the swing (122).

While the experimental evidence here reveals a facility with explanation of action, the ecological evidence is more telling. From a young age, children seek explanations. We see this for a wide range of non-psychological phenomena, e.g., "Why does it rain sometimes?"; "Why does Daddy, James (big brother), and me have blue eyes and you have green eyes?" (Callanan and Oakes 1992, 218, 221). But across a range of different ecological approaches, requests for explanations of *actions* loom large, and in particular, *psychological* explanations for actions are especially prominent. Researchers have used longitudinal techniques (Hood et al. 1979), directed parent-diaries (Callanan and Oakes 1992), and corpus data (Hickling and Wellman 2001). Hickling and Wellman summarize the state of the evidence: "all studies to date have revealed predominant discussion of causality involving persons' actions, intentions, and internal states" (2001, 679; see also Wellman and Liu 2007). Just as in the stochastic blicket study, children seem to presume that there will be an explanation for actions. Indeed, when we view the world through the lens of the explanatory compulsion, it's easy to have sympathy with Holbach's proclamation that the word "chance" is "void of sense.... Man uses the word chance to cover his ignorance of those natural causes which produce visible effects" (1889/1779, 37).

It's intuitive that a person's actual decision has to have an explanation. There has to be *some* explanation for why he made the choice that he did. There is a smattering of interview data on this. In his influential paper on the folk model of the mind, anthropologist Roy D'Andrade gives a summary report of interviews he conducted with Western subjects (D'Andrade 1987). When asked whether someone could do something for no reason at all, one subject answered, "Really no reason at all? I'd say there should be some reason somewhere." When asked if the reason could be trivial, the subject responded, "Could be trivial, could be anything. But there should be a reason" (133). D'Andrade also asked whether someone could fail to act on their desire in the absence of any competing desires: "If there wasn't a counterwish, could it be the case that he just didn't go even though he wanted to?" The subject responded, "That's like a contradiction. Because that doesn't make too much sense. There would have to be a reason why the person didn't do it if they wanted to do it. There'd have to be some reason. . . . It wouldn't be that they just wouldn't do it" (132). It's natural to construe these answers— "there has to be a reason"—as reflecting the explanatory compulsion that makes determinism so intuitively attractive.

We can see this explanatory compulsion in play in folk psychology if we present people with a task that focuses on explanation and prediction. In one study, participants were presented with a fanciful scenario in which they were to imagine 10,000 psychological duplicates scattered across 10,000 earthlike planets. The 10,000 people—all named "Jerry"— are specified to have minor physical differences, but no differences in psychology:

the physical differences are not readily detectible, and everything they have experienced throughout their lives has looked and sounded exactly the same. Indeed, at the psychological level, all of these different Jerrys have been exactly the same up until now. That is, they have all had the same beliefs, desires, thoughts, perceptions, and intentions (Nichols 2006, 69).

Each of the Jerrys wants to learn a new skill and each is currently trying to decide whether to learn to walk a tightrope; it is stipulated that one of them decides in favor. The participants were asked (i) how many of the rest of the people decided the same thing and (ii) to explain their answer. This is obviously a very complex task, and many subjects' explanations for their answers showed that they failed to abide by the condition of the thought experiment. Of those who did abide by the conditions of the thought experiment, the vast majority said that all the 10,000 individuals would decide the same thing. This, of course, conforms nicely with a deterministic view of the situation. But it's worth considering a bit further those who failed to abide by the conditions of the thought experiment. For the particular kind of failure exhibited is instructive.

The characteristic response of those who failed to abide by the thought experiment was to say (i) not all of the people would decide the same way and (ii) this is because the individuals probably had somewhat different beliefs, desires, etc. For instance, one subject wrote: "it is unlikely that they have all had the same experiences and encounters with others . . . that will alter their thought processes." Of course, this counts as a violation of the conditions of the thought experiment. But what's especially interesting is that this explanation fits in precisely with the idea that the explanatory compulsion applies to folk psychological efforts. When participants envisage that the people in the scenario make different responses, they try to provide a psychological explanation for why that is.[6]

Thus, there is some support for the view that people have an explanatory compulsion—they expect there to be an explanation for any particular event that is presented to them. And this compulsion is not restricted to billiard tables. Both children and adults expect *actions* to have explanations. Where two agents make different decisions, people expect that there must be some explanation for why they arrived at different decisions.[7]

This explanatory compulsion regarding actions seems to threaten libertarianism. For according to libertarianism, in many cases, there will be no deeper explanation for why two identically situated individuals make different decisions. It is telling that some sophisticated libertarians don't deny the explanatory compulsion. Instead, they refuse to accept its demands. Here is Campbell:

---

[6] In a follow-up study, a vignette described two psychologically type-identical individuals facing the same decision, and subjects were asked whether the two agents would definitely decide the same thing or whether it was *possible* that they would decide differently. Most subjects said that the two would definitely decide the same thing. Moreover, as in the other experiment, those who said it was possible that the two agents would respond differently gave *psychological* explanations for why the two might choose differently, violating the conditions of the thought experiment.

[7] There are delicate issues about the relationship between explanatory compulsion and causation. Of particular significance for the claim in this section, there is some controversy over whether *reasons* are causes. The story I'm telling is meant to be ecumenical. The evidence indicates that people assume that in order for two people to make different decisions, there must be difference makers. And at least in some cases, they assume the difference makers are reasons. Perhaps these reasons aren't causes, or perhaps they are special kinds of causes. In any case, the explanatory compulsion drives us to expect difference makers, whether they count as causes or not.

Repeatedly it is urged against the libertarian, with a great air of triumph, that on his view he can't say *why* I now decide to rise to duty, or now decide to follow my strongest desire in defiance of duty. Of course he can't. If he could he wouldn't *be* a libertarian. To "account for" a "free" act is a contradiction in terms. A free will is *ex hypothesi* the sort of thing of which the request for an *explanation* is absurd (Campbell 1957, 175; see also O'Connor, 1995, 188–9).

Campbell thus rejects the demand for an explanation of free action. Although the philosopher can take a stand here and refuse the question, *people* don't refuse the question. In everyday contexts, people naturally seek explanations for actions and they expect there to *be* one. If you turn on the explanation mechanism, you trigger a natural, deep process that is only satisfied by an explanation.

The compulsive nature of the explanatory system makes determinism intuitive and the cosmological argument compelling. The limitless thirst of the explanatory system is not so surprising when we consider the likely function of the system. Our explanation system is plausibly there because it helps us predict and manipulate the world (cf. Gopnik 2000). In this light, it makes sense that the system would have unrestricted ambitions. An explanation system that is willing to give up, cry "Uncle," would be less effective than an explanation system that won't take "brute fact" for an answer.[8]

1.2 Folk indeterminism

Although we are naturally disposed to expect an explanation, libertarians latch onto another natural disposition that conflicts with determinism, i.e., the sense that decisions *aren't* determined. A diverse body of evidence indicates that people have the intuition that choice isn't determined. The evidence comes from interviews with children, vignette tasks, and phenomenological studies. Let's start with the children. Young children are fluent with the idea that a person often *could have done otherwise* than she did. In one study, children observed an experimenter reach into a box and touch the bottom; the experimenter then asked the child, "Did I have to touch the bottom or could I have done

---

[8] This is not to deny that our explanatory urges can be suspended. Even though there is no satisfying answer to "Why is there something rather than nothing?", we set this aside to make lunch and babies.

something else instead?". Children overwhelmingly said that the person could have done something else (Nichols 2004b; see also Kushnir et al. 2009; Chernyak et al. 2013). Children did not, however, say the same thing after observing a physical event like a ball rolling into the box. Rather, in that case, children denied that the ball could have done something else.

Of course, one might wonder whether the notion of *could have done otherwise* that the child is deploying is really inconsistent with determinism. In a subsequent experiment, children were presented with scenarios of physical events and moral choices. In one of the moral choice scenarios, Mary chooses to steal a candy bar. After correctly answering some comprehension questions about the situation that immediately preceded Mary's choice, children were presented with a kind of roll-back question: "Okay, now imagine that all of that was exactly the same and that what Mary wanted was exactly the same. If everything in the world was the same right up until she chose to steal, did Mary have to choose to steal?" In a physical event scenario, a pot of water was put on a stove and boils. Again, after comprehension questions about the situation immediately prior to the boiling, the children were asked, "Okay, now imagine that all of that was exactly the same. If everything in the world was the same right up until the water boiled, did the water have to boil?" In this study, children were more likely to say that the water *had to boil* than that Mary *had to choose* to steal (Nichols 2004b).

It is hard to be confident that children really understand the roll-back set up here, but the same kinds of scenarios have been given to adults (Nichols 2012). Adults were presented with the water-boiling scenario and asked to imagine the moment right before the water boiled. They were asked to indicate the extent to which they agreed with this statement: "If everything was exactly the same up until the moment the water boiled, then the water had to boil at that moment." Adults tended to give high ratings of agreement for this case. Participants were also presented with a scenario in which a man stole a CD. They were asked whether the following would be possible: "Everything was exactly the same as it was (both inside and outside the man) up until the moment he chose to steal the CD, but the man didn't choose to steal the CD." To reinforce the critical feature, they were told that by saying that everything was "exactly the same up until the man chose to steal, this means *everything*. The store was the same, the CD was the same, what the man wanted was the same, and so on." For this case, participants were significantly more likely to disagree with the statement: "If everything was exactly the same up until the moment the man chose to steal the CD, then the man had to choose to steal the CD at that moment." This supports the idea that the participants are thinking of choice as indeterminist. In addition, many of the participants who gave different answers for the two cases explicitly invoked the nature of choice in explaining their responses. Here are a few examples:

"I think that it's most LIKELY that the people will not change what actions they take, but I think it's possible, whereas water doesn't choose to boil."

"For the water-boiling scenario, all things the same, water will boil in the same amount of time, each and every time. The scenario's dealing with choices, decisions could be made on a whim, with the outcome being random. So those answers could vary, even under the same exact circumstances."

"Regardless of circumstances, a person has a choice about their actions and may choose differently at any point. The water has to boil—it has no choice."[9]

Another method for investigating lay beliefs about determinism starts by presenting subjects with a description of a deterministic universe. Joshua Knobe and I presented subjects with a questionnaire that depicted both a determinist universe (A) and an indeterminist universe (B). The deterministic universe was characterized as follows:

everything that happens is completely caused by whatever happened before it. This is true from the very beginning of the universe, so what happened in the beginning of the universe caused what happened next, and so on right up until the present. For example one day John decided to have French fries at lunch. Like everything else, this decision was completely caused by what happened before it. So, if everything in this universe was exactly the same up until John made his decision, then it had to happen that John would decide to have French fries (Nichols and Knobe 2007, 669).

The other universe was indeterminist with respect to choice. In this universe, "almost everything that happens is completely caused by whatever happened before it. The one exception is human decision making." This difference was summarized as follows:

---

[9] There was, it should be noted, some variation in responses. One participant gave an explanation that seems to be explicitly determinist: "If everything was the same, then the result must be the same.... Otherwise, the circumstances surrounding the event must be different in some respect, possibly something to do with the time of the occurrence."

The key difference, then, is that in Universe A every decision is completely caused by what happened before the decision—given the past, each decision *has to happen* the way that it does. By contrast, in Universe B, decisions are not completely caused by the past, and each human decision *does not have to happen* the way that it does.

After this description, subjects were asked, "Which of these universes do you think is most like ours?" The vast majority of subjects answered that the *indeterminist* universe (Universe B) is most like ours. Note that the only feature of universe B that is indeterminist is choice. So, the responses indicate that people are committed precisely to the idea that choice is indeterminist (see also Roskies and Nichols 2008). This holds for populations studied in the U.S., China, Columbia, and India (Sarkissian et al. 2010).

Using yet another method, Deery et al. (2013) asked people about the phenomenology of their choices. First, the notion of determinism (dubbed "causal completeness" in the experiments) was explained to participants. After being given a general characterization of the notion of determinism, specific illustrations were offered, including the following: "According to causal completeness, if we could somehow replay the entire past right up until St. Helens erupted on May 18, 1980, then St. Helens would once again erupt at that time. Another way to put this is to say that all the events leading up to the eruption made it so that the eruption had to happen." To allay worries about comprehension of the materials, Deery et al. used the familiar psychological technique of *training to criterion*. Participants were asked critical questions to assess their understanding of determinism. If they answered incorrectly, they were given additional training and asked another set of questions to ensure that they understood the notion of determinism.[10] Following this training, participants were effectively asked whether their experience of decision-making was compatible with determinism. For instance, in one version, after selecting between two charities, participants were first asked whether they felt like they could choose either way. Most participants said that they did indeed feel that they could choose either charity. They were then asked to indicate agreement or disagreement with a statement that affirms incompatibilism: "Even though it felt like

---

[10] Most participants got the comprehension questions right the first time around, and a tiny fraction failed the training.

I could either choose to donate to *Castanea Dentata* or choose to donate to *Ulmus Dentata*, if causal completeness is true then I couldn't really have chosen differently than I did." Across several studies, the results were robust: participants reported that their experience of their ability to do otherwise was *incompatible* with determinism. It didn't matter whether they were merely imagining a decision or actually making a decision, whether the decision was morally salient or neutral, or whether the decision was present-focused or retrospective. In all conditions, people tended to report their phenomenology of choice as incompatible with determinism.

One last result is perhaps the most striking illustration of the anti-determinist streak in the commonsense conception of choice. In a recent experiment, David Rose and I presented participants with a deterministic scenario which explicitly included the statement "John decided to have French fries at lunch." They were subsequently asked whether they agreed that "In this universe, people make decisions." Nearly half of the participants said that in this universe, people didn't make decisions![11] Indeterminism seems to be so deeply entwined with a commonsense conception of decision-making that many people have trouble seeing how it is even possible for there to be deterministic decision-making (Rose and Nichols 2013).[12]

These results from experimental philosophy confirm what incompatibilists have long maintained—that the way people think about and experience their choices is at odds with determinism.

1.3 Summary

The psychology of philosophy is a messy business. The diverse range of philosophical problems that emerge from commonsense probably has

---

[11] We ran these studies in exploring provocative new work by Murray and Nahmias (2014) (see section 4.1.2 for a fuller discussion). Similar results were obtained by Sias (unpublished) and Chan et al. (forthcoming).

[12] In another study, Rose and I wanted to see whether this effect would emerge for any kind of human inference, whether practical or theoretical. We again presented participants with a deterministic scenario and compared judgments about decisions with judgments about simple theoretical inference. In the decision condition, participants were presented with an agent selecting French fries; in the theoretical inference condition, participants were presented with an agent answering an arithmetic problem. Again, all scenarios were deterministic; participants tended to agree that in the arithmetic scenario the person added numbers, but they were more likely to say that in the French fries scenario, the person did not make a decision.

an almost equally diverse set of psychological causes. In the case of free will, I've suggested that the problem is driven by the explanatory compulsion on the one hand and the indeterminist intuition on the other. On the one side, from a young age, we expect there to be an explanation for any particular event we encounter. This explanatory compulsion is a deep feature of the human mind. Most people don't have an articulated version of determinism pre-loaded into their minds, but they do have the compulsion for an explanation and this makes determinism an attractive view. The explanatory compulsion is also indiscriminate. Just as we expect there to be an explanation for why a fire started, we expect there to be an explanation for why two identically situated individuals behaved differently. When invited to explain why two identically situated people make different choices, people tend to think that there *should* be an explanation; in the context of the search for explanations, the idea that *there is* no explanation strikes people as a cop-out. However, from the first-person perspective, when we make decisions, it certainly seems otherwise. It seems like I can choose in different ways even given exactly the same features in place. With all of the same reasons in mind, with all of the same situational factors the same, it seems like I can make different choices. Recent work in experimental philosophy provides considerable evidence that people have this indeterminist view of their choices. The explanatory compulsion makes it seem like there must be some explanation for why I choose the tequila; but introspection makes it seem like I could have—with all of the same factors held constant—chosen bourbon. That's the fundamental conflict. The reason it's so hard to resolve the problem of free will in a satisfying way is that both the explanatory compulsion and the indeterminist intuition reflect deep parts of our ordinary way of thinking about ourselves and the world.

The explanatory compulsion explains half of the conflict at the heart of the problem of free will. If we press further and ask why we have the explanatory compulsion, I doubt that there will be a psychological answer. That is, there probably isn't a deeper psychological account of the acquisition of the explanatory compulsion. Presumably there is some non-psychological account for why we have the explanatory compulsion. For instance, there are plausibly evolutionary stories to be told about the adaptive benefits of being compelled to seek explanation. But for this book, I'm in the business of exploring psychological explanations, not evolutionary ones.[13] So I will rest content with the explanatory compulsion as the basic mechanism that drives a key part of the problem of free will.

The other driving force in the problem of free will is the intuition that our actions are not determined. Why do we have *that* intuition? The case there is, I think, is more amenable to psychological explanation, and I turn to that task next.

---

[13] Much of the interest in developing a naturalistic explanation of philosophical problems derives from the possibility of debunking various of the commonsense commitments that drive the philosophical problems. As I will set out in some detail in Chapter 5, it's extremely plausible that we can debunk the justificatory status of a belief by showing that the belief is solely the result of epistemically defective psychological processes. Debunking arguments based on evolutionary processes have proved more controversial.

2

The Indeterminist Intuition: Source and Status

As we saw in the previous chapter, people think that their choices are not determined. Most people have had no training on the notion of determinism. Yet people have definite—and converging—opinions on the matter, even across cultures. But this seems rather presumptuous given people's general ignorance about the nature of the universe. The bulk of this chapter will be devoted to discerning why people believe in indeterminist choice. I'll offer two slightly different explanations for why we believe in indeterminism. On both of these explanations, part of the explanation for the belief in indeterminism comes from a presumption about our access to our own mental states. The presumption is, roughly, that if our decisions *were* determined, we would be aware of it.

Providing an etiological account of the belief in indeterminism is part of the descriptive project of trying to chart the nature of our beliefs. But this etiological account can also contribute to substantive arguments. Given the state of knowledge in cognitive science, it would be manifestly premature to pronounce on whether choice is indeterminist (see, e.g., Nichols 2008a; Balaguer 2010; Roskies forthcoming). Rather than attempt to weigh in on that, I will focus on a substantive question that is more tractable given the current state of knowledge: to what extent are we justified in the belief that choice isn't determined? By knowing why we believe in indeterminism, we might be able to show that the belief isn't justified. The general debunking strategy here is familiar from Freud's work on religious belief. Freud argued that once we recognize the source of our religious beliefs, we will come to appreciate that they are unwarranted (Freud 1961 [1927]). Similarly we might find that the source of our belief in libertarian choice reveals that the belief is unwarranted. Indeed, that is exactly what I will argue at the end of this chapter.

2.1 Extant explanations for the indeterminist intuition

There is a long history of explanations for the belief in indeterminist choice. Libertarians and hard determinists, not surprisingly, offer rather different explanations. But none of the proposed accounts provides an adequate explanation for the acquisition of the belief in indeterminism.

2.1.1 Libertarian explanations for the belief in indeterminism

Libertarians tend to explain the belief in indeterminism in terms of the character of our experience. Here is Campbell:

> Let us ask, why do human beings so obstinately persist in believing that there is an indissoluble core of purely *self*-originated activity which even heredity and environment are powerless to affect? There can be little doubt, I think, of the answer in general terms. They do so, at bottom, because they feel certain of the existence of such activity from their immediate practical experience of themselves (Campbell 1967, 41).

So, according to Campbell, it is because of our *immediate practical experience* that we believe our choices aren't determined.

In explaining the virtues of libertarianism, Timothy O'Connor also adverts to experience:

> the agency theory is appealing because it captures the way we experience our own activity. It does not seem to me (at least ordinarily) that I am caused to act by the reasons which favor doing so; it seems to be the case, rather, that *I* produce my decision *in view of* those reasons, and could have, in an unconditional sense, decided differently. Such experiences could, of course, be wholly illusory, but do we not properly assume, in the absence of strong countervailing reasons, that things are pretty much the way they appear to us? (1995, 196–7)

While O'Connor is here pointing to experience as a reason to believe in indeterminism, it's natural to take this appeal to experience as simultaneously providing an explanation for why we in fact believe in indeterminism.[1]

The work in experimental philosophy suggests that the libertarians are right about the character of the experience. People's experience of choice

---

[1] Indeed, a particularly attractive package is that we believe in indeterminism because of our experience, and this is in fact good grounds for believing in indeterminism.

is at odds with determinism. But as an explanation for the belief in indeterminism, the direct appeal to experience is too anemic to be convincing. Start with the (apparent) fact that we have experiences that conflict with determinism. One natural explanation for why we have such experiences is that we have a prior *belief* that is at odds with determinism and this belief shapes our experience. If that explanation is right, then appealing to the experience itself is no help since we would still need to explain why we have the prior belief in indeterminism. Or, to put the problem a bit differently, it's possible that our experience of indeterminism is *theory laden*. That is, we might have the experience of indeterminism because of a background theory that denies determinism.[2] If such a background theory is what informs our indeterminist phenomenology, then the key question is how we ended up with such an indeterminist *theory*.

If experience is supposed to provide a noncircular explanation for our belief in indeterminism, then it has to be in virtue of experience that is *not* guided by an indeterminist belief or indeterminist background theory. It's plausible that some of our ideas do come directly from raw (i.e., non-theory-laden) experience. It doesn't take any conceptual sophistication or background theory to get the idea of pain from the raw experience of a toothache. The idea of indeterminism, however, is presumably much too complex to be directly given by raw experience. It is hard to see how such a sophisticated belief could be arrived at without some form of inference, whether explicit or (more likely) tacit.[3] At a minimum, the libertarians have not given a plausible explanation for how we could get the indeterminist belief from raw experience.

In characterizing the experience of agency, libertarians like Campbell and O'Connor emphasize the experience of the *self* as initiator. For instance, O'Connor writes, "it seems to be the case . . . that *I* produce my decision *in view of* those reasons, and could have, in an unconditional

---

[2] As elsewhere in the book, any internally represented body of information will count as a "theory" in the sense meant here. This leaves open whether the theory is revisable. It might turn out that the theory that feeds the phenomenology of indeterminism is incorrigible.

[3] One might promote a nativist view about the belief that choice is indeterminist. But if this is aimed at avoiding a role for inference, it is a dauntingly rich nativist proposal. It would require an innate concept of choice, an innate concept of indeterminism, and an innate belief that connects these concepts.

sense, decided differently." Perhaps then, the idea isn't that we have a raw experience of indeterminism, but that we have an experience of the self as originator of decisions, and it is this experience that explains why people believe in indeterminism. For present purposes, I want to grant part of the claim here. Let's allow that when we make decisions, it seems as if the self is the originator of the decision. This claim is also promoted by nonlibertarians. For instance, Terry Horgan maintains that we don't experience our actions as determined by our mental states; rather, the phenomenology is that the *self* is the source of action. Here's Horgan:

How . . . should one characterize the actional phenomenal dimension of the act of raising one's hand and clenching one's fingers . . . ? Well, it's the what-it's-like of *self as source* of the motion. You experience your arm, hand, and fingers as being moved *by you yourself*, rather than experiencing their motion either as fortuitously moving just as you want them to move or else as being transeuntly caused by your own mental states. (Horgan 2011, 79)

This all sounds phenomenologically quite right. So I am happy to agree with O'Connor that there is a phenomenology of self-as-source. But it's unclear how to leverage this into an explanation of the belief in indeterminism. One option is to hold that we experience the self as "purely" originating action in a way that isn't determined, as suggested in the passage from Campbell. That option, though, brings us back to the problem of theory-ladenness—it's hard to see how raw experience could deliver the content *self-originated activity isn't determined*. Recent work on the phenomenology of agency suggests a second option. Raw experience does plausibly allow us to distinguish self-generated actions from involuntary bodily movements, like being pushed (see, e.g., Blakemore and Frith 2003). Thus, there might be a kind of raw experience of self-as-source. It remains controversial whether this actually includes an experience of a *self* (Prinz 2011). More importantly, even if we have a raw experience that allows us to identify our self-generated actions, the libertarian would still need to explain how we move from that raw experience to the intuition that the self isn't determined. And this hasn't been done. Thus, while libertarians are right that we believe and feel that our decisions aren't determined, they have yet to provide a satisfying explanation for why we have the belief.

2.1.2 Hard determinist explanations
for the belief in indeterminism

Hard determinists have their own explanation for the belief in indeterminist choice. The leading motif in their explanation is *ignorance*. The basic strategy was put forward by Spinoza in the seventeenth century:

Men believe themselves to be free, simply because they are conscious of their actions, and unconscious of the causes whereby those actions are determined (Spinoza 1887 [1677], 134).

Men are mistaken in thinking themselves free; their opinion is made up of consciousness of their own actions, and ignorance of the causes by which they are conditioned. Their idea of freedom, therefore, is simply their ignorance of any cause for their actions (108).

Holbach promotes a similar view a century later:

Because [man] cannot perceive the chain of operations in his soul, or the motive principle that acts within him, he supposes himself a free agent . . . when he rather ought to say, that he is ignorant how or for why he acts in the manner he does. (Holbach 1889 [1770], 97)

For both Spinoza and Holbach, it is because we are ignorant of the causes of our actions that we think our actions aren't determined.

The ignorance-based explanation has long been attractive to hard determinists. But it is manifestly incomplete. In typical cases of ignorance, we do not draw grand conclusions about determinism. I currently have a headache; I am conscious of my headache; and I have no good idea about what caused it. I "cannot perceive the chain of operations" that led to my headache. Still, I don't infer an indeterministic source for my headache. Something similar can be said when I have an allergic reaction, nausea, achy joints, itches, and so on. Yet ignorance of the causes for these phenomena does not generally breed the belief that the phenomena aren't determined. So even if Spinoza is right that we are ignorant of the causes of our actions, that doesn't yet explain why we believe that our actions aren't determined.

Richard Holton offers a contemporary variant of the Spinozist approach. Holton begins by suggesting that what is available in our phenomenology isn't sufficient to determine our choices: "Our experience tells us that our choice is not determined by our beliefs and desires, or by any other psychological states—intentions, emotions etc.—to which we have access. Those could be the same, and yet we could choose differently" (Holton 2006, 15). I think Holton is right that, at least often, the psychological states we identify through introspection are not sufficient to determine our behavior.[4] Holton adverts to Buridan's ass style cases as one kind of example (6). I choose between two coins (or two piles of hay), even though my experience does not present me with any determinative set of considerations for taking one over the other. One might complain that Buridan's ass style scenarios are rare. But such cases point to a much broader phenomenon. Frequently (always?) the information to which I have access doesn't uniquely predict my action. Consider the timing of action. I want to turn on the stereo, and I am quite sure that I will eventually get up and do it. But when I actually get up is not uniquely predicted by the information that is introspectively available.

After noting that our *phenomenology* is such that our psychological states could be the same and yet we could choose differently, Holton goes on to write: "From there it is easy to move to the thought that we could be just the same in our entirety, and yet we could choose differently: that the world is indeterministic" (Holton 2006, 15). Why is it easy to move? How do I go from the lack of an introspectively available set of factors that determine my action to the conclusion that there is no set of factors that determine my action? It would be a kind of scope fallacy to move from "I don't experience my actions as determined" to "I experience my actions as not determined." Now, people surely do commit scope fallacies. But notice we don't seem to commit the scope fallacy when it comes to headaches. That is, the phenomenology of headaches doesn't present us with a set of deterministic headache-causes, but we don't leap to indeterminist conclusions there. Like Spinoza's account, Holton's is at least incomplete. For it remains unclear how we move from the fact that we don't perceive deterministic psychological causes to the conclusion that our choices aren't determined.

---

[4] Holton also writes: "If I am right that choice is not determined by one's prior beliefs and desires, then there is an important sense in which, phenomenologically, it is not determined" (Holton 2006, 5). I'm less sure about this. Consider again my headache. My headache is not determined by my prior beliefs and desires, nor by the other factors that are introspectively available to me. I could have the same introspectively available features and not have a headache. Does that mean that there is an important sense in which phenomenologically my headache is not determined? If so, then it doesn't seem so meaningful to say of an event that "phenomenologically it is not determined." If not, then we need an explanation of the asymmetry between headaches and choices.

2.2 How to make inferences about determinism

Setting aside the folk, scientists and philosophers obviously have views about determinism. It's hard to find compelling evidentiary arguments for the ambitious claim that the entire universe is deterministic. But there are perfectly legitimate ways to make inferences about whether a more restricted system is deterministic or not. The key is that one must be able to assess all of the inputs to the system.

If we know the boundaries of a system, and we can monitor all of the inputs, then we can be in a position to assess whether the system is deterministic. Neuroscientific research on the release of neurotransmitters provides a nice example. Neurotransmitters are released from the end of a neuron into the synaptic cleft. Researchers have explored the relation between neural activation and the release of neurotransmitters by activating a single neuron in a fixed way and monitoring the release of neurotransmitters. Apparently the release of neurotransmitters into the synaptic cleft can differ even given the same activation of the neuron. This has been used by some to argue that the behavior across the synapse is indeterminist (Glimcher 2005, 48). For it seems that given the same input, the mechanism can produce different outputs. The empirical details here are vexed, for it's not clear that all the factors were controlled for across conditions (Roskies forthcoming). But the argumentative strategy is perfectly sensible. If we have a closed system and we know all of the inputs, then if the system behaves in different ways given the same inputs, that constitutes evidence that the system is not deterministic.[5]

2.3 Back to Buridan's ass

The neuroscientific argument for indeterminism in synaptic release provides a model for how to argue for indeterminism. And this kind of argument, I suggest, was deployed by Medieval libertarians. A number of Medieval philosophers, including Peter Olivi, Duns Scotus, and William

---

[5] Of course, there is the complication that the system might have hidden variables that are deterministic but produce apparently indeterminist behavior. Such possibilities bedevil inferences about determinism even in physics. So these arguments are not foolproof. But they still provide perhaps the best approach we have for assessing whether a system is deterministic.

of Ockham, used Buridan's ass cases to argue for indeterminist choice (see Rescher 2005). Here is Olivi:

> When there is some number of equal things that are equally useful, nothing explains the will's adoption of one or the other of them except the freedom by which one is equally able to do this or that. . . . It often happens that we want to take one of two coins. We deliberate and ascertain that there is just as good reason to take the one as the other. In these circumstances, we rightly think that we would be able to take and keep the one coin just as well as the other. Then, when we take one of the two, we manifestly feel that we do this from freedom of the will alone and not from some greater satisfaction in the one as opposed to the other (quoted in Kaye 2004, 23).

The argument seems to be that (i) the factors that inform my decision are equibalanced between the two options, but (ii) I make a choice. Thus, the choice isn't determined.

Leibniz famously rejected the possibility of Buridan's ass, insisting that: "a perfect equality on two sides is never to be found" (see Rescher 2005, 27). And Leibniz availed himself of the unconscious states—*petites perceptions*—to maintain that there are unconscious tie-breakers in all such cases. He criticizes earlier philosophers of free will for "ignoring these insensible impressions which can suffice to tilt the balance" (1765/ 1981, II, i., 15). Now, Leibniz had no empirical evidence that there are always tie-breakers. However, his remarks draw out a tacit assumption of the Medieval argument for indeterminism—the argument presumes that *we can tell* that there are no tie-breaking factors in Buridan's ass cases.

A similar kind of presumption seems to be implicit in a key discussion of free will in Ockham. Ockham first defines free will as "that power whereby I can do diverse things indifferently and contingently, such that I can cause, or not cause, the same effect, *when all conditions other than this power are the same.*" He then goes on to claim that we can know that we have this free will through experience: "the thesis can be known evidently through experience since a human being experiences that, no matter how much reason dictates a given thing, the will is still able to will that thing or not to will it" (Ockham 1980, 88). But how do I know that I can engage in this kind of free action *when all conditions are the same*? At a minimum, I must be able to tell whether *all the conditions are the same.*

Ockham's case here plausibly depends on the assumption that I have access to the proximal factors that impinge on my decisions. The texts do suggest that Ockham presumes that all of the relevant factors are consciously available (see Brower-Toland, forthcoming). Given that assumption, we can piece together an argument for indeterminism:

1. The factors that are introspectively accessible do not determine my choice.
2. I have introspective access to all the (proximal) factors that influence my choice.
3. My choice is not determined.

The argument closely resembles the kind of argument we find in neuroscience. The first premise is quite plausible to this day. And, at least in Ockham's time, the second premise was perfectly reasonable. It is a powerful argument for indeterminism.

2.4 Philosophy recapitulates ontogeny

We have already granted that—at least often—the introspectively accessible features of our current states don't uniquely fix a decision. Let's assume that this is something that people are aware of on the slightest reflection. That is, assume that people know that what is introspectively accessible doesn't fix a decision. If people also presume that they have access to the proximal influences on their decisions, then they would have the materials to draw a reasonable inference to indeterminism. So, do people assume that they have such access?

On some contemporary accounts, people presume that they have access to *everything* in their minds (e.g., Carruthers 2008). If people really presupposed such introspective transparency, that would obviously suffice to move from the belief that *the factors available to introspection do not determine my choice* to the conclusion that *my choice is not determined*. There is, however, little evidence to support such a strong claim. At least at the explicit level, many people acknowledge the possibility that they might not be able to access various aspects of their current mental lives (Kozuch and Nichols 2011).

Although people don't assume complete mental transparency, such a strong assumption is not necessary to fund the inference to indeterminism. All that is required is a kind of default (but defeasible) assumption that the causal influences on decisions are introspectively available. And there is evidence that people do have such a default assumption. For instance, people report that they *usually* know what leads them to make the decisions they do. And people tend to expect that subjects in a psychology experiment would be aware of the influences on their decisions. Kozuch and I presented participants with the following description of an experiment by Nisbett and Schachter (1966):

Researchers asked subjects to take a series of shocks that increased in intensity. Before they were given the shocks, some subjects were administered a pill and told that the pill would lead to heart palpitations, irregular breathing, and butterflies in the stomach. In fact, the pill was phony, but these symptoms are also the most common symptoms experienced by people when undergoing electric shocks. The researchers predicted that the subjects who were told the pill would produce these symptoms (heart palpitations, irregular breathing, etc.) would take more intense shocks than other subjects. The researchers were right. Subjects who were told that the pill would produce heart palpitations, irregular breathing and butterflies in the stomach accepted far more intense shocks.

In the original Nisbett and Schachter experiment, the subjects clearly thought that the pill was causing heart palpitations and irregular breathing, and this affected how much shock the subjects took. As a matter of fact, the researchers report, subjects were unaware of the influence of their thoughts about the pill. Kozuch and I wanted to know whether our participants would anticipate this. We asked our participants whether the subjects in that experiment would have been aware that they attributed some of their physical symptoms (e.g., butterflies and heart palpitations) to the pill. Our participants maintained that the subjects would indeed have been aware of this.

Although participants were thus inclined to presume access about decision making, it turns out that participants do not treat all mental events alike in this respect. In another task, we presented participants with a description of a different experiment (Nisbett and Wilson 1977) in which subjects memorized a series of word pairs and then were given a word association task. The original experiment found that people who had memorized the word pair "ocean–moon" were more likely to name "Tide" when asked for the name of a laundry detergent. Again, what Kozuch and I wanted to know was whether our participants would expect the subjects to be aware that memorizing "ocean–moon" influenced their association to "Tide." We found that our participants did *not* expect subjects to be aware of this influence. In another task, we asked participants about the extent to which one is typically aware of the factors that produce urges, and participants showed significantly less agreement with the claim that one is typically aware of the influences on urge-formation, as compared to decision-formation. Our results do not support the idea that people have an unqualified presumption of introspective transparency. However, they do suggest that people have a kind of default presumption that the influences on decisions are introspectively available. Moreover, decisions seem to be special in this regard. The factors influencing associations and urges are regarded as less introspectively accessible than those influencing choice.

The data here are really quite limited, and so it's hard to draw any very precise conclusions about the extent of the presumed access. But I think we can make a bit of headway by coming at this from another direction: *why* would we think that we have good access to the factors implicated in decision making?

There are prominent areas of our psychology in which we have an exaggerated sense of our ability for detection. Change blindness offers a striking example. In change blindness studies, participants take a very long time to notice large differences in flashing presentations of a doctored photo. When asked to estimate how quickly they would (or did) notice the change, people vastly overestimate their performance (Levin et al. 2000; see also Scholl et al. 2004). Why do subjects presume that they would notice the changes? Levin and colleagues suggest that it is because of the salience of the successes we have in perception:

A large body of research shows that subjects attend to "hits" more than "misses" when considering their success at everyday tasks (see for example, Gilovich, 1991; Hearst, 1991), and that these highly available instances exert a powerful effect on reasoning and decision making (Tversky and Kahneman, 1973) (Levin et al. 2000, 408).

Our attention is drawn to factors that are *present*, rather than to the possibility that there are hidden factors (Hearst 1991). Of course, often this is quite appropriate. There are typically indefinitely many things that we don't see when we make evaluations. It would be excessively demanding to try from the beginning to accommodate the possibility of hidden factors. Instead, in both science and life, we proceed in a more tractable fashion.

The role of salient successes in generating an exaggerated sense of one's knowledge is elaborated in work by Rozenblit and Keil (2002).

They explored the factors that lead people to have a sense of "explanatory depth" for a system. What they find is that people take themselves to have a high level of understanding for mechanisms like locks, toilets, and zippers. When pressed to explain these devices fully, people tend to be flummoxed and subsequently downgrade their self-reported level of understanding. What, then, gives them the initial sense of a deep understanding? Rozenblit and Keil suggest that it is in part because there are discrete, visible parts to these devices (538). The visible parts are also manifestly causally implicated in the workings of the device. Compare this to devices for which we typically *don't* have access to any of the causal parts, like touch screens or flashdrives. Because we don't have access to any of the causal factors, we have (I suggest) no sense of explanatory depth at all, and so we are quite prepared to acknowledge our ignorance of the causal factors. It's only because we have seen the causal parts of locks and zippers that we have the sense of a fairly complete understanding.

With this background in place, we can start to piece together an explanation for why people tend to expect access to factors implicated in decision making (Kozuch and Nichols 2011). When we introspect, we do plausibly find discrete states (e.g., thoughts and intentions) that are causally implicated in our decisions. We succeed in explaining and understanding much of our behavior in terms of these introspectively available states. In addition, we virtually never get disconfirmation of these explanations of our own behavior (Nisbett and Wilson 1977, 256; see also Levin et al. 2000). In light of this, it is not at all surprising that we have a sense of a deep understanding of the factors implicated in our decisions. The fact that there *might* be hidden factors that we aren't accommodating in our explanations is of no more significance in this domain than elsewhere. Until you show me the factors I'm neglecting, I'm unlikely to incorporate them into my explanations. Indeed, even after we acknowledge the theoretical possibility of hidden factors influencing choice, we rarely bring that fact to mind. It takes great vigilance to keep in mind that there are (right now!) introspectively unavailable factors influencing my decisions.

More empirical work is sorely needed on the extent of presumed access to decision making. But if the foregoing sketch is right about the default presumption of introspective access, then we have what it takes to explain the inference to indeterminism. We are granting that people believe (1):

1. The factors that are introspectively accessible do not determine my choice.

I've proposed that people also have a default assumption that we have access to the proximal factors that influence our decisions. Given these assumptions, it would be natural, indeed appropriate, to conclude that choice is—at least often—not determined.

I've argued that this account can explain why people believe that decisions aren't determined. The account can also accommodate the fact that people *don't* think that about other mental events. People have no idea about how semantic memory works. If asked, "What is your mother's maiden name?", people have no trouble responding; at the same time, people have little to say when asked, "How did you retrieve that?" (Nisbett and Wilson 1977, 232). But this isn't very surprising to anyone. People don't presume to know the operations of semantic memory. Similarly, we have no good sense of discrete causal factors implicated in getting (endogenously produced) headaches. In these cases, we don't have a sufficiently powerful causal story to begin with, and so we have no sense of explanatory depth. So there is no presumption of broad-scale access to the causally relevant factors in the generation of headaches.[6] As a result, there is no basis for drawing indeterminist conclusions about headaches from the fact that we can't detect a deterministic set of causes.

2.5 A statistical learning explanation of the belief in indeterminism

The previous explanation relied on a deductive structure for explaining the acquisition of the belief in indeterminism. In recent work on acquisition in cognitive science, statistical learning has turned out to provide extremely powerful models for a number of domains (see, e.g., Perfors et al. 2011). And, as it happens, such an inductive learning framework provides a slightly different way to explain why people believe in indeterminist choice. A bit of background is required to tell the story.

Principles of probabilistic inference challenge the old chestnut that "absence of evidence is not evidence of absence." To illustrate the basic idea, imagine that a friend has eight cards—four Kings and four Aces. He

---

[6] In this respect, headaches are like flashdrives and decisions are like zippers.

shows you this, then turns them all face down, shuffles them up, then randomly separates out two of them, destroying the other six. You don't know whether there are now two Kings, two Aces, or one of each. He randomly picks one, peeks at it and reports that it's a King. He replaces it with the other, shuffles, again randomly picks one, and peeks at it: King. Imagine this process of random sampling with replacement occurs ten times and each time the result is a King. Do you think that one of the two cards is an Ace? You shouldn't! The fact that there is no evidence in favor of there being an Ace counts as evidence that there isn't an Ace. If there were an Ace in the set of two, it would be a suspicious coincidence that the Ace never showed up. Indeed, on standard Bayesian approaches to probabilistic inference, each data point with no Ace exponentially decreases the odds that there is an Ace.

One important feature of this example is that we actually have a lot of relevant evidence that informs our inference about whether there is an Ace. If we were shown no card at all, that would be an absence of evidence, but it would not count towards showing that there isn't an Ace. Thus, we need to have the relevant kind of negative evidence. Turning to choice now, we have been granting, with Spinoza, Holbach, Holton, and Horgan, that when we make decisions, we often do not have introspective access to a set of causes that deterministically predicts our decisions. However, as noted in the previous section, even in cases where we don't introspect deterministic causes, we do have introspective access to numerous discrete mental states—thoughts, urges, concerns—that influence our decisions. So we have a good deal of introspective evidence on factors influencing our decisions.

Although my proposal is likely pretty evident already, before I lay it out, it will be helpful to return to cards for a slightly different example. Now imagine two decks of cards. One deck consists of 26 unique pairs; the other has no pairs. One of the decks is selected at random; the other is destroyed. From the surviving deck, ten sets of five cards are randomly selected (leaving two cards over) and laid out face down. You need to determine whether this deck is the one with pairs or the one without pairs. You are simply told, for each set of five cards, whether there is a pair in that set. Now suppose that none of the ten sets of five cards has a pair. If none of the sets contains a pair, that counts as evidence that the deck that was selected was the deck without pairs—it counts as evidence that there are no pairs of cards. As before, if it had been the deck with pairs, it would be a suspicious coincidence that no pairs occurred in ten observed sets of five.

We can think of the agent as in a situation comparable to the person trying to determine whether the deck is the one with pairs. Let's suppose that the agent is tasked with assessing whether decisions that fall into a certain class are determined. The class of decisions we'll focus on are "difficult decisions." This will include decisions in which it is very unclear which way to act, like Buridan's ass cases and cases of incommensurable values.[7] The agent has made lots of these decisions. For each of those decisions, the agent has knowledge of a set of mental states that influences his decisions. (On the previous analogy, this would be akin to the knowledge of whether there is a pair in a certain set of five cards.) However, we are granting (again with Spinoza and company) that in each of these cases, the set of states of which he is aware does not provide a deterministic explanation of his decision. Given the relevant evidence that he does have (i.e., evidence of the influence of sets of states) and the evidence that he doesn't have (i.e., evidence of sets of states that determine his decision), the agent infers that difficult decisions are not deterministically produced. The fact that we are never aware of a set of deterministic causes for our difficult decisions provides evidence that those decisions aren't determined. As with the sets of cards, if difficult decisions did have deterministic causes, it would be a suspicious coincidence that none of the sets of states in our evidence base is a deterministic set.

The foregoing provides an account of how rational probabilistic inference would lead an agent to think that he makes undetermined decisions. There are, of course, a *lot* of assumptions built in to the proposal: (1) It assumes that the inference is made over a restricted class of decisions—

---

[7] I choose this class of decisions partly because this is a class of decisions that is often treated as the key class of undetermined decisions (see, e.g., van Inwagen 1989, 417; Kane 2002, 228) and partly because it's uncontroversial that we lack introspective access to deterministic causes for these decisions. (Indeed, it's plausible that for many such decisions there *aren't* deterministic causes at the psychological level. That is, the class of difficult decisions might well contain genuine counterexamples to psychological determinism.) However, it is not implausible that introspection never reveals a deterministic set of causes for *any* of our decisions. For instance, as noted earlier in the text, we seem to lack access to enough information to predict the exact timing of our intention formation. If we are, in fact, never aware of a set of deterministic causes for our decisions, this would ground a much more expansive argument for indeterminist choice.

difficult decisions. This assumption makes it easier to claim that in the target cases, we never have access to deterministic sets of causes. (2) That, however, is another assumption—that none of the sets of accessible states provides a deterministic story of the decision. (3) The proposal also assumes that the agent has access to some evidence which is taken as relevant to showing evidence of absence. That is, the evidence of causal influences is being assumed to be relevant to showing the absence of causal determinism. This is akin to the case with the cards—the fact that your friend keeps turning over Kings is relevant to your inference about whether there are Aces. (4) Finally, the inference is only rational if the set of sets—and the states within each set—are randomly selected and representative. Again, this is built into the cases with cards. If you found out that your friend was *not* randomly sampling the cards, then you should be reluctant to draw the inference that there are no Aces. In the case of decision making, the assumption of random sampling of representative sets is such that if there *were* deterministic causes, they would have shown up in our samples of sets.

We should distinguish two different claims here. One claim concerns proper rational inductive inference and the other concerns what people actually do. Our current interest is primarily in what people actually do. But it bears noting that this proposal, given assumptions like 1–4, does provide a rational inductive basis for inferring indeterminism about decisions. Furthermore, a reasonable case might be made for the propriety of the first three assumptions. Whether this is actually how people come to believe that there are undetermined choices is unknown. But the kind of probabilistic reasoning involved seems to be available in normal humans. An emerging body of evidence indicates that children learn in ways that approximate probabilistic inference (see, e.g., Xu and Tenenbaum 2007; Gerken 2010; Dawson and Gerken 2011; Xu and Kushnir 2013). So although the statistical learning explanation of the belief in indeterminism is still a how possible story, it's a how possible story that has some roots in the actual. Furthermore, in the absence of any other explanation, this how possible story is a good candidate for a how actual story.

Obviously the account of the indeterminist intuition I've offered in this section and the previous one share a common core. On both accounts, the belief in indeterminism is inferred from the fact that we do not perceive a set of deterministic causes for our decisions. Despite this commonality, the accounts have different advantages as hypotheses about why people believe in indeterminism. An advantage of the inductivist account is that it doesn't require a strong assumption of transparency. So long as we think that the sets are randomly selected and representative, the fact that we don't find a set of deterministic causes in any of the sets counts as reason to think that difficult decisions aren't determined. Unless you think that the deterministic sets of causes are being systematically hidden from you, the right statistical inference is that decisions aren't determined. An advantage of the deductivist account in the previous section is that it can generate an inference to indeterminism from a single decision. Given a relatively strong default assumption of introspective transparency, one can infer indeterminism from inspecting just one decision. All one need do is examine the features of a single decision and if one fails to find a deterministic set, then one can infer that indeterminism holds for that decision.

Just as the two accounts have a common core, they have a common vulnerability. And if either of these accounts is the right account for why we believe in indeterminism, then the belief isn't justified. Or so I will now argue.

2.6 Debunking the belief in indeterminist choice

Let's start with the deductivist account. If this is the right story about the origin of the indeterminist intuition, how does it reflect on the epistemic status of the belief in indeterminist choice? The answer depends on the epistemic status of the default assumption that we have access to the causal factors that influence our decisions.

While we do plausibly have access to *some* causal factors in our own decision making, we are ignorant of many of the proximal factors that play a crucial role in generating our decisions. Social psychology has been chronicling the limitations of introspection for decades, and there is a large catalog of effects. Here's a small sampling. In one study, participants primed with words related to rudeness were more likely to interrupt an experimenter than were those primed with words related to politeness. But none of the participants showed any awareness of the effect of the prime (Bargh et al. 1996, 234). In a quite different paradigm, participants were asked to write down the last two digits of their social security number and subsequently given a chance to participate in an auction of fancy chocolates and fine wines. Those for whom the last digits were high made higher bids than those for whom the last two digits were low (Ariely et al. 2003). In yet another paradigm, subjects filled out a questionnaire in a room that either had or lacked a citrusy cleaning smell. They were subsequently moved to another room where they were told to eat a biscuit. Those who had just been exposed to the citrus smell were more likely to clean up the crumbs (Holland et al. 2005). When then asked about whether the smell had affected their decision to clean up the crumbs, none of the subjects said that it had (691). This just scratches the surface of such effects (see, e.g., Doris forthcoming). There are entire traditions of research, like cognitive dissonance, that focus on unconscious influences on thought and action (see Cooper 2007).

There is little dispute, at this point, that there are unconscious influences on our decisions. We do not have complete access to the causal influences on our decisions. How does this bear on the epistemic propriety of the belief in indeterminist choice? Let's return for a moment to Ockham's argument for indeterminism. Ockham seems to have inferred indeterminism from the fact that the introspectively available factors don't determine decisions. However, he only took into account the introspectively available influences on decision making. Was he also expected, on pain of epistemic impropriety, to anticipate introspectively unavailable factors in decision making? Presumably not. In general, until we have reason to think that there *are* hidden factors, it's plausible that we are justified in forming beliefs as if there aren't hidden factors. We now think that sunburn is caused by ultraviolet rays. In the eighteenth century, the prevailing view was that sunburn was caused by the sun's heat (Roelandts 2007). Eighteenth-century heat theorists had neglected the possibility that invisible light caused sunburns. Does that mean that they weren't justified in believing in the heat-theory of sunburn? Light beyond the visible spectrum wasn't even discovered until 1800. It is a harsh epistemology that impugns the justification of eighteenth-century heat theorists on the grounds that they failed to consider the effects of invisible light. Similarly, for Ockham, it seems epistemically harsh to charge him with being unjustified in believing in indeterminist choice on the grounds that he neglected introspectively invisible influences on decision.

Today we know that there are important limits on introspection. At least *some* of the factors that influence our choices are introspectively unavailable to us. This puts us in a much different epistemic situation. Of course, the libertarian might maintain that there are cases of choice in which we do introspect all the causally relevant factors and that in these cases, our belief in indeterminism is true. The extant data don't obviously exclude that possibility.[8] However, given the limits of introspection, we are not justified in trusting introspection on these matters. For we know that introspection misses out on causally important influences. Thus, even if there are deterministic factors that cause our decisions, we cannot expect introspection to tell us. So the fact that we don't introspect a set of deterministic factors doesn't provide grounds for believing that there are not deterministic factors.

A very similar problem attends the epistemic propriety of the belief if it's based on the proposed statistical inference. On the statistical account, our belief in indeterminism derives from inferring the absence of deterministic sets of causes from the absence of evidence of any deterministic sets. As we saw, that inference depends on the assumption that the candidate sets of causes are randomly sampled and representative. This assumption is clearly violated. The entire space of unconscious and lower-level causes is neglected. Again, that neglect wouldn't necessarily impugn the inference for our ancestors and children who are ignorant of psychological science. But for the scientifically literate, it is beyond dispute that there are unconscious psychological factors that influence our decisions; and it is quite possible that our decisions are also causally influenced by neural processes that do not correspond to any psychological kinds. Insofar as unconscious and lower-level factors are systematically excluded from the introspectively available sets of causal influences, we know that it is unwarranted in this case to infer indeterminism from the lack of evidence of determinism.

I've offered two candidate explanations for why we believe in indeterminist choice. The accounts aren't actually in competition with each other, but if either of these explanations is the right account, we can

---

[8] Determinists like Leibniz insist that there must be hidden factors that take up the slack. But this is driven by a prior commitment to determinism and begs the question against libertarians.

mount a debunking argument against the common belief in indeterminist decision making. For on both accounts, our belief in indeterminism arises from false presuppositions about the evidence we get from introspection. As a matter of fact, we don't perceive a deterministic set of causes for many of our decisions. If people use this to infer that our decisions aren't determined, then the inference is defective. For we now know that introspection systematically fails to detect important proximal influences on decisions. So if the belief that our choices aren't determined really does come from processes like the ones I've described, then we are not justified in believing that choice is indeterminist. Our intuition of indeterminism counts for nothing.[9]

---

[9] Obviously this debunking argument is targeted at the beliefs of ordinary people. If philosophers or scientists have some other way of inferring that choices are indeterminist, that would not be threatened by the debunking argument. At the same time, philosophers are also *people*, and many of our philosophically significant intuitions likely have the same sources as the intuitions of non-philosophers.

3

Free Will and Error

A growing body of empirical evidence (reviewed in section 1.2) indicates that people think that their choices aren't determined. It is not just that they don't have the belief that their choices are determined. Rather, they positively think that their choices are not determined. And this belief is implicated in their thoughts about free will. For instance, when presented with a description of a deterministic universe, most participants say that in that universe, people don't have free will (Roskies and Nichols 2008; Rose and Nichols 2013). This provides reason to think that the everyday conception of free will is not compatible with determinism.

Libertarians hold that we do make free indeterminist choices. But this is a minority view in philosophy. Perhaps the most enduring traditional philosophical critique is Hobbes' libertarian dilemma. On the one hand, libertarians say that an agent's decision isn't free if the decision is the product of deterministic processes. But on the other hand, if the decision is *not* determined, then it isn't determined by the agent either! That, critics maintain, leaves the libertarian fresh out of intelligible options (for discussion see Kane 1996, 11).[1] As the libertarian dilemma illustrates, libertarian free will can seem decidedly mysterious and counterintuitive (see also Strawson 1986, 1994). These kinds of considerations have always struck me as powerful reasons for doubting libertarianism. Of course, as evidenced by quantum mechanics, some mysterious and counterintuitive views are apparently true. However, our belief in quantum mechanics is based on good independent reasons. This is not the case for the lay belief in indeterminist choice. The lay belief in indeterminist choice, I've suggested

---

[1] Libertarian philosophers, including Kane himself, have developed sophisticated responses to arguments like the libertarian dilemma. I can't engage those responses here. My point is just that arguments like the libertarian dilemma succeed in revealing counterintuitive aspects of libertarian free will.

(Chapter 2), is based on flawed inferences. This debunking argument supplements traditional objections to libertarianism. If we had a good independent reason to think that we have libertarian free will, then the fact that it's mysterious could be viewed as something we simply need to accept. However, our commonsense belief in indeterminist choice is not grounded on good independent reason. Thus, in the absence of some other reason for thinking that our choices are undetermined, we should take the traditional objections to pose a very serious threat to libertarianism.

The foregoing doesn't count as a rigorous argument against libertarianism, but I hope that it suffices to motivate the assumption guiding this chapter. Many philosophers think that libertarian free will doesn't exist—that there is no such thing as libertarian free will. These are obviously *substantive* claims about the metaphysics of free will. I want to explore such eliminativist conclusions, and to do so, I will assume that libertarianism is false. The issue of interest concerns the consequences of folk error on free will, so the issue can only be joined if we grant that there is something interestingly mistaken about the folk view. There are many ways that the folk view might be mistaken. For instance, it might be that the folk view falsely assumes that agents have free will of a sort that contravenes event causation. But to keep things as simple as possible, let's just assume that determinism is true.[2] That means that the folk falsely believe in indeterminism. One last stipulation is required. People use the term "free will" in lots of different ways. For the purposes of this chapter, the term "free will" will be taken to pick out the kind of choice that is presumed to be in conflict with determinism.[3] To summarize: we are assuming that the notion of free will is in error because it falsely presupposes that indeterminism is true. With that large set of assumptions, we can frame the key question: Does free will exist?

---

[2] The main points in this chapter can be made if we assume instead that (i) in addition to the presupposition of indeterminism, people also have a presupposition that choice isn't random and that (ii) all events are either determined or random (cf. Russell 1995, 14; Kane 1996, 11). For the sake of readability, I am taking the simpler assumption that determinism is true.

[3] For this chapter, I'm suspending my usual practice of not using the term "free will" when characterizing lay views. The reason for the suspension is that it facilitates the discussion of free will eliminativism. The eliminativist argument *can* be presented without using the term. For instance, one might frame the argument using the word "choice" rather than "free will." However, since arguments for eliminativism are traditionally framed as philosophical arguments concerning the existence of free will, I give precedence to the traditional terminology.

3.1 Eliminativism and reference

It might seem that I have so thoroughly stacked the deck that it trivially follows from my assumptions that free will doesn't exist. If we take on all those assumptions, then eliminativists can claim an easy victory. However, does the fact that the ordinary notion of free will has a false presupposition entail that there is no free will? Over the last several decades, it has become clear that this is no trivial matter at all. The basic theme has played out over and over in contemporary philosophy. In ethics it appears in the debate over error theory (Mackie 1977; Blackburn 1985); in social–political philosophy, it's found in disputes over the existence of race (Appiah 1995; Andreasen 2000; Mallon 2006); in philosophy of science, it's endemic to debates about scientific realism (Feyerabend 1962; Laudan 1984; Boyd 2002); and in philosophy of mind, we find the theme in debates about eliminative materialism (e.g., Stich 1983; Lycan 1988). In each of these debates, eliminativists maintain that *K doesn't exist* (where *K* might be morality, race, belief, etc.). Typically shortly after an eliminativist claim of this sort is made another group of philosophers adopts a *preservationist* position. In effect, they say, *Ks aren't what we thought they were.*

To set out the problematic, I'll focus on the debate over eliminative materialism, since the critical themes to be discussed here were carefully charted in that debate (see esp. Stich 1983, 1996; Lycan 1988; Bishop and Stich 1998). One central argument for eliminativism went roughly as follows:

   (i) "belief" is a term (or concept) in a folk theory;
   (ii) that folk theory is massively mistaken;
   (iii) therefore, beliefs don't exist.

Stich was characteristically pellucid in his presentation of the argument. He begins by setting out David Lewis' (1972) descriptivist account of how theoretical terms get their meaning and reference from the theory in which they are embedded (Stich 1983, 17–21). A theoretical term refers to whatever object or class of objects satisfies some critical set of claims in the theory. Stich then argues that the folk psychological theory that gives meaning and reference to "belief" is deeply erroneous; from this he concludes that beliefs don't exist. Lewis himself approves of a key component of this argumentative strategy. He writes: "If the names of mental states are like theoretical terms, they name nothing unless the theory . . . is more or less true" (Lewis 1972, 213). The salient difference between Lewis (1972) and Stich (1983) concerns the extent to which the folk theory is true. Unlike Lewis, Stich thinks the folk theory is deeply mistaken and this enables the eliminativist conclusion.

William Lycan reacted to these eliminativist arguments by calling into question the Lewisian account of how the reference of theoretical terms gets determined. Lycan writes:

I am at pains to advocate a very liberal view . . . I am entirely willing to give up fairly large chunks of our commonsensical or platitudinous theory of belief or of desire (or of almost anything else) and decide that we were just wrong about a lot of things, without drawing the inference that we are no longer talking about belief or desire. To put the matter crudely, I incline away from Lewis's Carnapian and/ or Rylean cluster theory of the reference of theoretical terms, and toward Putnam's . . . causal–historical theory. As in Putnam's examples of "water," "tiger," and so on, I think the ordinary word "belief" (qua theoretical term of folk psychology) points dimly toward a natural kind that we have not fully grasped and that only mature psychology will reveal. I expect that "belief" will turn out to refer to some kind of information-bearing inner state of a sentient being, . . . but the kind of state it refers to may have only a few of the properties usually attributed to beliefs by common sense (1988, 31–2).

Lycan promotes a "liberal" view of reference fixing. On the approach to reference fixing adopted by Lycan, the reference of a theoretical term can succeed even if the theory is radically mistaken. For on this theory, (again very roughly) the reference of a theoretical term is the entity or kind that was "baptized" when the term was introduced. As people transmit the term to others, the term continues to refer to the entity or kind that was baptized at the end of that causal–historical chain of transmission. As a result, people can have massive misconceptions about the objects that their terms (or concepts) refer to.[4]

Thus the core of the dispute between eliminativists and preservation-ists seems to be over what is required for a term or concept to refer

---

[4] Although Lycan's liberal view of reference fixing is causal–historical, a descriptivist can be more or less liberal about reference fixing. It all depends on how much of the theory has to be true in order for the term to refer. So the key distinction of interest is between theories of reference that are liberal and those that are conservative. However, for ease of discussion, I will often focus on the causal–historical theory as the key example of a liberal theory and a restrictive descriptivism as the key example of a conservative theory.

successfully (see, e.g., Stich 1996; Bishop and Stich 1998).[5] For instance, the eliminative materialist (e.g., Stich 1983) says,

> There are no such thing as *beliefs*. Of course there are causally efficacious psychological states that are semantically evaluable, but there are no psychological states that have their causal efficacy *in virtue of* their semantic properties.

The preservationist replies:

> There are such things as *beliefs*. After all, even though there are no psychological states that have their causal efficacy *in virtue of* their semantic properties, there are causally efficacious psychological states that are semantically evaluable.

The eliminativist maintains that the fact that the concept of belief has a false presupposition about semantic causal efficacy means that beliefs don't exist. If a descriptivist theory of reference is right, then the fact that the concept of belief is critically associated with a false presupposition provides reason to think the eliminativist is right. The preservationist maintains that the fact that there is this false presupposition isn't enough to entail that beliefs don't exist. The concept of belief can allow for this amount of associated error. If a causal–historical theory of reference is right, then there is reason to think that "belief" continues to refer despite the fact that it is associated with a critical presupposition that is false.

The same kind of analysis applies to debates about eliminativism in the free will literature (e.g., Hurley 2000; Vargas 2005; Pereboom 2009). Grant that determinism is true but that indeterminism is an important element of our folk notion of free will. The free will eliminativist might say:

> Free will doesn't exist; of course there is preference-guided information processing, but everything is determined.

And the preservationist might say:

> Free will does exist; after all, even though everything is determined, there is still preference-guided information processing.

Who is right in this exchange? It seems to depend on how liberal the reference-fixing relation is. If the causal–historical theory is right, then

---

[5] Bishop and Stich (1998; Stich 1996) argue that the appeal to reference in these arguments only works if one assumes a substantive rather than a deflationary account of reference. Since this chapter is already technical enough, let's just assume that the right theory of reference is a substantive one.

it's plausible that "free will" refers successfully despite the false presupposition. If descriptivism is right, then the fact that the concept of free will is critically associated with a false presupposition provides reason to think that "free will" fails to refer and consequently that the eliminativist is right.

3.2 The geography of error

The philosophical space we've been exploring starts with the assumption that some concept is enmeshed in significant error. In the philosophy of free will, the two most prominent reactions to this situation are eliminativism (e.g., Vargas 2005; Pereboom 2001) and "revisionism" (Vargas 2005, 2011, 2013). But these two views do not exhaust the space of possibilities. In this section, I will lay out the philosophical geography more fully (see Figure 3.1). Let's say we agree that some concept has, as part of its associated content, an error. In some cases, the error might be specified. For instance, in metaethics, Mackie maintains that folk morality falsely presupposes that moral statements are objectively true. One might agree that Mackie has identified an error in the folk concept of morality and then proceed to consider whether moral eliminativism follows. That would be a case in which we have a specified error. But in other instances, we might acknowledge that there is an error

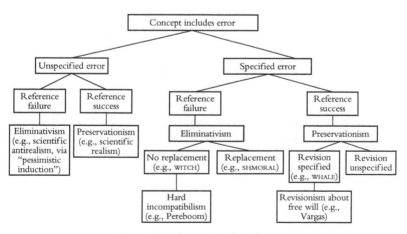

Figure 3.1 The geography of error

associated with a concept, even though we do not know what the error is. Often in science, we have reason to think our theories have errors even when we don't know what the errors are. For instance, current theory surrounding neurotransmitter reuptake channels likely contains significant errors, even though we haven't yet identified them. Thus, the error can be *specified* or *unspecified*, and that provides the first branch in our tree.

For our purposes, the more important issue is whether to draw an eliminativist or a preservationist conclusion. If the associated error yields a failure of reference, then the argument sketched in section 3.1 suggests that eliminativism follows for the kind under consideration. If, however, the associated error does not stand in the way of successful reference, then the preservationist position stands. Let's start with the *unspecified error* branch. Philosophers of science typically acknowledge that current theories likely have a great deal of unspecified error. This admission is a first step in broad-scale anti-realist arguments based on the "pessimistic induction." Prominent versions of this argument explicitly appeal to reference failure. Laudan observes that many theories that were successful in their time are now acknowledged to contain "central terms that (we now believe) were nonreferring" (Laudan 1984, 121). It's widely agreed that the entities posited by those terms, e.g., *phlogiston, caloric, humors,* don't exist. The anti-realist then notes that since our current theories are acknowledged to contain significant error, it's likely that current science is in the same boat—the theoretical terms fail to refer and the posits don't exist. Scientific realists reject this picture. They maintain that the fact that there is a great deal of error in a theory doesn't entail that the theoretical terms fail to refer, and they use this stratagem to defend preservationism. Like Lycan, scientific realists can draw on causal–historical theories of reference to defend the claim that a term can refer successfully even if it is embedded in a theory rife with error (Boyd 1983).

Let's turn now to the *specified error* branch. If we know what the error is, and the concept continues to refer despite the error, then preservationism holds. If we follow the preservationist branch and promote a revised concept, then we have a *revisionist* theory (Vargas 2011).[6] This

---

[6] Revisionism in Vargas' sense requires (1) that the errors are specified and (2) that a specific revision of the concept is offered (Vargas 2011, 460). Preservationism is thus a broader category, since one can be a preservationist even if (1) or (2) doesn't hold. In this chapter, I use the term "revisionism" in Vargas' sense.

approach is familiar. To take a folksy example, in earlier times, the concept WHALE falsely presupposed that whales were fish. Taxonomy kept the label and adjusted the concept, moving WHALE onto the mammal branch. In the free will literature, Manuel Vargas has been the most systematic (and tireless) advocate of revisionism. He argues that the folk notion of free will is error-ridden, but the concept continues to refer; in addition, he proposes a revisionist account of free will on which the critical feature of free will is the capacity to respond to moral considerations (Vargas 2013).[7]

Because of Vargas' careful work, revisionism is the preservationist view that has received the most attention (Fischer et al. 2007; McKenna 2009; Pereboom 2009). But it's possible to be a preservationist even if one doesn't proffer a revision. One might know that a given concept has a specific error associated with it, and preserve the concept without having a revisionist proposal. Call this node "revision unspecified" (Figure 3.1). If we know that the reference relation permits at least the amount of error associated with the concept of interest, then we might promote preservationism even in the absence of a revisionist proposal.[8] For instance, a causal–historical theorist will likely take preservationism as the default position regardless of whether one has developed a specific proposal for a revised concept. This is an important option for contested kind terms like "free will." For it's perfectly sensible to hold a preservationist view about *free will* even if one does not side with any particular revisionist proposal.

On to the eliminativist branch. If the error associated with a term (or concept) yields a failure of reference, then eliminativism seems to follow. In the most familiar cases, eliminativism holds that the target concept is empty and should be entirely discarded. For instance, the concept WITCH falsely presupposed the existence of certain supernatural powers and, on the standard narrative, we have abandoned commitment to the kind picked out by "witch" without looking for a replacement. Hard determinists typically take a similar approach to FREE WILL, maintaining that

---

[7] Vargas' position is actually more nuanced. He proposes two different ways to run revisionism, and I'm focusing on what he calls "connotational revisionism" (Vargas 2013).

[8] This seems to be Lycan's attitude about *belief* when he writes: "I think the ordinary word 'belief' (qua theoretical term of folk psychology) points dimly toward a natural kind that we have not fully grasped and that only mature psychology will reveal" (1988, 32).

there is no such thing as free will and that we should not seek a replacement concept but face the truth. It is, however, available to the eliminativist to proffer a replacement for the empty concept. In *Ethics: Inventing Right and Wrong*, Mackie famously maintains that because moral beliefs falsely presuppose objectivity, the concept of morality is empty and all moral claims are false. Almost equally famously, in that same book, Mackie proceeds to promote what looks very much like a moral philosophy. The apparent inconsistency can be avoided if we suppose that Mackie is replacing our concept, MORAL, with a closely related concept, SHMORAL, that doesn't carry the problematic presupposition of objectivity (see Blackburn 1985, 150).[9] (See Figure 3.1.)

That concludes my cartography of error. But with the map before us, the contrast between replacement-eliminativists and revisionists might seem rather precious. After all, the replacement theorist is free to adopt whatever proposal the revisionist offers for FREE WILL, and the replacement theorist can say that while FREE WILL is an empty concept, the revisionists describe a related concept that is not empty. Indeed, the replacement theorist is even at liberty to adopt a *homonym* to pick out his replacement concept. So what is the fuss about between eliminativists and revisionists? Well, the eliminativist (including the replacement theorist) maintains that there is *no such thing as* free will and that everyone is under the illusion that there is free will. The preservationist (including the revisionist) says that there *is* free will and that everyone has merely been under some misapprehensions about its nature. This seems to be a fundamental ontological disagreement.

3.3 Reference conventions and ontology

It is a tacit assumption behind these eliminativist debates that there is a single correct reference relation to be discovered for a class of terms. Once we figure out the reference relation for the relevant class of terms (e.g., natural kind terms), we can simply apply the theory to the terms and thereby find out whether *belief, race,* and *free will* exist. However, this might just be a mistake. It might be a mistake to assume that there is

---

[9] On Vargas' latest presentation of revisionism, the replacement view would count as "denotational revisionism." As noted earlier, I reserve the term "revisionism" for his "connotational revisionism" (Vargas 2013).

a single reference relation for kind terms. Instead, in different contexts, different reference relationships might be operative. This is a heterodox idea, but it has an advocate in the philosophy of science, and there is a smattering of experimental evidence for this pluralist view. In attempting to explain discourse in the history of science, Philip Kitcher maintains that different reference relations are in play in different contexts. He writes:

> Different tokens of the same type [of term] may be associated with different modes of reference...
> A token's mode of reference is of the *descriptive type* when the speaker has a dominant present intention to pick out something that satisfies a particular description and the referent of the token is whatever satisfies the description. The *baptismal type* is exemplified when the speaker has a dominant present intention to pick out a particular present object (or a set of objects, one member of which may be present) (Kitcher 1993, 77; see also Bishop 1999).

Kitcher goes on to use this approach to reference to analyze episodes in the history of science (101). In some cases, when phlogiston theorists use cognates of "phlogiston," the term is naturally read as tied to a particular description. Priestley writes that if he had burned a pipe "in the open fire, the phlogiston would have escaped" (Priestley 1775 (vol. 2), 251). Here we naturally interpret the reference of "phlogiston" to be fixed by the description *the substance released in combustion*. That description, we now know, is not satisfied by anything—there is no substance released in combustion. Hence, in those contexts, the reference of "phlogiston" is determined by the associated description and the term comes up empty. However, there are other times when Priestley uses cognates of "phlogiston" that seem more naturally interpreted in causal–historical ways. For instance, Priestley reports breathing in "dephlogisticated air" after he had tested its effects on mice. He writes, "I fancied that my breast felt peculiarly light and easy for some time afterwards... Hitherto only two mice and myself have had the privilege of breathing it" (Priestley, 162). We now know that what Priestley and the mice were breathing was *oxygen*, and it's natural to think that *oxygen* is precisely what the term "dephlogisticated air" refers to in this context (Kitcher 1993, 100).[10]

---

[10] In many cases, the presence of systematic ambiguity will not affect the truth of existence claims. For instance, in contemporary chemistry the concept OXYGEN likely refers successfully under both descriptivist and causal–historical reference conventions.

In a recent paper, Ángel Pinillos, Ron Mallon, and I defend this kind of pluralistic approach to reference (Nichols et al., forthcoming). We provide experimental evidence that natural kind terms are systematically ambiguous. In some cases, the reference of a token term is fixed by a descriptivist convention; in other cases, the reference of a token term (of the same type) is fixed by a causal–historical convention. To support the ambiguity theory, we presented participants with descriptions of contested kind terms from natural history, drawn from medieval bestiaries. As we explained to the participants, the cases were real cases. In several different experiments, participants were presented with the following sketch:

In the Middle Ages, animal researchers described a distinctive kind of mammal. They called it catoblepas. The catoblepas was said to be like a bull but with a head so heavy that the animal had to keep its head down at all times. It was also thought that the catoblepas had scales on its back. Of course there is nothing that meets this description, but researchers think that it was based on reports of encounters with wildebeests.

After reading that description of *catoblepas*, participants were presented with some questions that were expected to elicit a descriptivist interpretation and some that were expected to resist a descriptivist interpretation.

Our hypothesis was that if the participants are asked about the *existence* of a kind, this will lead people to apply a descriptivist convention to the kind term. It's a familiar point that the causal–historical theory of reference has difficulties accommodating empty terms (e.g., Devitt and Sterelny 1999). For instance, if the modern use of "Santa Claus" causally traces back to the historical Saint Nicholas, the causal–historical account suggests that "Santa Claus" is Saint Nicholas, and hence Santa Claus exists. By contrast, descriptivism claims that the meaning of a term like "Santa Claus" is given by the associated description, and so it's easy for such a theory to accommodate the sad truth that Santa Claus doesn't exist. The fact that questions about existence make more sense under a descriptivist framework led us to predict that people would be likely to respond as descriptivists when presented with an existence statement. Thus, following the description regarding *catoblepas*, participants were asked to indicate their level of agreement with the sentence "Catoblepas exist." As predicted, people tended to *disagree* with this statement (for related results, see Machery et al. forthcoming).

One reaction to the corroboration of our prediction is that descriptivism is simply the right theory of reference. But we suspected that people could be led to make judgments that are more naturally taken as causal–historical. Given that the description associated with *catoblepas* isn't satisfied by anything, descriptivism entails that the term doesn't refer to anything and thus suggests that *catoblepas* don't exist. Again, the previous result suggests that people did in fact interpret "Catoblepas exist" in this descriptivist way. But there are some sentence forms that actually presuppose existence. When a term occurs in the subject position with predication, there is a presupposition of existence. If I say, "Cannonball's solo on 'So What' was lovely," this presupposes that Cannonball had a solo on "So What." (To say "I disagree" would typically imply that Cannonball had a solo but it wasn't lovely.) However, if I say, "Miles listened to Cannonball's solo on 'So What'," this does not presuppose that Cannonball had a solo on that song. (To say "I disagree" would typically not imply that Cannonball had a solo.) (Cf. Strawson 1950.) Thus, our prediction was that if we placed "catoblepas" in the subject position and predicated something of it, people would be more likely to respond in concert with a causal–historical convention. To test this, after the description regarding *catoblepas*, participants were asked to indicate their level of agreement with the sentence "Catoblepas are wildebeest." As predicted, people tended to *agree* with this sentence (which predicates "are wildebeest" of *catoblepas*). Indeed, even when participants were given *both* sentences, "Catoblepas exist" and "Catoblepas are wildebeest," they agreed more with "Catoblepas are wildebeest" than with "Catoblepas exist."

Thus, ordinary people seem to shift how they think about the reference relation depending on subtle features of discourse. This doesn't mean that people are confused. It can be perfectly right to say that (1) is false and (2) is true:

1. "Catoblepas exist";
2. "Catoblepas are wildebeests."

The different statements are naturally associated with different conventions of reference, so there is no inconsistency.

We used simple statements for our experiments, to keep the design as clean as possible. And we find that existence statements attract descriptivist interpretations of the kind term. But of course we don't mean to suggest that it is impossible to produce an existence statement that attracts a causal–historical interpretation. For instance, if a speaker says, "Catoblepas are wildebeests, so catoblepas exist," the fact that existence statement (1) is part of the statement doesn't make the statement contradictory. Rather, in the context of that utterance, it's plausible that the causal–historical convention is in play and we would want to accept the existence claim (Nichols et al. forthcoming).

Now we can finally get to the issue concerning eliminativism and preservationism about free will. We have been assuming that the folk conception of free will contains significant error. If the foregoing story about the diversity of reference conventions is right, how should we interpret Galen Strawson when he says, "Free will doesn't exist"? Descriptively, of course. He is keying on the false description associated with "free will," and pointing out that nothing meets that description. To interpret Strawson's use of "free will" causally–historically would be manifestly uncharitable. What reference-convention is in place when Manuel Vargas says, "Free will isn't what we thought"? Presumably *not* restrictive descriptivism, or what he says is, by his own lights, false.[11] This allows us to say that Vargas is right and Strawson is also right. It's just that the term "free will" operates with a different reference convention in the different contexts.

This pluralist approach yields a pacifistic answer to the metaphysical debate over the existence of free will. The eliminativist is assuming a demanding convention of reference and so, given that an important presupposition about free will is false, the eliminativist is right to say (under that convention for reference) that there is no such thing as free will. The preservationist, on the other hand, is adopting a more liberal convention of reference, and so the preservationist is right to say (under that convention for reference) that there *is* such a thing as free will despite the false presupposition. This pluralism deflates somewhat the importance of the metaphysical dispute between eliminativists and preservationists. There is no univocal answer on whether eliminativism is true.[12]

---

[11] One option would be to interpret Vargas' statement as deploying a causal–historical reference convention. Another possibility is just that the reference convention in play is descriptivist but is very liberal about how much of the description must be satisfied for reference to succeed.

[12] An obvious way to reject my pacifism is to insist that there is a single correct theory of reference for kind terms, and hence there must be a univocal answer to the eliminativist question. That maneuver reestablishes the battle, but it's a rather different battle—one about the univocal nature of reference.

The pacifistic answer I'm promoting should not obscure the fact that, regardless of which standard for reference we adopt, in giving up the indeterminist dimension of choice, we are rejecting an important and perhaps incorrigible part of the way we ordinarily think of ourselves. It is self-deception to deny that our normal understanding of our decisions is vertiginously problematic. That is the point stressed by the eliminativist. Still, as with other genuine philosophical perplexities (like skepticism), the fact that there is genuine perplexity here doesn't mean we need to obsess on it, and the preservationist can be seen as offering an alternative to obsession.

3.4 Practical interests and illusions

In his classic essay, "Deconstructing the Mind," Stich makes a provocative argument that socio-political factors have shaped metaphysics. His leading example is witches. Stich points out that some contemporary scholars maintain that witches do exist and that they also existed during the Inquisition (e.g., Luhrman 1991). However, witches, according to these theorists, don't do black magic or have pacts with the devil. Stich says that in the comfort of liberal democracies, this is a fine and interesting thing to say. But when faced with witch trials that led to torturing and executing innocent people, Stich suggests that eliminativism provides a more politically effective position:

In sixteenth-century Europe ... people who held the view that none of the women accused of being witches had made a pact with the devil or caused any harm, and that these women ought not to be tortured or put to death, might be much more effective if they insisted that witches are myths—that they simply do not exist—and thus that all of the women accused of being witches are falsely accused. That, near enough, is what many of them did say and what most of us say as well. (1996, 69)

It was a politically powerful move to deny that witches exist, and this might explain how our cultural forebears arrived at witch eliminativism.

I will attempt to build on Stich's insight. But the history is somewhat complicated. In England, the early witch skeptics (e.g., Scot 1584; Ady 1656) were not eliminativists. It's easy to see why: the term "witch" was commonly thought to be used in the Bible, and many of the skeptics did not want to defy scripture (see, e.g., Notestein 1911, 132). Thus, many of the early skeptical attacks did in fact promote the view that witches were not what people thought they were—in particular, witches did not have compacts with Satan. The most important of the early skeptics, Reginald Scot, held that the witches of the Bible included poisoners and illusionists (Scot 1584, 136–7; see also Thomas 1971, 572–3), and he explicitly maintains a preservationist view: "My question is not (as manie fondlie suppose) whether there be witches or naie: but whether they can doo such miraculous works as are imputed unto them" (Scot 1584, 15).[13]

Within a society deeply committed to scripture, to defend witch-eliminativism required arguing that the Bible did not quantify over witches. This was overtly done in the later seventeenth century. The first chapter of John Wagstaffe's book is entitled "That the Bible hath been falsely translated in those places which speak of witchcraft" (1671, 1). Rejecting any biblical witches makes available the option of denying the existence of witches outright, and that's exactly what Wagstaffe (83–4) and later skeptics (e.g., Hutchinson 1718, 229) did. These later skeptics, of course, won the day and witch-eliminativism prevails (Notestein 1911, 343).

It remains unclear whether the success of witch-eliminativism was facilitated by the political effectiveness of eliminativism for abolishing witch trials. To be sure, all of the skeptical writings (both preservationist and eliminativist) reflected a deep concern about the welfare of those accused of being witches. In any case, what is quite clear is that both eliminativism and preservationism were in play in the seventeenth century. And it's not hard to imagine history having played out in the preservationist fashion, retaining commitment to non-supernatural witches. Indeed, the term "magician" provides a closely related counter-point to "witch." In the Middle Ages, *magicians* were regarded as individuals with supernatural powers (e.g., Thomas 1971, 41).[14] Yet we now use that term with no supernatural commitment. For *witch*, we fixed the

---

[13] Scot thinks that people accused of being "witches" in England are not witches in any biblical sense at all: "But as for our old women, that are said to hurt children with their eies, or lambs with their lookes, or that pull downe the moone out of heaven, or make so foolish a bargaine, or doo such homage to the divell; you shall not read in the bible of any such witches, or of any such actions imputed to them" (137).

[14] For uses of "magicians" as supernatural, see King James I (1597, 31), Casaubon (1670, 111), and Boulton (1715, 33). For uses of "magicians" in roughly the modern sense, see Wagstaffe (1671, 23) and Webster (1677, 166–7).

reference convention such that the supernatural component is essential, affording an eliminativist view; for *magician*, we adopted a much more liberal reference fixing convention.[15]

Although the actual historical role of practical interests is unclear, it is very plausible that practical interests can have important effects on ontological claims about witches and magicians. Nonetheless, although practical interests can plausibly affect which statements about free will (or witches) are true, it would be more constructionism than I can credit to think that this settles a deep metaphysical question about free will (or witches). When we apply practical interests to fix a reference convention, we are affecting which sentences are true, but we are not descrying the structure of reality.

I've been arguing that there are different reference conventions available for kind terms. History provides examples in which we have taken a restrictive reference convention (e.g., *witch*) as well as examples in which we have taken a liberal reference convention (e.g., *magician*). It is a matter of considerable historical interest why we adopt one convention rather than another. But, borrowing from Stich, it does seem likely that practical considerations can impact which conventions we adopt. In addition, if Pinillos, Mallon, and I are right about the availability of different reference conventions, then there need be no mistake in adopting one convention or the other (Nichols et al. forthcoming). As a result, we might appeal to practical interests in deciding which convention to adopt and impose.

To return to free will, Strawson says, "Free will doesn't exist" or "Free will is an illusion." Vargas says, "Free will does exist" or "Free will is no illusion." Each is right, under the appropriate reference fixing convention.

---

[15] This parallels examples from the history of science. Historically, we have come to associate "phlogiston" with "the substance emitted in combustion." We have fixed that description as the reference convention. Since nothing is emitted in combustion, it follows (given this way of fixing reference) that "phlogiston" doesn't refer. We went exactly the opposite direction with "atom." In keeping with earlier atomic theories, Dalton maintained that atoms are indivisible. (As Kitcher has it, "Almost everything Dalton maintained about atoms is wrong" (1993, 106).) When chemists like Rutherford discovered that Dalton's "atoms" were divisible, one option would have been to claim that atoms don't exist, adopting the reference convention that welds indivisibility to "atom" (it is the etymology after all). Alternatively, Rutherford could have said that even if there are atoms, atoms are not what Dalton and co. were studying. Instead, Rutherford opted for a preservationist view on which one says, "Atoms aren't what we thought they were. Turns out they're divisible."

If practical concerns can be recruited to determine which reference convention to adopt, this might provide a new kind of argument for preservationism or eliminativism.

There is a growing body of work that suggests that telling people that they don't have free will has negative social consequence (e.g., Vohs and Schooler 2008; Baumeister et al. 2009). The experiments have their limitations, but they are certainly suggestive enough to merit consideration. In one study, participants in the *no free will* condition were told things like the following: "Science has demonstrated that free will is an illusion" and "Like everything else in the universe, all human actions follow from prior events and ultimately can be understood in terms of the movement of molecules." These participants indicated that they were less willing to engage in prosocial behavior (e.g., let a classmate use their cellphone) than participants who were either given no information on free will or information that affirmed the existence of free will (Baumeister et al. 2009). More generally, telling myself that there is no free will is likely to interfere with my productivity (there is practical benefit in the chant of the Little Engine that Could). By contrast, telling myself "it's my free choice whether I do it" is plausibly productive, even when I think that the notion of "free choice" is enmeshed in error.

These considerations are far from decisive, but they provide some reason to think that it can be in our practical interests to be preservationists about the notion of free will. Proclaiming, "Free will is an illusion!" will likely impede the production of valued behavior. And, as noted, we can proclaim instead, "Free will is no illusion!" without running rationally afoul. Since a liberal reference convention is available, we can simply adopt such a convention for the reference of "free will."[16] We can do this, it should be emphasized, even if we refrain from embracing a specific revisionist proposal. We can just maintain that our ordinary notion of free will can successfully refer despite the associated error (cf. Lycan on *belief*).

[16] Some of Vargas' arguments for revisionism also work as practical reasons for adopting a preservationist-friendly reference convention. For instance, Vargas maintains that the affirmation of free will tends "to contribute to our better perceiving and appropriately responding to moral considerations" (2007, 155–6). Insofar as we want to facilitate perceiving and responding to moral considerations, this would provide a practical reason for preservationism. (Vargas actually makes this point about the "responsibility-characteristic practices, attitudes, and judgments," but he would include the affirmation of "free will" among that set of practices, attitudes, and judgments.)

There is thus some evidence of practical advantages to sustaining preservationism about free will. But there are also practical advantages to adopting eliminativism. As Tamler Sommers notes, the denial of free will can undercut an ugly self-righteousness: "Recognizing that all the people whom we love, respect and cherish, including ourselves, do not deserve praise for being who we are may help to lessen the disdain and contempt we sometimes feel for those who are not fortunate enough to make it into this charmed circle" (Sommers 2007, 15). Sommers also suggests that denying free will can help to assuage pathological guilt, "the kind of morbid hand-wringing that keeps us awake all night thinking about what might have been" (Sommers 2007, 14). Indeed, invoking determinism is an explicit strategy in some prominent behavioral therapies. Wolpe and Lazarus (1966) write, "Since the patient has had no choice in becoming what he is, it is incongruous to blame him for having gone awry." Patients wracked by self-blame should, on this view, be counseled that "human behavior is subject to causal determinism no less than that of billiard balls or ocean currents" (Wolpe and Lazarus 1966, 16; see also Wolpe 1990, 59; Robertson 2010). Although self-blame might sometimes be beneficial, at the neurotic end of the spectrum, it is a powerful hindrance to well-being. The recognition that we lack ultimate control might well moderate those reactions.

These practical considerations favor adopting the eliminativist view and proclaiming, "Free will *is* an illusion!" The refrain is familiar now—this proclamation is rationally available to us as a function of adopting a particular reference convention for "free will." Just as eighteenth-century English scholars came to identity the reference convention of "witch" as fixed by the description *human with satanically derived supernatural powers*, so we might decide to fix the reference convention for "free will" with the description "indeterministic choice" or perhaps "causa sui." Given our assumption that determinism is true, that reference convention would ground eliminativism.

Thus, practical interests can be brought to bear on both sides of the free will debate. There are practical advantages to preservationism and also to eliminativism. Where next? Do we just calculate which view has the greatest practical advantage and then adopt and impose the appropriate reference convention? Perhaps we don't need a univocal answer. We might be *discretionary* in whether we adopt compatibilism or incompatibilism. When it serves our interests to affirm free will, we can do so; when it serves our interests to deny free will, we can do that. There need be no inconsistency here. We have available different ways of thinking about reference conventions; in some contexts we think liberally, in others, restrictively. As a result, we can be strategic about the conventions we adopt when it comes to "free will," adopting preservationism in some contexts and eliminativism in others.

Can we sustain this kind of two-faced strategic approach to free will? Maybe not. But given how much we excel at hypocrisy (e.g., Valdesolo and DeSteno 2007), it seems like we are quite capable of keeping two books, shifting according to what serves our interests. Indeed, people's beliefs concerning free will change depending on whether they want to punish a person (Clark et al. forthcoming). This kind of motivated reasoning is no doubt morally inappropriate in some contexts. But what's important for our purposes is that it reveals *flexibility* in free will beliefs. And that gives reason to think that a strategic discretionary approach is psychologically possible. In the case of free will, I've argued, our interests are sometimes best served by eliminativism and other times best served by preservationism. So if we can manage to be elastic in our practices, it would serve our interests to do so.

In this chapter, I've argued that the statement "Free will exists" is true under some available reference conventions and false under others. As a result, in some contexts, the statement is true—because in some contexts the right way to think about the reference of "free will" is liberal about associated mistakes; in other contexts, the statement is false—because the right way to think about the reference of "free will" in some contexts is restrictive about associated mistakes. Since it's reasonable to interpret the eliminativist as adopting a restrictive convention for fixing reference, his claim that free will *doesn't exist* is true; it's reasonable to interpret the preservationist as adopting a liberal convention, so his claim that free will *does exist* is true. My secondary objective in this chapter has been to promote a discretionary (in)compatibilism on which we can be strategic in embracing eliminativism in some contexts and preservationism in others, based on what serves our practical interests. We have good practical reasons for embracing preservationism in some contexts and eliminativism in others. The diversity of reference conventions makes this expedient possible.

PART II

Moral Responsibility

4

Incompatibilism: Intuitive and Isolated

The first half of this book focused on agency: lay views about agency, whether those views are well grounded, and possible ontological implications of concluding that agency isn't what we thought. I now turn to issues about moral responsibility. As before, we will begin with the purely descriptive project. What are the lay commitments surrounding moral responsibility? This chapter aims to address that question. I will argue that people tend to be committed to the incompatibilist view that determinism undermines moral responsibility. But this is hardly the only plank in the folk theory of responsibility. There are numerous considerations that moderate our attributions of responsibility. Moreover, these additional considerations do not derive, psychologically, from the incompatibilist commitment. Rather, I'll argue, the other moderators of blame are independent strands in our moral thought.

The path through this chapter is somewhat twisty. I begin by arguing that incompatibilism is intuitive. But this is just one element of our folk view of responsibility. Another salient element is the intuition that manipulated agents aren't responsible. This intuition that manipulation is exonerating provides the basis for an argument for incompatibilism. I'll argue that it's problematic to rely on this intuition to support incompatibilism since the intuition is in fact driven by the presence of a third-party manipulator. Thus, there is no straight inference from this intuition to incompatibilism. More generally, I will argue that the incompatibilist intuition is isolated from the rest of the folk theory of responsibility. The fact that incompatibilism is isolated matters because it means that deleting incompatibilism from our theory of responsibility need not carry with it the deletion of any of the other elements.

4.1 Folk incompatibilism

Much work on free will seeks to establish that moral responsibility is incompatible with determinism. The arguments typically appeal to intuitions. In professional philosophy, the intuitions are typically not direct intuitions of incompatibilism. For instance, Van Inwagen appeals to intuitions about the transfer of non-responsibility, and Pereboom appeals to intuitions about manipulation. But if incompatibilism is intuitive, that itself counts as an important consideration in favor of the incompatibilist thesis. We might want to debunk it, or we might want to overthrow it. But if incompatibilism is intuitive, then we have to reckon with it in some way.

4.1.1 Natural incompatibilism

A number of studies have indicated that people do indeed regard determinism as undermining moral responsibility. I'll start with the briefest review of some of the findings, but we will see a broader array of results as we consider objections to the initial studies.

Several years ago, Josh Knobe and I presented participants with a description of a causally determinist universe, A, and a description of another universe, B, that was very similar to A, except that in Universe B, human decisions are not causally determined. After the description of the universes (see section 1.2), participants read a summary of the difference:

The key difference, then, is that in Universe A every decision is completely caused by what happened before the decision—given the past, each decision *has to happen* the way that it does. By contrast, in Universe B, decisions are not completely caused by the past, and each human decision *does not have to happen* the way that it does.

Following this, participants were asked, "In Universe A, is it possible for a person to be fully morally responsible for their actions?" Most participants gave an incompatibilist response—they denied that people could be fully morally responsible in that universe (Nichols and Knobe 2007). Indeed, incompatibilist responses were even found in a cross-cultural study with participants from India, Hong Kong, Colombia, and the United States (Sarkissian et al. 2010). In all four of these cultures, the majority of subjects claimed that it is not possible for people to be fully morally responsible in a deterministic universe. Nor is this basic finding just a peculiar effect of the words "fully morally responsible"—participants also say that in a deterministic universe, people should not be morally blamed (Roskies and Nichols 2008; see also Misenheimer, 2008; Feltz et al. 2009; Pacer 2010). It's surprising that people have intuitions about this at all. Many, perhaps most, of these participants have never heard of causal determinism before being exposed to the vignettes. And yet people converge—even across cultures—on the view that determinism precludes moral responsibility. The flat-footed interpretation of the results is that people really do have some commitment to incompatibilism, and describing determinism to them affords them the opportunity to express that commitment. I think this flat-footed interpretation is the right one. But we should consider some alternatives.

4.1.2 Challenging the interpretation

The evidence indicates that, when presented with a description of a causally deterministic universe, people tend to respond as incompatibilists—they deny that agents are morally responsible in such a universe. But it's possible that these responses should not be taken at face value. The issue, at this juncture, is whether these responses should be taken to reflect what people really think. It is not, at this point, to evaluate whether people *should* think that. Is there reason to think that the apparently incompatibilist responses are really superficial, such that we shouldn't take the responses to reflect any real commitment to incompatibilism? There are several ways to challenge the flat-footed interpretation that the results show that people are incompatibilists. I'll canvas the three most significant challenges and argue that none of them is convincing.

4.1.2.1 HOT VS. COLD COGNITION

Numerous studies have shown that descriptions of determinism elicit incompatibilist responses. However, for some kinds of questions, people give compatibilist responses. For instance, people tend to give compatibilist responses if they are presented with a case of a horrifying moral violation.[1] In one study, participants were presented again with the

---

[1] People also tend to give compatibilist responses when determinism is characterized in ways that do not emphasize causal inevitability. For instance, the scenarios in Nahmias et al. (2006) emphasize perfect predictability, and they get generally compatibilist responses (see also Nahmias and Thompson forthcoming). In work that emphasizes causal inevitability we generally find incompatibilist responses (e.g., Nichols and Knobe 2007; Feltz et al. 2009; Sarkissian et al. 2010; Rose and Nichols forthcoming).

descriptions of the two universes and then told that in Universe A, a man named Bill deliberately burns his family to death. In that case, most people claim that Bill *is* fully morally responsible for killing his family, even though the scenario is set in a determinist universe.

There are, of course, many differences between the question "Is it possible for people to be morally responsible?" and "Is Bill [the family murderer] morally responsible?" One plausible explanation for the different responses is that the latter question is emotionally freighted. If that candidate explanation is right—that the emotional response drives the compatibilist judgment—does that mean that the responses in the unemotional cases should be dismissed?[2]

There is no *general* conclusion about the propriety of a judgment to be drawn simply on the basis of whether or not emotion affected the judgment. In some cases, emotions plausibly improve response. Emotions can increase personal engagement with a task, and when material is more personally engaging, people process it more deeply. In one representative study, undergraduate subjects were shown arguments that advocated decreasing privileges in dorms. One group was told that the arguments were for a policy that would apply to their own university; the other group was told that the policy was for another university. Those who thought the issue concerned their own university were significantly more successful at evaluating the quality of the arguments than those in the group with less personal involvement (Petty and Cacioppo 1979). Thus, insofar as emotions increase one's involvement in a task, emotion can lead to less superficial responses.

Although emotions can sometimes enhance decision making, emotion can also be the source of bias. One particularly compelling demonstration of this comes from Jennifer Lerner et al. (1998). They first induced anger in participants by having them watch a movie clip of a bully beating up a school kid. The participants were then taken to another room and given a completely unrelated questionnaire with vignettes concerning a parking attendant, a construction worker, and a used car salesman. These agents were all blameworthy in some way. For instance, the used car salesman withheld information from a customer, leading to costly repairs for the purchaser. The details are less interesting than the

---

[2] I am just assuming for present purposes that the murderer case is more emotionally arousing and that this amplifies blame, though this has not been tested.

result. Despite the fact that the vignettes were completely unrelated to the movie clip, the participants who had been induced to feel anger allotted more blame and punishment to the characters in the vignettes. In this case, it's extremely plausible that the emotion is operating as a bias. Indeed, Lerner et al. found that they could make the bias disappear by telling participants that after completing the surveys, they would have to explain their judgments. Apparently, when participants expect to have to justify their evaluations, considered judgment prevails over the affective bias.

The preceding cases illustrate that the mere fact that emotions affect a judgment does not tell us whether the judgment is appropriate. In some cases, emotions improve judgment; in other cases, emotions distort judgment. How should we think about the suggestive evidence on emotions and compatibilist judgment? Should we dismiss the incompatibilist responses to the emotionally flat presentation? Should we dismiss the compatibilist responses to the emotionally freighted presentation?

There are empirical reasons to think we should dismiss the compatibilist responses to the emotionally freighted cases. These same sorts of cases trigger blame judgments even when most of us (including compatibilists) would not regard the agent as blameworthy. Mandelbaum and Ripley presented participants with a case in which a person's behavior is determined by a "neurological illness" outside of the agent's control. When asked an emotionally bland question about the agent's responsibility for "a certain behavior," people tend to rate the agent as not being responsible. But when presented with the emotionally freighted case of rape, participants are much more likely to say that the agent is responsible (reported in De Brigard et al. 2009). Most of us, when calm, cool, and collected, would not think this agent blameworthy. And so it seems to be a feature of this kind of emotional case that it generates blame judgments in a way that neglects exculpating factors. That is, it's plausible that, just as in the Lerner studies, the elicitation of emotion by these cases biases our normal evaluative judgments, leading us to blame in cases where—by our own lights—blame is inappropriate. There are different ways this can occur. One possibility is that emotions just overpower our judgment, such that we give a ballistic blame response. A quite different possibility is that the emotions lead us to reinterpret the situation in ways that defy the description of the case. That is, because we feel anger at the agent, this might lead us to disbelieve that

the neurological illness *really* caused the harmful behavior. Much motivated reasoning has this kind of character—our motivation leads us to
biased reinterpretations of situations (see, e.g., Kunda 1999). In either
case, the emotions are leading us away from our considered judgments.
   The foregoing gives some reason to reject the current challenge. The
fact that highly emotional cases elicit attributions of responsibility under
determinism does not show that we should take these responses as
reflecting our true moral commitments. For the very same kind of highly
emotional cases elicit attributions of responsibility even in cases where
our true moral commitments deny responsibility. In addition, there is no
positive evidence that when cases are less emotional this leads to defective judgments. That is, there is no explanation of exactly how the low-
emotional content leads to inaccurate judgment.[3] There might be other
reasons to think that the judgments in the emotionally bland cases are
defective (see the following subsection), but the fact that strong emotions
are not implicated does not, by itself, look like a reason to dismiss these
judgments.

4.1.2.2 ABSTRACT VS. CONCRETE

In the previous section, I focused on the possible role of emotion in
explaining responses to deterministic scenarios. But there is another
distinction between the emotionally bland and the emotionally loaded
cases. The former cases are *abstract*—they ask a very general question
about the propriety of blame in a deterministic universe. The question about
the family murderer, on the other hand, is more concrete—a particular
individual and action is specified. Does the fact that incompatibilist
responses are elicited by abstract formulations provide reason to discount it?
   As with the presence vs. absence of emotion, there is no general
answer about whether abstract or concrete presentations elicit more
informative and reflective responses. In some cases, abstract formulations are less likely to trigger errors. Consider Tversky and Kahneman's
notorious Linda example (1983). In their study, participants are given a
description of Linda as a single, outspoken woman who majored in
philosophy and was concerned with discrimination. After reading the

---

[3] A longer treatment of these issues can be found in the discussion of "affective
competence" in Nichols and Knobe 2007.

description, people rated the statement "Linda is a feminist bank teller" as more probable than the independent statement "Linda is a bank teller." But of course A & B cannot be more probable than B: if Linda is a feminist bank teller she must also be a bank teller. Tversky and Kahneman dub this the "conjunction fallacy," and on their model, people make this mistake because the case triggers the "representativeness heuristic." The description of Linda is seen as representative of feminists, and people then judge a feminist bank teller as a better match for Linda than a bank teller. Obviously in order for the representativeness heuristic to get triggered, concrete details are required. The content of the case sets up judgments that Linda's description is representative of feminists. Without that concrete association, people shouldn't make the error. If you just ask people whether A & B is sometimes more likely than B, few people will commit the conjunction fallacy. As a result, by providing a more abstract formulation of the question, fewer errors of this sort can be expected. And once this way of presenting the case is brought to people's attention, responses to the Linda case are revised. The concrete details of the Linda case trigger a probability assessment that is—by the subjects' own lights—a mistake.

So, in some cases, people will be less error-prone when given a more abstract description. In other cases, however, concrete cases likely elicit the responses that we take to reflect a basic competence. Stock examples come from judgments about grammar. Consider an abstract statement like the following: "A proper name must come before any pronoun that is linked to it." Many English speakers would likely assent to this abstract claim. But competent speakers also tend to think that the following sentence is well formed: "Before he gave the lecture, Mark prepared the microphone." The judgment about the abstract principle is at odds with the intuition about the concrete sentence. Linguists would maintain it is the intuition about the concrete sentence that reflects the fundamental grammatical competence; the opinion about the abstract principle reflects a superficial thought about grammar, and this superficial thought should be disregarded.

Again, it's impossible to make any general claims about whether we should favor responses to an abstract or concrete question. Fortunately, in the present case we don't need to decide. We've seen that several studies attract incompatibilist responses from abstract questions. There are also several studies that use concrete cases and still get incompatibilist responses. For instance, in one study, participants were given a concrete case involving a tax cheat. When the case is set in an indeterminist universe, people judge the agent to be morally responsible, but when the case is set in a determinist universe, people judge that the agent is *not* morally responsible (Nichols and Knobe 2007; see also Feltz et al. 2009).[4] The fact that people give incompatibilist responses to both abstract and concrete cases counts against the idea that incompatibilism is a superficial response to abstraction.

4.1.2.3 BYPASSING

The most important challenge for a flat-footed interpretation of incompatibilist responses is that people aren't affirming incompatibilist responses at all (Nahmias et al. 2007; Nahmias and Murray 2010; Murray and Nahmias 2014). Instead, when people deny responsibility it's because they misunderstand the description of determinism. In particular, people mistakenly interpret the description of determinism to mean that our mental states lack causal efficacy. Nahmias and colleagues call this "bypassing," and characterize it as follows: "An agent's mental states are bypassed when she ends up doing what she does regardless of what they are" (Murray and Nahmias 2014, 440). The proposal is that people conflate determinism with bypassing, and this is what leads people to deny responsibility in deterministic scenarios.

Of course, if people's mental states have no impact on their behavior, that is an excellent reason to think that people aren't morally responsible for their behaviors. So, if people interpret determinism as entailing bypassing, it is perfectly rational for them to infer the lack of responsibility from bypassing. However, it seems to be a flat-out confusion to think that determinism entails bypassing. Even if determinism is true,

---

[4] In our original task, Knobe and I treated the tax-cheat case as "low affect" and compared it with a "high affect" case involving a serial rapist. We found that people were more likely to give a compatibilist response to the rapist case (Nichols and Knobe 2007, 676). Subsequent studies have found that people give incompatibilist responses even to the rapist case (Feltz and Cova forthcoming). It's unclear what explains the different responses in these different studies. One possibility is that the original result was just a fluke. Another possibility is that although the "high affect" case was sufficiently upsetting for the original group we studied (University of Utah undergraduates), it is not sufficiently upsetting for the other groups that have been studied. But in any case, the point of the present section is actually reinforced by Feltz and Cova's analysis. For they find that people tend to give incompatibilist responses to an even wider range of concrete cases than previously thought.

our behavior might be caused (not bypassed) by our mental states. Thus, if people give incompatibilist responses because they think determinism entails bypassing, then people's responses don't reflect a real commitment to incompatibilism. It isn't the contemplation of *determinism* that leads people to deny responsibility; rather, it is the contemplation of *bypassing*.

Strikingly, people *do* make bypassing judgments when given a description of causal determinism. For instance, when presented with a description of a determinist universe, many participants agreed that in that universe, "what a person wants has no effect on what they end up doing." In addition, bypassing responses are correlated with the denial of moral responsibility and free will (MR/FW) (Murray and Nahmias 2014). This provides support for the *Bypassing Model*, which we can depict as follows:

Description of Determinism → Bypassing Judgment → Denial of MR/FW

On this model, apparently incompatibilist responses are really a product of the mistaken interpretation of the description of a determinist universe. The only reason people deny moral responsibility is because they conflate determinism with bypassing.

Although the Bypassing Model presents an important alternative, the situation turns out to be more complicated—and more interesting—than the model suggests. First, people do not make a global bypassing confusion about determinism. When it comes to natural processes like volcanoes, people don't take determinism to mean that the prior physical events have no effect on whether a volcano occurs (Deery et al. 2013). In effect, people say even if determinism is true, the occurrence of a volcano depends on physical processes that precede the volcano. Moreover, people don't even make bypassing judgments about computers. Participants were presented with a description of a deterministic universe and asked to imagine that the universe includes computers that operate with programs and data; participants were then asked to indicate whether in that universe "the computers' programs and data have no effect on what they end up being caused to do." People tended to *disagree* with that statement, suggesting that they do *not* think that bypassing holds for computer programs. Similar results obtain for questions about facial expressions. Participants tended to deny that in the deterministic universe, "people's emotions have no effect on what facial expressions they end up making" (Knobe forthcoming). People recognize that even if determinism is true, emotions causally influence facial expressions.

The pattern of effects poses a puzzle. People don't globally confuse determinism with bypassing—they don't make bypassing mistakes for physical events, computers, or facial expressions. So why do people make the bypassing judgments about mental states and decision? David Rose and I recently tried to answer this question. First, we propose an alternative to the Bypassing Model—the Incompatibilist Model:

Description of Determinism→ Denial of FW →Bypassing Judgment

On this model, the bypassing judgments occur downstream from judgments about moral responsibility and free will. That is, people don't draw an incompatibilist conclusion because they confuse determinism and bypassing; rather, they draw a bypassing conclusion as a result of denying free will.

These models are *causal* models. The Bypassing Model says that judgments of bypassing cause denials of free will and responsibility; the Incompatibilist Model says that denial of free will cause bypassing judgments. One prominent approach to adjudicating between such models is to subject the data to causal modeling algorithms. There have been major advances in causal modeling over the last 20 years (e.g., Pearl 2000; Spirtes et al. 2000). The algorithms take statistical data and determine which causal model "fits" the data better. Rose and I conducted a version of the Murray and Nahmias bypassing experiment and used a standard causal modeling algorithm to analyze the data.[5] When we ran the algorithm, we found that the best fitting model was—by far—the incompatibilist model (Rose and Nichols 2013; see also Björnsson forthcoming; Chan et al., forthcoming). Indeed, the Bypassing Model didn't fit the data at all. This indicates that judgments of bypassing are caused by the denial of free will rather than the reverse.

The fact that the Incompatibilist Model is the best fitting model helps to rebut the claim that incompatibilist responses are a confusion born of misinterpreting determinism. But we are still left with a major question—why does imagining determinism have this series of effects

---

[5] We used the Greedy Equivalence Search algorithm in Tetrad IV (<http://www.phil. cmu.edu/projects/tetrad/>). For details, see Rose and Nichols 2013.

that culminates in an affirmation of bypassing? Rose and I thought that perhaps it's because determinism poses a much deeper threat (see also Sias unpublished). A recurring feature of teaching the problem of free will is that introductory students will often say that if determinism is true, then no one makes *choices*. Perhaps, then, many people take determinism to undermine the possibility of decisions. They might tend to think of decisions as fundamentally indeterminist. If that's right, then it would make sense to say that under determinism, your mental states have no effects on your decisions—for under determinism, you don't *make* decisions. To test this, we ran another study in which we presented participants with a description of a deterministic universe and just asked them whether people make decisions in that universe. For a contrast case, we also asked whether people add numbers in that universe. We found that almost half of the participants claimed that people in that universe *don't* make decisions, which was significantly greater than the proportion of participants who said that people don't add numbers in the deterministic universe. Indeterminism seems to be built into the way many people conceive of decision making.[6]

As philosophers, we are so accustomed to thinking of decision making in compatibilist ways that it is tempting to think that the results I've reviewed show that people are even more mistaken about determinism than we thought—if they think determinism precludes decision making, then they are profoundly confused. However, this is far too uncharitable. People can, of course, think about decisions the way philosophers and economists do. The basic idea of expected utility theory is surely available to ordinary people. So the point is not that people are incapable of thinking about compatibilist forms of decision making. Rather, the point is that the way people ordinarily think of decisions—of choice— is deeply at odds with determinism. In light of this, it actually makes sense for people to endorse bypassing under determinism. To see why, consider a different case. Assume that determinism is true. Now consider the following statement: "Random processes have no effect on people's behavior." That statement seems right, under the assumption of

---

[6] We used causal modeling to explore the relation between bypassing judgments and judgments about existence. We found that the best fitting model was one in which judgments about the nonexistence of decisions drive judgments of bypassing rather than the reverse. For details, see Rose and Nichols 2013, study 2.

determinism. If determinism is true, then behavior isn't affected by random processes since there *are no* random processes. Similarly, people claim that under determinism, decisions have no effect on behavior because there *are no* decisions. This pattern of results also explains why people *don't* make bypassing judgments about volcanoes, computers, or facial expressions. The occurrence of volcanoes, information processing, and facial reactions is not challenged by determinism. The challenge is much more specific; it applies distinctively to decision making. The bypassing experiments—far from showing that people aren't really incompatibilists—serve to indicate just how deep incompatibilism goes.

The Incompatibilist Model that Rose and I defend is focused on free will, not moral responsibility. But this model might help explain why people also think determinism undermines moral responsibility. For *decisions* are a primary target of our practices of allocating blame and moral responsibility.[7] And the results we've seen in this section indicate that the very notion of decision is in tension with determinism. Thus, insofar as we hold people responsible for decisions, determinism is in tension with holding people morally responsible. We hold people responsible for their decisions, and we conceive of decisions as indeterminist. But if determinism is true, then they aren't making decisions as we conceive of them. We are holding them responsible for something—indeterminist decision making—that they aren't doing if determinism is true.

The aim of this section has been to provide a descriptive account of folk views about determinism and moral responsibility. The extant results provide support for the view that there is a deep strand of incompatibilism in folk views of free will and moral responsibility. The most powerful challenge to this idea—the evidence that people infer bypassing from determinism—turns out to provide some of the most surprising evidence in favor of folk incompatibilism. People's incompatibilist responses don't emerge from some arbitrary fluke about the cases. Rather, determinism threatens the very notion of decision. This finding in turn can help explain why people think that determinism threatens moral responsibility. Insofar as determinism threatens the idea that

---

[7] As philosophers since Hume have observed, we do make normative evaluations even when no decisions are involved, e.g., with natural talents and defects. However, this does not alter the fact that (at least) much of our practice of attributing moral responsibility is keyed to decisions.

people make decisions, it would, a fortiori, undermine the idea that they can be morally responsible for their decisions.

4.2 Other aspects of folk responsibility

Incompatibilism is one aspect of folk attitudes about responsibility. But it is hardly the only one. P. F. Strawson, in discussing the various considerations that blunt our moral reactions, provides a list of reasons for withholding or attenuating blame. He distinguishes two groups:

> To the first group belong all those which might give occasion for the employment of such expressions as "He didn't mean to", "He hadn't realized", "He didn't know"; and also all those which might give occasion for the use of the phrase "He couldn't help it", when this is supported by such phrases as "He was pushed", "He had to do it", "It was the only way", "They left him no alternative", etc. . . . The agent was just ignorant of the injury he was causing, or had lost his balance through being pushed or had reluctantly to cause the injury for reasons which acceptably override his reluctance.

For the second group, he distinguishes two subgroups:

> In connection with the first subgroup we may think of such statements as "He wasn't himself", "He has been under very great strain recently", "He was acting under post-hypnotic suggestion"; in connection with the second, we may think of "He's only a child", "He's a hopeless schizophrenic", "His mind has been systematically perverted", "That's purely compulsive behaviour on his part". Such pleas as these do, as pleas of my first general group do not, invite us to suspend our ordinary reactive attitudes towards the agent, either at the time of his action or all the time.

Before Strawson begins this long list, he writes, "It needs no saying now how multifarious these considerations are." But it is precisely their multifariousness that I want to stress. Here is a partial summary of the factors that Strawson lists as mitigating blame: lack of intent, ignorance, coercion, countervailing values, situational pressures, insanity, and compulsion. There is a smattering of evidence that people do indeed moderate blame in light of these factors[8], but it is not at all controversial that these factors mitigate blame reactions, so I don't propose to review the empirical evidence. I'll ultimately argue that incompatibilism is

---

[8] For example, there is empirical evidence that coercion (Woolfolk et al. 2006), lack of intent (Shaver 1985), and lack of knowledge (Young et al. 2010) moderate attributions of blame.

independent of these multifarious factors. But there is a further factor that Strawson doesn't mention, and it's one that plays a central role in debates about free will: manipulation. Given its importance in contemporary debates about responsibility, the role of manipulation in ordinary thought requires more extended discussion.

4.3 Manipulation

4.3.1 Manipulation arguments

Imagine that John commits some stereotypically wrong action— mugging an elderly woman. Most people would say that John deserves considerable blame. But now suppose it turns out that all his life, John was a person of upstanding character dedicated to helping others. Yesterday, however, he was kidnapped by the Society Against Senior Citizens and brainwashed so that what he most wanted was to mug old people. In that case, it seems like we don't want to blame John anymore. John was manipulated and this provides prima facie grounds for absolving him from blame. In such cases, the agent seems to be a mere puppet of another agent (Taylor 1983, 44), and how can it be right to hold a puppet responsible?

The raw intuition that manipulation undercuts blame in such cases drives a prominent argument for incompatibilism. Manipulation arguments for incompatibilism have become increasingly sophisticated, but for our purposes, a simple version will suffice.[9] The basic argument is (1) if an agent is manipulated to have the character that he does, he isn't responsible, and (2) there are no morally relevant differences between such manipulated agents and ordinary agents in a determinist universe, thus, (3) agents in a deterministic universe aren't responsible. There is a large literature on manipulation arguments (e.g., Fischer 2004; Mele 2005; Pereboom 2001). But for present purposes, I want to focus just on the initial intuition that the manipulation of an agent absolves him of moral responsibility.

---

[9] One key feature of these arguments is that they attempt to describe manipulated agents who meet all of the compatibilist conditions on moral responsibility (see, e.g., Pereboom 2001, 114). That is essential to making the arguments effective against compatibilists.

4.3.2 Hard compatibilism

In the face of the manipulation argument, many compatibilists bite the bullet and maintain that, contrary intuitions notwithstanding, the manipulated agent really is responsible. This "hard compatibilism" strategy is found in Hobbes and Skinner (see, e.g., Kane 1996, 67). But the view has been resuscitated with a vengeance. Frankfurt is the advocate most forceful and prominent. According to Frankfurt, what matters for responsibility is (in part) one's character. And it doesn't matter how that character was formed. He writes:

A manipulator may succeed, through his interventions, in providing a person not merely with particular feelings and thoughts but with a new character. That person is then morally responsible for the choices and the conduct to which having this character leads. We are inevitably fashioned and sustained, after all, by circumstances over which we have no control. The causes to which we are subject may also change us radically, without thereby bringing it about that we are not morally responsible agents. It is irrelevant whether those causes are operating by virtue of the natural forces that shape our environment or whether they operate through the deliberate manipulative designs of other human agents (Frankfurt 2002).

McKenna explicitly embraces this: "I believe that the compatibilist should make this point her ally" (McKenna 2008, 158). So does Watson, who maintains that it's the gentler horn of a dilemma:

We can put this in the form of a dilemma. One alternative is to "bite the bullet," as Kane puts it, insisting that free agents might indeed be the products of manipulation by designers. Many would agree with Kane that this is "a hard line indeed, and one that ... is also hard to accept" (67). Or else free agency must be admitted to be at least partly an historical concept: agents are free if and only if they meet conditions C ... (perhaps inter alia) and C is not determined by the design of another agent. But this admission is the thin edge of a wedge that inevitably makes way for the full force of historical considerations. So this option is theoretically unstable. The intuition to which it responds is incompatibilist (Watson 1999, 361).

The hard compatibilist thus rejects altogether the import of the manipulation intuition. On Watson's view, accepting the manipulation intuition puts the compatibilist on a steep slope to incompatibilism. That's why Watson says that the intuition behind the manipulation argument is incompatibilist.[10] The hard compatibilist evades the argument by refusing to accept the manipulation intuition.

4.3.3 Puppeteer

A very different response to the manipulation argument is to claim that the manipulation intuition trades on the fact that there is another *agent* doing the manipulating. For instance, in discussing manipulation cases, Lycan writes, "What we object to in these cases is precisely that the victim is the puppet of another person" (1987, 117). It's because there's a puppeteer, on this view, that we take manipulation to undermine responsibility. *Pace* Watson (1999, 361), this response rejects the idea that the manipulation intuition is fundamentally an incompatibilist one.

The puppeteer response is widely dismissed in the contemporary literature on compatibilism. Pereboom writes, "the claim that this is a relevant difference is implausible" (Pereboom 2001, 115). Pereboom proposes that if the manipulator is replaced with a spontaneously generated machine that produced the same effects, this would make no difference to the responsibility of the affected agent. Similarly, Mele writes, "the responsibility undermining effects of intentional manipulators can be matched by blind forces." For instance, Mele suggests that the same effects could be produced by a brain disorder or by "a spontaneously generated magnetic field" (Mele 2006, 241; see also Mele 1995, 168).[11]

It's unclear how persuaded we should be by these examples. It would be easy enough for the puppeteer advocate to point out problems with each case. Mele is probably right that appealing to a brain disorder will

---

[10] McKenna develops a related line of response against the manipulation argument. Like advocates of the manipulation argument, McKenna actually agrees that there is no morally relevant difference between (certain) cases of agents manipulated into having a certain character and agents who develop the character through familiar deterministic processes. But in contrast to the incompatibilist, McKenna uses it to argue that manipulation needn't undermine responsibility. The fact that a determined agent can be responsible forces us to acknowledge that the manipulated agent can be responsible too (so long as the manipulation leaves intact all of the pertinent compatibilist conditions for freedom) (McKenna 2008).

[11] "Suppose that a brain disorder has this result in Beth, although it does not deprive her of the capacity for critical reflection and identification—or that the change in Beth is a result of her passing through a strange, randomly occurring electromagnetic field at the center of the Bermuda Triangle" (168). Mele's point is different from Pereboom's, since Mele is concerned with bypassing, not compatibilism. Nonetheless, his examples, if right, count against the puppeteer response.

facilitate exculpation. But this might be because of something special about the invocation of "brain-disorder" and not something that plays on the same kinds of intuitions as the manipulation cases. When we turn to Pereboom's spontaneously generated machine, the very thought of this machine that behaves in ways indistinguishable from an agent invites thinking that it *is* an agent (cf. Arico et al. 2011; Fiala et al. 2012). As for Mele's spontaneously generated magnetic field, the case is pretty thinly described, and it is likely that intuitions about the case would depend a great deal on how the case is filled out. Without further elaboration, it will not be convincing to the advocate of puppeteer response.

So these examples are not devastating to the puppeteer critique of the manipulation argument. But what is really needed is a positive reason to think that the puppeteer response is right. Does the presence of an agent make a critical difference to the intuitions in classic manipulation cases?

Thanks to recent work by Jonathan Phillips and Alex Shaw, we now know that people really are sensitive to the presence of a manipulating agent when making responsibility assessments. Phillips and Shaw presented participants with cases in which agents behave immorally. In some versions, a third-party (the manipulator) puts in place mechanisms expected to lead the agents to behave immorally; in other versions, the same mechanisms emerge without any involvement from a third-party. In one of the third-party cases, participants were presented with the following:

In the 1960s the government of a small Eastern European country plotted to secretly start a war using industrial workers, in order to get revenge on the wealthy citizens of the Shaki village. For the first part of their plan, the government intentionally destroyed farm machinery and set fire to several food stores on purpose. As a result, there was a serious lack of food in the country. Soon the people living in the city couldn't get enough food to feed themselves. The whole city shut down, crime skyrocketed and a small but violent uprising broke out.
The government knew their plan was working perfectly. Right at that time, a group of industrial workers heard through the government news channel that the Shaki village had a surplus of food. After hearing the news, the group of industrial workers raided the Shaki village, stealing food from the farmers in that village and killing innocent people. The government had known this would happen all along and it was exactly what they planned.

So in this manipulation case, the government created a food shortage by burning down several food stores. In the no-manipulator case, the food stores are destroyed by a wildfire. Participants attributed significantly more blame to the workers when the manipulator was absent. Moreover, the judgments of blame closely tracked judgments of *causal responsibility*. If a manipulator is involved, the manipulator is regarded as largely causally responsible for the outcome, and the agent is judged less causally responsible (Phillips and Shaw forthcoming).[12]

Thus, the experiments show that people do indeed attribute less blame when there is a third-party manipulator, as compared to the case where there is no agent. Of course, the vignettes are designed so that, from the agent's internal angle, the cases are indistinguishable. The agent we are evaluating doesn't know whether he has been manipulated by a third-party. As evaluators of the cases, we know whether there has been third-party manipulation, and if there was a third-party manipulator, our attributions of blame are greatly diminished. This suggests that the presence of a puppeteer really does have a significant impact on manipulation intuitions.

4.3.4 Against the manipulation argument

The experimental results indicate that the intuition that drives manipulation arguments largely depends on the presence of a third-party manipulator—a puppeteer. If we take away the puppeteer, we substantially weaken (and perhaps eliminate) the reduction in blame associated with manipulation cases. So, while Pereboom and Mele maintain that the presence of an agentive manipulator is irrelevant to the mitigation of responsibility, the evidence suggests that our intuitions really are sensitive to this feature of the cases.

As philosophers, we might maintain that the distinction between the agent and the no-agent cases is theoretically arbitrary. But this move cannot be made lightly by the advocates of the manipulation argument.

---

[12] Strikingly, Phillips and Shaw found that the effect of manipulation even depends on the extent to which the third-party's intention is congruent with the outcome. In another study, the third-party does exactly the same thing—destroys the equipment and food of the workers—but instead of attacking the Shaki village (as the government intended), the workers attack a completely different village. The workers get blamed significantly more in that condition than when they attack the village that the government intended them to attack.

One feature of the empirical work is that some kinds of third-party actions mitigate responsibility without eliminating it. This would fit with the view that the right way to think about responsibility is as scalar rather than dichotomous (see, e.g., Tierney 2013).

If we take the experimental findings at face value, they suggest that there really is an asymmetry in our lay intuitions that conforms neatly with the claims of the puppeteer response. So we cannot rely on lay intuitions about manipulation cases to generalize to cases that have no manipulating agent. Lay intuition does not treat the cases as morally equivalent. On the other hand, if we take the experimental findings to show that lay intuitions are confused (because they are inappropriately sensitive to the presence of an agent), it's not obvious that we can then *use* lay intuitions about manipulation cases to argue for incompatibilism. Insofar as one is relying on common intuitions about manipulation, it's likely that those intuitions are driven by the presence of a third-party. So it seems unprincipled to maintain that the intuition is right when it's applied to cases with a puppeteer but that the intuition is wrongly sensitive to a puppeteer. If it weren't for the third-party, the intuition would not have such power. So the empirical results give new vigor to the puppeteer response, and this provides the compatibilist with additional ammunition against the manipulation argument. Apparently, in ordinary moral thought, there really is something special about third-party manipulation and, at least as far as those intuitions go, it seems to be a mistake to assimilate determinism and manipulation.[13]

4.3.5 Should manipulation be mitigating?

I've been arguing that the compatibilist's hand isn't forced. The (lay) manipulation intuition does not provide the basis for an argument for incompatibilism. That does not yet, however, settle whether a person should not be held responsible if his character was produced by malicious brainwashers. That is, the fact that the manipulation intuition doesn't ground an argument for incompatibilism doesn't tell us whether manipulated agents should be held responsible.

Hard compatibilists reject the manipulation argument by dismissing the manipulation intuition. But if, as I've suggested, the manipulation argument fails on other grounds, then what hard compatibilism

---

[13] Most discussions of manipulation arguments rely—at least tacitly—on intuitions. But perhaps there is a way to run the manipulation argument that doesn't appeal to intuitions at all. In that case, the empirical results on intuitions would be irrelevant. The point in this paragraph is that insofar as the manipulation argument relies on exculpating intuitions about manipulation, the empirical results support the puppeteer response.

proposes to buy us, we already get for free. In the absence of pressure from the manipulation argument, it's unclear why one would want to adopt this hardline view that rejects outright the prevalent intuition that manipulation is exculpating.

Hard compatibilists don't simply reject the manipulation intuition, of course. They also promote theories of responsible agency on which manipulation is not a mitigating factor. For instance, "hierarchical" and "mesh" theories of responsibility focus on the structure of the agent's psychology and are silent on the relevance of the history of how structure came about (see McKenna 2009 for a review). But even if one favors such theories, it doesn't immediately follow that we should conclude that manipulation is irrelevant to responsibility. Manipulation might just be another factor that matters to responsibility, even if it doesn't organically follow from one's theory of responsible agency.

One way to reject the normative import of manipulation is to debunk the manipulation intuition. Vargas (2013) takes this strategy. He suggests that intuitions about manipulation (and other historical factors) are vestiges of the kind of folk libertarianism that we need to give up. Here's Vargas: "I am inclined to think they are generated by an unwarranted conviction we have about the requirement that we be ultimate sources of our own actions" (2013, 299). This leads Vargas to conclude that the intuitions are unreliable: "I don't yet see that we have sufficient reason to think that those intuitions—however widespread they may be—are reliable or truth-guiding" (301). The empirical work on manipulation intuitions suggests that what drives the intuitions is not primarily our mistaken libertarian commitments, but the presence of a third-party. In addition, though, as I'll argue in Chapter 5, it's a very tricky matter to land debunking arguments in normative ethics.

Even if we can't provide independent justification for our intuition that manipulation is exculpatory, we might just embrace our brute attitude. As I will stress in subsequent chapters, normative commitments come to an end somewhere (sections 5.5 and 6.5). The fact that we can't give a justification for the norm *causing suffering is wrong* doesn't make us suspend our commitment. We might take the same attitude about our commitment to the role of manipulation as an excusing condition. We find it intuitively compelling that those who are brainwashed shouldn't be blamed. The fact that we are naturally committed to the idea that manipulation undermines responsibility might accord that commitment a prima facie authority which does not depend on providing some further justification for the commitment.

4.4 The explanatory limitations of folk incompatibilism

The previous section attempted to undercut the manipulation argument for incompatibilism. This is only a pyrrhic victory for the compatibilist. For even if the manipulation intuition is inadequate to fund an argument for incompatibilism, there remains the fundamental incompatibilist intuition itself (section 4.1). That seems to provide an important consideration in favor of incompatibilism. I began this chapter by arguing that it's a deep fact about us that we find determinism to undercut blameworthiness. But determinism is hardly the only factor that we take to undermine responsibility. As Strawson notes, all of the following factors seem to mitigate blame: lack of intent, ignorance, coercion, countervailing values, situational pressures, insanity, and compulsion. We've seen that manipulation is yet another factor that diminishes blame attributions.

I went to some lengths to argue that manipulation intuitions are sensitive to the presence of a puppeteer and hence that they do not support an inference to incompatibilism. If that's right, then a further conclusion becomes plausible: people's intuitions about manipulation do not *explain* their intuitions about incompatibilism. That is, it's not the case that incompatibilist intuitions are an inference from intuitions about manipulation. Descriptively, manipulation is yet another separate item on the list of responsibility-undermining considerations, along with ignorance, coercion, compulsion, etc. In addition, these are plausibly *separate* items, each with its own history. There is no reason to think that there is a common psychological ground for all of these excusing factors. These considerations are not children of a single parental principle.

This point is especially important when we turn to the explanatory power of the fact that incompatibilism is intuitive. Our commitment to incompatibilism is a dispositional or *implicit* belief; that is, it is not explicitly represented in our minds consciously or unconsciously (see, e.g., Fodor 1987; Lycan 1988). Prior to philosophical education, to a first approximation, no one ever formulates the thought. That is, people do not have an explicit representation with the content *determinism precludes moral responsibility*. That doesn't mean that folk incompatibilism is superficial or false or trivial to abandon. I have long had the implicit belief that $10^4 > 1,498$. Prior to constructing the example, I had never explicitly thought it. And yet, I think it's absolutely true. It's not superficial since it follows from basic principles of arithmetic. *Rejecting* it is out of the question. So the fact that a belief is implicit does not entail that it is superficial, false, or negotiable. But it does entail something of significance. If a belief is implicit, it cannot give rise to explicitly represented beliefs. My implicit belief that $10^4 > 1,498$, while true and nonnegotiable, cannot be the causal source of any of my explicitly represented beliefs.

The set of explicit commitments we have about moral responsibility is extensive. People routinely excuse agents under conditions of coercion, ignorance, compulsion, and manipulation. And often enough those excusing factors are explicitly invoked. Since the incompatibilist commitment is implicit, that means that it cannot explain the explicitly represented commitments concerning responsibility. Our beliefs that ignorance, lack of intention, coercion, manipulation, etc. are exculpatory cannot be explained by the commitment to incompatibilism.

The claim here is a descriptive claim, of course. The idea is that as a matter of fact, people have multiple different rules of exculpation. Many of these rules likely have different developmental trajectories and different learning contexts. But the fact that we can learn exculpating rules about coercion, ignorance, and manipulation before having a thought about incompatibilism shows that we don't derive these considerations from incompatibilism. More importantly, the fact that these explicit rules do not grow out of the commitment to incompatibilism suggests that even if one gives up incompatibilism, that need have no effect on our commitments to the exculpatory nature of coercion, ignorance, or manipulation.

In this chapter, I've argued that incompatibilism is part of commonsense. However, as I've stressed in this last section, it is an *implicit* part of commonsense. That doesn't render incompatibilism philosophically insignificant. But it does have an important implication. If, as will be considered in Chapter 7, we should abandon incompatibilism, this needn't interfere with our moral practices. We can forego that element of commonsense without disrupting the rest of our moral framework.

5

Debunking Arguments

The rise of experimental philosophy has been accompanied by a rise in debunking arguments.[1] I have already discussed two debunking arguments (in sections 2.6 and 4.3.5). But it is time to investigate the nature and propriety of debunking arguments more systematically. I will start by distinguishing different forms of debunking arguments, and I will adopt a particular, psychologically oriented approach to debunking. On the type of debunking argument that I will promote, one attempts to undercut the justificatory status of a belief by showing that the belief was formed by an epistemically defective psychological process. There are promising applications of such debunking arguments in metaethics, I'll contend. In normative ethics, debunking arguments face greater obstacles. This will be important for the subsequent discussion of normative principles like retributivism that are bound up with responsibility (Chapter 6).

5.1 Varieties of debunking

Debunking arguments don't aim to show that a belief is false; rather, they aim to undermine the justificatory status of the belief. These kinds of arguments afford the opportunity to wring philosophically interesting conclusions from empirical findings. Philosophers working at the intersection of ethics and cognitive science tend not to commit a simple naturalistic fallacy. Rather they use empirical results to leverage arguments against the epistemic credentials of various ethical beliefs. There are several prominent debunking arguments in the recent literature, (e.g., Singer 2005; Joyce 2006; Street 2006; Greene 2008), but Richard Joyce

---

[1] A century ago, prominent debunking arguments were offered by Nietzsche and Freud.

has been perhaps the most explicit in offering a characterization of debunking. He writes:

I contend that on no epistemological theory worth its salt should the justificatory status of a belief remain unaffected by the discovery of an empirically supported theory that provides a complete explanation of why we have that belief while nowhere presupposing its truth (Joyce 2006, 219).

Joyce applies this approach to debunking to the case of morality, with the following provocative conclusion:

our moral beliefs are products of a process that is entirely independent of their truth, which forces the recognition that we have no grounds one way or the other for maintaining these beliefs (Joyce 2006, 211).

There are various worries one might have about Joyce's formulation of debunking. Consider my beliefs about future probabilities. I believe that Hume will still be taught at universities in a hundred years. But presumably the explanation of that belief doesn't presuppose its truth. And yet it seems rash to say that my belief is unjustified as a result. Even worse, consider my beliefs about my own future action. I believe that I will go to the train station at 10 a.m. That belief is not debunked by the fact that we can explain my belief without presupposing the truth of my belief. Consider that if I *don't* make it to the station because, say, there is a huge protest blocking my access, it wouldn't be fair to say that this undermines the justificatory status of my earlier belief.[2]

One way to address these problems is by incorporating probability into the account. Folke Tersman does exactly that in his characterization of debunking:

Consider a fact F that is offered as evidence for a theory T. A debunking explanation of F is an explanation that does not entail that T is true or significantly likely (2008, 395).

Tersman's account avoids impugning the justificatory status of my belief that I will go to the train station. A complete explanation of why I have that belief—one that goes beyond citing F—might entail that the truth of the belief is significantly likely.

---

[2] Cf. Goldman 1967.

Tersman's account of debunking improves upon (or perhaps clarifies) Joyce's account. But there is a critical commonality between Tersman's account and Joyce's. Both accounts construe debunking in terms of whether the *best explanation* of a belief implicates the truth of the belief.[3] Recall that Joyce claims on any credible epistemology, if we can explain a belief without presupposing the truth of the belief, then this undermines the justificatory status of the belief. That is, if the best explanation of the belief that P doesn't involve the truth of P, then the justificatory status of the belief is undermined.[4]

The best-explanation account seems sensible, but if intended to provide a necessary condition for justified belief, it is too demanding. Consider Lavoisier's belief in the caloric theory of heat. Since caloric theory is false, the best explanation of Lavoisier's belief in caloric theory will nowhere presuppose the truth of his belief. Does that impugn the justificatory status of the venerable chemist's belief? Or consider a case from mathematics. Frege's set theory relies on the axiom of comprehension, which leads to inconsistencies exposed by Russell's paradox in 1901. Given that Frege's set theory leads to inconsistencies, we know that a complete explanation of Frege's 1900 belief will not presuppose the truth of Frege's set theory. On the best-explanation approach to debunking, that suffices to undercut the justificatory status of Frege's 1900 belief in set theory.

Lavoisier's belief in caloric was false, but few epistemologists would say that Lavoisier's belief was unjustified as a result of being disconnected from truth. It is common wisdom in epistemology that false beliefs can be very well justified. But presumably the best explanation of a false belief will not presuppose the truth of the belief. Hence, the best explanation

---

[3] Wielenberg (2010) argues that several recent evolutionary debunking arguments (e.g., Ruse 1986; Joyce 2006; Street 2006) all depend on an apparent disconnection between belief and truth.

[4] For this chapter, I am focusing on debunking arguments that aim to show that an agent is unjustified in his belief that *P*. Often the appeal to best-explanation arguments has a more global target than an agent's justification. For instance, Harman's argument against moral facts is that the best scientific explanation for moral thought will not invoke moral facts (1977). This is offered as an argument that there is no good reason to posit moral facts. Wielenberg calls Harman's argument a "metaphysical debunking" argument (2010, 452–3). I have no objection to calling this a "debunking" argument, but importantly, the conclusion of the argument does not imply that people who believe in moral facts are unjustified.

approach to debunking doesn't accord well with prevailing views of justification.[5]

Although this best-explanation approach to debunking has controversial epistemic implications, there is a much less controversial characterization of debunking available. One way to challenge the epistemic propriety of a person's belief is by attacking the propriety of the psychological process that leads to the belief. If we determine that the process that led to (and sustains) a person's belief is epistemically defective, that will count as challenging the justificatory status of the belief. The class of epistemically defective processes is heterogeneous, but a familiar example is wishful thinking. If the reason a student thinks the exam will be easy is because she hopes it will be, then the student's belief in the easiness of the exam is unjustified. Maybe the exam will be easy, but the student's belief is in terrible justificatory repair if the process that generated the belief is wishful thinking. Indeed, the student is unjustified even if she is unaware of the fact that her belief was generated by wishful thinking. In contrast to best-explanation debunking, we might call this *process debunking*. The focus of process debunking is the epistemic propriety of the belief-formation process. A process debunking argument aims to show that an agent's belief that P is generated by a process that does not yield justified belief.[6]

While the best-explanation approach to debunking would undercut Lavoisier and Frege's beliefs in their areas of expertise, the process approach is much more charitable. So long as the processes that led to Lavoisier and Frege's beliefs were epistemically appropriate, the

---

[5] An alternative way to develop best-explanation debunking is in terms of second-order beliefs. If one comes to realize that the best explanation of one's belief that P does not presuppose the truth of P, then at that point, one is no longer justified in believing that P (see, e.g., Kahane 2011, 105). Perhaps this is the best interpretation of Joyce. But my interests here are not to refute Joyce. Rather, as will become clear, the point is to explicate a kind of debunking argument that is quite different from the best-explanation variety.

[6] Unlike Kahane's characterization of debunking (see previous footnote), the kind of process debunking I've sketched is not tied to the presence of second-order beliefs. An agent's belief can result from a defective process even if they have no second-order beliefs.

There are, however, ways to frame best-explanation debunking that will overlap with process debunking. Tersman's best-explanation account of debunking is unqualified, but one could advance a version of his account that keys on the best *belief-formation-process* explanation: if the best *processing* explanation for how a belief was formed doesn't entail that the belief is significantly likely, this might be a process debunking explanation (depending on what makes a process epistemically defective).

justificatory status of those beliefs is not challenged by process debunking. This charity seems fitting. Lavoisier's belief in caloric theory was the product of scientific reasoning that was more reputable than most of the inferences most of us draw. Process debunking provides no reason to criticize the justificatory status of Lavoisier's belief in caloric.

The Lavoisier case illustrates one way in which best explanation debunking and process debunking come apart—the former will sometimes impugn the justificatory status of a belief while the latter remains neutral. The two approaches to debunking can also dissociate in the other direction. For in some cases a belief will be generated by an epistemically defective process even though the best explanation of the belief will presuppose the truth of the belief. Imagine that John believes that there are electrical impulses in his brain, and the sole basis for his believing this is a deranged paranoia that the government implanted a chip in his head. On the process approach to debunking, the fact that John's belief comes from a deranged-paranoia process impugns the justificatory status of John's belief. But at the same time, it's plausible that a complete explanation of John's belief will presuppose the truth of his belief—after all, if John's brain *didn't* have electrical impulses he'd be dead and bereft of beliefs altogether. As a result, the belief does not fall prey to best-explanation debunking, even though it is debunked by the process approach.

5.2 Process debunking

While best-explanation debunking courts epistemic controversy, process debunking is on solid ground. If process Q is an epistemically defective basis for coming to believe that P, then insofar as people believe that P as a result of process Q, their belief that P is unjustified. That conditional licenses the following schema for debunking arguments:

1. S believes that *P* because of process *Q*.
2. Process *Q* is an epistemically defective basis for coming to believe that *P*.
3. S is not justified in believing that *P*.

This schema is framed in an unqualified fashion, but such arguments can obviously be developed in more qualified ways as well. So, if we know that S's belief that P depends *to some extent* on defective process Q, then we can conclude that S's belief that P is unjustified *to the extent* that it depends on process Q. To put this in terms of credence: whatever amount of credence in P is uniquely contributed by defective processes, that amount of credence is unjustified.[7]

Freud (1927/1961) provides the canonical case of a process debunking argument. He maintains (with little evidence) that people believe in God because of wishful thinking. Freud is very clear that this does not entail that God doesn't exist—Freud doesn't commit the genetic fallacy of concluding that a belief is false because it has an epistemically defective origin. But Freud does think that showing that theism comes from wishful thinking has important epistemic consequences:

> our attitude to the problem of religion will undergo a marked displacement. We shall tell ourselves that it would be very nice if there were a God who created the world and was a benevolent Providence, and if there were a moral order in the universe and an after-life; but it is a very striking fact that all this is exactly as we are bound to wish it to be (1927/1961, 42).

Plantinga credits Freud's argument as an important challenge to theistic belief, characterizing Freud's argument as follows: "the... complaint is that theistic belief is not *rational* and lacks *warrant*. Unlike memory beliefs, *a priori* beliefs, or perceptual belief, theistic belief does not originate in the proper function of processes aimed at the production of true belief" (2000, 194). To put this in terms of the schema, Freud's argument is as follows:

1. People believe that God exists because of wishful thinking.
2. Wishful thinking is an epistemically defective basis for coming to believe that God exists.
3. People are not justified in believing that God exists.

---

[7] This formulation allows us to accommodate the fact that a person might initially believe P because of a defective process, which causes a subsequent epistemically upstanding process that provides a good and sufficient basis for believing P. In that case, we would want to say that the agent is now justified in believing that P. Thanks to an anonymous referee for raising this issue.

One further note about the schema. It is flexible about the class of individuals who are targeted by the argument. A process debunking argument only applies to people who have the belief as a result of the defective process; the argument itself does not preclude the possibility that some people believe from a defective process and others believe from an epistemically proper process.

Plantinga ultimately rejects Freud's argument, but he doesn't reject the *form* of argument.[8]

In typical cases, wishful thinking counts as an epistemically defective process for forming beliefs. That's the backbone of Freud's epistemic critique of religious belief. Just as the student is unjustified if she thinks the exam will be easy simply because she hopes it will be, so too the theist is unjustified in believing in God if wishful thinking is the sole source of his theistic belief.

Wishful thinking is a familiar example of an epistemically defective process, but several types of processes are widely regarded as epistemically defective. Goldman offers this list of epistemically defective processes: "confused reasoning, wishful thinking, reliance on emotional attachment, mere hunch or guesswork, and hasty generalization" (1979, 9). Epistemologists disagree about what makes these belief-formation processes defective. Goldman suggests that the processes are defective because they are unreliable, i.e., they lead to false beliefs a large proportion of the time. Cohen (1984) challenges the reliabilist explanation of what makes the processes defective; instead, he maintains that the processes are defective because the resulting beliefs aren't "conditioned by the evidence" (283). Although Cohen and Goldman disagree about what makes the processes defective, it is important to note that they agree that the processes *are* defective (e.g., Cohen 1984, 282–3). So we can often register that a process is defective without taking sides on what makes the process defective.

Of course, sometimes processes are defective in some contexts and not others. Logical contraposition is appropriate for material conditionals, but not for counterfactual conditionals (Lewis 1973, 35). So it would be a mistake to make a global pronouncement on the epistemic propriety of contraposition. As a result, in evaluating the epistemic propriety of a process, we need to be careful to assess whether the process is epistemically defective in the context of interest.

---

[8] Instead, Plantinga challenges Freud's psychological claim that theistic belief comes from wishful thinking. Plantinga also raises the possibility that God designed us to have the wishfulfillment mechanism as a means to lead us to theistic belief. In that case, Plantinga says, wishful thinking would be an epistemically proper basis for theistic belief (2000, 195–8).

5.3 Metaethics and debunking

Now that we have a rough characterization of process debunking in hand, we can turn to applications. Debunking arguments apply very differently, I will argue, in metaethics and normative ethics. I will illustrate this by contrasting debunking arguments on the belief in moral objectivity with debunking arguments on the propriety of retribution. Our ultimate interest will be in the normative ethical questions. But issues about moral objectivity will be important for how we frame the issue of debunking in normative ethics. As a result, I will set out the issues concerning the belief in moral objectivity in some detail.

5.3.1 Are people moral objectivists?

Over the last several years, there has been a growing body of empirical work on whether ordinary people think morality is objective (Nichols and Folds-Bennett 2003; Nichols 2004a; Wainryb et al. 2004; Goodwin and Darley 2008; Wright et al. 2008; Sarkissian et al. 2011). Giving a precise characterization of objectivity is itself a major philosophical endeavor. I will not attempt such a project here. But roughly speaking, the operative notion of objectivism in the experimental literature is that the truth conditions for objective claims are independent of the attitudes and feelings people have toward the claim (see Shafer-Landau 2003).[9] On this notion of objectivism, if an objective claim is true, then anyone who denies the claim is mistaken. As a result, if two individuals disagree about some objective statement, then at least one of them must be wrong. There are uncontroversial examples of claims that are objective in this sense, including claims about matters of fact (e.g., a chlorine atom has 17 protons) and matters of logic or math (e.g., $2*7 = 14$). The truth of $2*7=14$ holds independently of anyone's attitudes about that proposition. And if an alien denies that $2*7=14$, then at least one of us is wrong. We can't disagree and both be right about objective matters.

A number of contemporary philosophers maintain that ordinary people presuppose that morality is objective. Joyce is particularly clear on the matter:

---

[9] The kind of objectivism under discussion here is thus stronger than some views labeled as "realist" (e.g., Railton 1986).

Moral values are exactly those values which are *not* relative: they are the ones that apply to an agent regardless of that agent's desires or cultural placement. Our ordinary use of the concept of *motion* is not much affected when we let go of absolutism; our ordinary use of the concept of *moral rightness*, by contrast, is completely undermined without absolutism (Joyce 2002, 97; see also Mackie 1977, 33).

Several studies suggest that ordinary people do, at least in some cases, take moral claims to be objective.[10] As noted, if moral statements are objective, then when people disagree about a moral statement, at least one of them has to be wrong. That has been the entry point for experimental studies on folk objectivism.[11] In one of the most important recent studies, Goodwin and Darley (2008) presented participants with a variety of statements, falling into several different classes:

Factual statements, e.g., "The earth is not at the center of the known universe."
Social-conventional statements, e.g. "Calling teachers by their first name, without being given permission to do so, in a school that calls them 'Mr.' or 'Mrs.' is wrong behavior."
Ethical statements, e.g., "Robbing a bank in order to pay for an expensive holiday is a morally bad action."
Taste, e.g., "Frank Sinatra was a better singer than is Michael Bolton."

For each statement, participants were asked whether they agreed or disagreed with the statement. They were then asked, "According to you, can there be a correct answer as to whether this statement is true?" (1351). After answering this question, the participant is told that another respondent has disagreed with their answer. The participant is asked about whether they think that "the other person is surely mistaken" or that "it is possible that neither you nor the other person is mistaken." Responses were coded as "fully objectivist" if the participant said that there can be a correct answer and that the other person (who disagrees with the participant) is surely mistaken (1352).

The main result of this experiment is that people were much more likely to give objectivist responses for the ethical statements than for the statements about taste or social convention (1352–3). Indeed, in this

---

[10] See Sarkissian et al. (2011) for a dissenting view.
[11] Objectivism entails that if two people disagree, one of them must be wrong. But such a view about disagreement is consistent with other views like a universal intersubjectivism. Studies like the ones discussed here do not tease this apart. But there is no reason it could not be done in future studies.

experiment, people's responses about the ethical statements were no less objectivist than their responses about the factual statements. As Goodwin and Darley summarize it, "individuals seem to treat core ethical beliefs as being almost as objective as scientific or plainly factual beliefs, and reliably more objective than beliefs about social convention or taste" (1354).[12]

5.3.2 Why are people moral objectivists?

There is thus some reason to think that people are inclined to believe in objectivity about moral claims. The experiments don't actually ask participants whether morality is objective but instead ask about particular moral claims. However, for ease of exposition, I will forego precision and follow the empirical literature in characterizing these results as indicating a lay belief in moral objectivity. The next question is *why* people believe in moral objectivism. No doubt there are lots of factors that contribute to the lay belief in moral objectivity. But this is a chapter on debunking, and so I will focus on factors—emotional and motivational—that might support debunking arguments.

5.3.2.1 AFFECT, OBJECTIVITY, AND DEBUNKING

There is a small but diverse body of evidence suggesting that emotions contribute to the belief in objectivity (see Nichols 2014 for review). Just to take one example, in a recent study, researchers explored the role of incidental disgust in judgments of objectivity (Cameron et al. 2013).

---

[12] As is often the case in psychology, each experiment on moral objectivism is limited in its own way. In the Goodwin and Darley study, it's possible to give responses that would be coded as "objectivist" even about something that you know to be conventional. I think that driving on the right side of the road is a convention, certainly not objectively prescribed. But if given the Goodwin and Darley questions about driving on the right, I might interpret the questions as asking *what the local convention is*, and in that case, I would give "objectivist" responses—I would say that there is a correct answer about what the convention is, and if others disagree, they are mistaken. However, the fact that people tended not to judge the social–conventional statements as "objective" suggests that they are not generally interpreting the objectivity question as asking about what the local convention is. For if people were generally interpreting the questions as asking about the facts concerning local conventions, they should have given "objectivist" answers for the social–conventional items too. This gives Goodwin and Darley a first line of defense against the worry. Recent work by Jen Wright et al. helps shore this up by showing that the explanations people give for their objectivity judgments are appropriate, as evaluated by independent coders (Wright et al. forthcoming).

Participants were presented with a range of cultural practices, e.g., "The family of a murderer can be killed by the victim's family." For each practice, they were asked a version of an objectivity question: "To what degree is the behavior morally wrong regardless of the culture in which it is practiced?" (Cameron et al. 2013, 721). To induce disgust, participants were shown a disgusting image, and then a textbox describing the cultural practice. In the control condition, non-disgusting images were used. The disgust induced by these images is obviously incidental disgust—not disgust that is integrally related to the cultural practice. Yet participants in the disgust condition agreed more strongly that the practice was wrong regardless of the culture, indicating that the induction of disgust increases judgments of objectivity.

Thus, there is some reason to think that emotion facilitates judgments of objectivism. In addition, we know that judgments of moral wrongdoing are characteristically accompanied by reactions of anger or disgust (e.g., Scherer 1997; Rozin 1999). Let's go beyond the suggestive data and suppose that these emotional processes are critical in generating and sustaining the belief in objectivity. If so, will that fund an argument debunking the belief in objectivity? Whether morality is objective is a metaphysical issue, and emotions seem like a poor guide to metaphysics. Metaphysicians rarely train their students to have heightened emotional sensitivities. However, the mere fact that emotions are critical to the belief in objectivity would not be enough to ground a debunking argument. Emotions tend to increase attention and focus. In that way, they can facilitate good reasoning. To fund a debunking argument, it has to be the case that the operative emotional process is epistemically defective in the context of interest. Is there any reason to think that this holds in the case of emotions and objectivity? The disgust induction experiment looks promising on this score. For it suggests that emotional mechanisms that lead to objectification are defective *when it comes to whether something is objective*. The emotional processes apparently lead—in a non-evidentiary fashion—to false beliefs about objectivity. Judgments of the objectivity of moral claims were inflated when participants were shown a disgusting image completely unrelated to the content of the moral claim. Strikingly, the effect disappears when participants are antecedently instructed, "While you are viewing the images, pay attention to the subtle differences between the feelings you are having toward the images" (2013, 722). This finding serves to corroborate the epistemically inappropriate role that the incidental disgust plays in the simple study (where there is no instruction to attend closely to differences in feelings). When people are led to attend closely to the fact that what they are feeling is *disgust*, they discount the negative value of this emotion when evaluating the question about objectivity.

Thus there is a tiny bit of evidence suggesting that emotional processes inflate judgments of objectivity in epistemically defective ways. A prevailing approach in emotion theory might help explain these results. According to the appraisal-tendency framework, emotions like anger and disgust are associated with increased certainty (Smith and Ellsworth 1985; Lazarus 1991). When people are led to feel anger, this generates a greater sense of certainty or confidence about their interpretation of the situation before them (see, e.g., Lerner and Tiedens 2006). This increased certainty makes sense when we think about the ecological function of emotions like anger and disgust—these are emotions that are designed to trigger action. In ecologically typical circumstances, when these emotions are activated, taking action is important for the organism, and it is counterproductive to second guess. The sense of certainty associated with anger and disgust provides a hint of an explanation for what happens in the case of judgments of objectivity. Moral violations trigger anger and disgust. So the emotions concomitant with moral condemnation would also facilitate certainty about the wrongness of the violation—certainty that one has diagnosed the situation correctly as wrong. Tolerance for other views gets pushed aside. While the increased certainty associated with anger and disgust might be ecologically beneficial, these benefits don't extend to epistemic propriety. Insofar as we believe in moral objectivity because the associated feelings of anger and disgust trigger greater certainty in one's assessment, the belief in objectivity is not justified.

5.3.2.2 MOTIVATION, OBJECTIVITY, AND DEBUNKING

Another potential contributor to the belief in objectivity is motivation: we might believe that morality is objective because we want it to be (cf. Mackie 1977, 43). David Rose and I have recently started exploring the possibility that the desire to punish partly explains judgments of objectivity (Rose and Nichols forthcoming). In one study, participants were presented with a case known to trigger high ratings of objectivity (racial discrimination). One group of participants received a version of the case in which the wrongdoer was severely punished; the other group received a version in which the wrongdoer was not punished. The prediction was that those who read that the wrongdoer was punished severely would be less motivated for punishment and accordingly give lower ratings of objectivity. This is exactly what happened, suggesting that the desire to punish does affect objectivity judgments.[13] This in turn makes it somewhat plausible that the belief in objectivity is partly generated by the desire to punish.

The results on punishment and objectivity point to a prima facie debunking argument that resembles Freud's. Just as wishful thinking is a prima facie defective basis for believing in God, the desire to punish is a prima facie defective basis for believing in moral objectivity. To the extent that people believe in objectivity because of their desire to punish, their belief is prima facie unjustified. Of course, this is just the barest sketch of a debunking argument. Perhaps the desire to punish is an epistemically appropriate basis for coming to believe in objectivity (cf. Plantinga on wishful thinking and religious belief [2000, 195–8]). Or perhaps there is some other epistemically proper process that generates the belief in objectivity, such that this process secures the epistemic propriety of the belief regardless of the influence of the desire to punish. These remain open possibilities, but in light of the evidence on punishment and objectivity, these possibilities must be elaborated and defended if they are to defuse the debunking argument.

I'm under no illusions that the preceding debunking arguments are decisive. We currently have only a smattering of evidence suggesting that the belief in moral objectivity is facilitated by epistemically defective processes. But these are very early days. Metaethics stretches back for millennia; the empirical study of objectivity beliefs is barely a decade old. We can reasonably expect a much richer picture of the psychological basis for the belief in objectivity in the future. In any case, the aim of this chapter is to get clear on how experimental work *might* contribute to debunking arguments in ethics. And if the thrust of the foregoing is right, we can articulate a plausible debunking argument:

---

[13] A closely related study used causal modeling to explore the relationship between judgments of objectivity and attitudes about punishment. The results indicated that attitudes about punishment drove judgments about objectivity rather than the reverse.

To some extent, lay people's belief in moral objectivity depends on emotional and motivational processes that are epistemically defective for forming beliefs about objectivity. To the extent that the belief in moral objectivity depends on such processes, that belief is unjustified.

As noted earlier, there are presumably other factors that influence the belief in moral objectivity (see, e.g., Mackie 1977, 42–5). And perhaps some of those other factors have better epistemic credentials than the processes already considered. But it remains to be seen. In any case, we now have a sketch of a process debunking argument in metaethics. Whether the argument can support a strong conclusion that the lay belief in moral objectivity is unjustified will depend on what science reveals about why we have the belief.

5.4 Interlude

The previous section sketched an argument that attempts to debunk the lay belief in moral objectivity. Before we turn to debunking in normative ethics, we need to pause to consider how undermining the belief in moral objectivity would affect the status of lay normative beliefs. Joyce maintains that we are unjustified in believing in objectivism and that it follows that all of our moral beliefs are unjustified (2006, 211). This is because, according to Joyce, objectivism runs so deep in the practice that it is entwined with our moral concepts (2006, 202–9).

Is the belief in objectivism so critical to ordinary moral practices? As we've seen, Joyce maintains that the answer is *yes*, and he maintains that the effect of giving up moral objectivity (or "absolutism") will be profound: "Our ordinary use of the concept of *motion* is not much affected when we let go of absolutism; our ordinary use of the concept of *moral rightness*, by contrast, is completely undermined without absolutism" (Joyce 2002, 97). We now have a modicum of evidence on how abandoning objectivity affects people's normative judgments, and, as I'll explain, the effects seem far from profound.

The evidence I've reviewed might give the impression that people are uniformly objectivists about morality. However, I haven't told the whole story. One of the recurring findings in the empirical work on objectivism is that many people respond as *non*objectivists, and not simply because they are confused about the question (Nichols 2004a; Feltz and Cokely 2008; Goodwin and Darley 2008). To take one example, in Goodwin and

Darley's study, a sizable minority of people say that robbery is wrong, but not objectively so. More interestingly, even within the domain of ethics, we find variation in the extent to which particular statements are treated as objective (Goodwin and Darley 2008, 1346). For instance, as compared to their responses on whether robbing a bank is wrong, participants were more likely to say that whether abortion or euthanasia is wrong is a matter of opinion (1347, Table 1) or an issue about which there is no correct answer (1351, Table 2). Indeed, people will classify issues like the death penalty and euthanasia as *both* moral and nonobjective (Wright et al. forthcoming). Furthermore, whether or not a person responds as an objectivist makes little difference to other central features of their moral judgments. In particular, people who explicitly reject objectivism about a canonical moral violation (e.g., pulling hair) continue to treat such violations as different from conventional violations (e.g., talking out of turn): pulling hair is still regarded as more serious, wrong because it hurts the person, and wrong independent of authority (Nichols 2004a). Apparently, giving up objectivity isn't such a big deal.[14] The basic moral rules that are at the heart of folk morality persist in much the same way.

5.5 Normative ethics and debunking

Metaphysical beliefs, including beliefs about the objectivity of morality, are true or false depending on the way the world is. Arguments that attempt to debunk such beliefs can thus target processes that are epistemically defective ways of forming beliefs about the world. But many philosophers hold that, unlike metaphysical beliefs, normative ethical beliefs are not objectively true or false (e.g., Harman 1977; Joyce 2002; Prinz 2007; Doris and Plakias 2008; Gill and Nichols 2008; Greene 2008; Timmons 2008; Sarkissian et al. 2011). For those views, one must say more about what it is for an ethical belief to be the product of an epistemically defective process. In the remainder of this chapter, I want to explore the prospects for debunking under the assumption that the

---

[14] Joyce says that an essential feature of our moral concepts is that they carry a practical clout that would be defeated if one thinks of moral strictures as merely contingent. In effect, he suggests that if morality were not regarded as objective, it would be treated in much the way that etiquette is (2006, 202–9). The results described earlier cast some doubt on this.

right philosophical view of morality is relativist. Since this philosophical view is embraced by many philosophers, especially in naturalistic moral psychology, this focus will still have broad relevance.

In the previous section, we saw that even people who give up moral objectivism otherwise treat ethical claims much the same as before. This will be our starting point for investigating debunking arguments in normative ethics. The focus is thus narrowed further. The question is about *folk* normative beliefs, and it concerns what we might consider *post-objectivist* folk ethical beliefs.[15] If we as philosophers embrace moral relativism, how might we debunk these lay ethical beliefs?

5.5.1 Folk moral relativism

The first question concerns how to interpret people's post-objectivist statements that it's wrong to rob banks and wrong to hit innocent people. Normative relativism in some form offers the most flat-footed way to interpret these statements.[16] Thus, I will explore how normative ethical beliefs might be debunked, under the assumption that the beliefs are best interpreted as relativistic. For these purposes, let's adopt a standard characterization of moral relativism. Here's Mark Timmons' textbook rendition of moral relativism:

What is right and what is wrong for the members of a culture depends on (is ultimately determined by) the basic moral norms of their culture (Timmons 2013, 44).

Two important features about this characterization of moral relativism need to be stressed:

(i) the basic moral norms exhaust the moral domain. There are no moral facts or principles that are independent and external to the set of basic moral norms.
(ii) the basic moral norms are a set of moral rules or principles, but not *metaethical* doctrines. Nonetheless, the moral norms can be quite varied, and might include such principles as: *it is wrong to steal; it is right to punish wrongdoers; it is good to help the suffering.*

---

[15] For convenience, I will retain the term "ethical," even though I have not tried to rule out error theory. What I say can be recast in terms of "pseudo-ethical" principles, should error theory be right.

[16] The main alternative is some form of noncognitivism. I focus on relativism partly because lay people often explicitly avow a form of relativism about ethics. By contrast, I'm not sure lay people can even articulate noncognitivism.

On this characterization, when people say that stealing is wrong, but not objectively so, we should interpret this as saying something like this: "according to the basic moral norms of my community, stealing is wrong (for members of my community)."

A similar kind of relativism is independently plausible for how people typically think about etiquette. Thus, we can characterize etiquette relativism as follows:

What is polite and what is impolite for the members of a culture depends on (is ultimately determined by) the basic etiquette norms of their culture.

When I tell my child that it is wrong to put the knife to the left of the plate, I am relying on a set of etiquette rules about which I do not presume cultural universality. Nor do I think that there is some independent font of etiquette rules, external to the set that I've inherited in my culture.

Relativists can certainly identify epistemically defective processes that give rise to ethical beliefs. Many of our ethical beliefs depend on inferences from other norms and facts, and these might involve epistemically defective processes. Suppose that Joe believes that capital punishment is wrong, and this is solely because he thinks that only God should decide matters of life and death. If it turns out that Joe's belief in God is entirely based on wishful thinking, then this undermines both his belief in God and the consequent belief about capital punishment. This is a kind of debunking argument, but it is not a very deep result for normative ethics. The more ambitious and familiar debunking arguments target basic moral norms that are not the product of consciously available inference.

It is a familiar point in ethics that reasons have to give out at some point, and it's plausible that at the bottom of the pile will be a set of basic normative principles. Consider, for example, the *retributive principle* that a person should be punished because and only because of his wrongdoing. People in our culture reliably make assessments of punishment in accordance with this principle, and they explicitly endorse the principle. In many cases, people's punishment judgments are guided by the retributive principle and not by other normative principles or values that people hold. For instance, in a recent experiment in behavioral economics, participants monetarily punished an unfair player even though the player would never even know that he had been punished.

There was no opportunity here for moral education, rehabilitation or communication of any sort, but participants were no less inclined to punish (Nadelhoffer et al. 2013). Famously, there are utilitarian defenses of retribution (e.g., Rawls 1955), but it is unlikely that people's commitment to the retributive principle issues from such abstract reflections. Rather, as will be discussed in greater detail in Chapter 6, the retributive principle seems to be basic, one of the principles at the bottom of the normative pile.

Let's explore how a debunking argument might be marshaled against basic normative principles, using the retributive principle as an exemplar of such principles. We've been working with the following process debunking schema:

To the extent that people believe that P as a result of an epistemically defective process, their belief that P is unjustified.

In the present case, what we need to know is whether people believe the retributive principle because of an epistemically defective process. We saw that the belief in objectivity might well be the product of epistemically defective processes. Might something similar hold for the belief in retributivism?

Normatively basic principles like the retributive principle are not the product of consciously available inferences. That alone does not make them unjustified, of course. For something similar holds for basic beliefs like perceptual beliefs (e.g., my belief that there is a table in front of me), and few epistemologists think those beliefs are unjustified. To evaluate whether the retributive principle is the result of epistemically defective processes, we need to say more about epistemic propriety. Epistemologists differ, of course, in their opinions about what makes for epistemic propriety. For instance, some internalists hold that epistemic propriety supervenes on mental states alone, whereas externalists deny this (though see Comesaña (2005) for an argument against that kind of externalism). Everybody, however, should agree that *evidence* of unreliability is evidence of epistemic impropriety (for instance, see Feldman (2003) for an example of an internalist who accepts this). Thus, if we have evidence that our commitment to a normatively basic principle was formed by unreliable processes, this will provide reason to think that our commitment is unjustified.

The critical question for the would-be debunker will concern the reliability of the belief formation process. Given a relativistic interpretation of folk normative ethics, what determines whether a process is reliable? That is, what determines whether a process generally produces true beliefs (in the target domain)? Broadly speaking, there are two options. Reliability might be determined *internal* to the framework or *external* to it. Let's start outside the framework.

5.5.2 Framework-external debunking

To debunk the belief in the retributive principle from outside the frame-work would be to show that our belief in the retributive principle was produced by a process that generates a large proportion of false beliefs in the target domain. What will our yardstick be for saying that the process produces false beliefs in the domain of normative ethics? Note that it cannot be a *moral* yardstick, because we are assuming moral relativism. So we can't appeal to framework-external moral truths as the basis for debunking from outside the framework.

Perhaps the most prominent debunking arguments in normative ethics in recent years are due to Joshua Greene (2008) and Peter Singer (2005). The arguments are based on findings that certain characteristic-ally deontological judgments seem to be driven by emotional responses. The best-known findings involve presenting participants with a scenario in which one can save five innocent people by pushing one innocent person in front of a train. People who have deficits in emotional respon-siveness are more likely to say it's okay to push the person in front of the train (Koenigs et al. 2007; see also Valdesolo and DeSteno 2006). Thus, there's some reason to think that emotions are implicated in the judg-ments about these cases. Greene tells a similar story about retributivism—we promote retributive punishment because of our "retributivist feelings" (2008, 71).

Greene draws on the fact that emotions play a critical role in facilitat-ing retributivist judgments to marshal a debunking argument against retributivism. If we interpret this as a framework-external debunking argument, we need a framework-external specification of why the emo-tional processes are epistemically defective. This has not been done in any detail, but one natural approach is to invoke rationality as the relevant framework-external factor. Consonant with this, Singer suggests that the emotional processes that underlie the deontological judgments are not "reasoned" or rational and hence are deficient for forming beliefs about right and wrong (Singer 2005, 350).[17]

Although this debunking argument has some appeal, it threatens to be a doomsday argument for normative ethics. For it's quite plausible that the entire moral framework we have is built upon arational emotional responses (see, e.g., Nichols 2004c; Prinz 2007). If we'd had other emotions, or no emotions at all, our normative framework would be unrecognizable.

Not only does a broad-scale debunking of emotion-based normative principles put normative ethics in a precarious spot, we would likely reject this form of argument in other normative domains. Musical preferences, for instance, are presumably grounded in arational emotional processes. Most people regard Mozart's music as more beautiful than Schoenberg's. And it's likely that this depends on a kind of primitive emotional response to Mozart over Schoenberg. Even rats show a distinct preference for Mozart over Schoenberg (Cross et al. 1967). There is apparently something within our mammalian brains that biases us towards Mozart, and it's likely that this is not grounded on anything remotely rational. But it would be rash to conclude from this that people are unjustified in thinking that Mozart's music is more beautiful than Schoenberg's. Aesthetic judgments are not debunked by the fact that ultimately they have an arational emotional source. So the mere fact that a normative judgment is the product of emotions doesn't fund a framework-external debunking argument. And if this kind of framework-external debunking fails for aesthetics, we need an argument for why the situation is different for normative ethics.

The foregoing rationality-based debunking argument is hardly the only possible framework-external debunking argument. To avoid the doomsday scenario, a debunker could attempt to give a more discriminating account of why selective arational emotional processes are epistemically defective. However, one might think that this entire approach is wrong. If we assume moral relativism and also interpret people as normative relativists, the appropriate site for a debunking argument is

---

[17] "Rationality" isn't precisely defined by Singer, but for present purposes let's grant that the implicated emotional processes are not rational. It should also be noted that while Singer recruits debunking arguments in normative ethics, he does not do so for moral objectivity.

within the moral framework. For if there are no framework-independent moral truths, then it's plausible that the factors that are relevant to assessing the propriety of basic moral principles will not come from the exclusively non-moral facts outside of the framework. What matters morally is not given outside the framework, but within it.

5.5.3 Framework-internal debunking

To determine whether a process is unreliable from within the framework, we need a framework-internal notion of truth. Moral relativists can accommodate a kind of ethical truth, so long as it is couched within the relativistic framework. Harman provides a useful formulation:

For the purpose of assigning truth conditions, a judgment of the form *it would be morally wrong of P to D*, has to be understood as elliptical for a judgment of the form, *in relation to moral framework M, it would be morally wrong of P to D*. Similarly for other moral judgments (Harman 1996, 4).

Given this account, we can say that a moral judgment is the result of an unreliable process if that judgment comes from a process that produces a large portion of false beliefs, by the lights of the framework. So, suppose I come to believe that I am morally entitled to be paid more than many of my colleagues. Perhaps this belief is true. But if it turns out that the belief is generated entirely by self-interest, then there is a clear basis for debunking the belief. For ethical beliefs generated by self-interest will very often be false beliefs, by the lights of the basic norms of my culture. Thus my self-interest-generated belief that I should be paid more is not justified, from within the moral framework of my culture.

From within the framework, this kind of debunking of judgments about cases is available, but it doesn't go very far. It can be used to impugn specific judgments, but it yields no general conclusions for normative ethics. The more interesting debunking questions target not specific judgments about cases, but rather basic normative principles like the retributive principle.[18] So, from within the moral framework, how might debunking work for such principles?

---

[18] One might draw on psychological evidence to argue that for certain allegedly basic moral principles, there really *is* no such principle guiding our judgments. For instance, people's judgments about cases seems to conform to the principle of double effect, but this can be explained as a function of the confluence of different psychological processes rather than any representation of the principle of double effect. This approach might provide part

To debunk the commitment to the retributive principle, we would need to show that the retributive principle is produced by an unreliable process, a process that leads to a high proportion of false beliefs. However, there is an obvious kink. Within the moral framework, what counts as true is *given* by the principles in the framework. That it is right to punish the guilty is one of the (prima facie) truths of the moral framework. Whatever process led us to the belief in the principle is thus a process that leads us, again by the lights of the framework, to a greater proportion of true beliefs. For the process led us to the belief that partly constitutes which ethical beliefs count as true. As a result, from within the set of first-order normative principles, it is not at all clear how to debunk the basic normative principles that ultimately determine what is right and wrong.[19]

This is not to say that the standing principles of folk ethics are sacrosanct within the moral framework. Within a moral framework, principles often come into conflict. Many philosophers hold that a basic retributive principle comes into conflict with the principle that one should maximize utility. Some philosophers argue that the principle of utility shows that we should abandon the retributive principle. But this conclusion would not be reached by debunking; rather, this would count as a *conflicting* moral consideration, not a debunking one. The argument would be that the retributive principle conflicts with other, more important, principles within the framework. This is part of a perfectly respectable enterprise. Indeed, it constitutes an enormous part of normative ethics, but it shouldn't be confused with debunking.

---

of a debunking argument. But for many of our apparently basic moral norms, it's independently plausible that there *is* a represented principle guiding judgment (Gill and Nichols 2008; Mallon and Nichols 2010).

[19] One way to develop a debunking story would be to maintain that there is, within the framework, a second-order moral norm that claims that certain processes (e.g., processes of implicit racism) are defective bases for forming first-order moral norms. If that second-order norm were sufficiently important to the community, then it might be used to debunk first-order norms that derive from the despised process. (Thanks to Mark Timmons for suggesting this kind of case.) This would be a debunking argument, but since none of the arguments in the literature has been developed in this way, I won't consider it further.

6

Brute Retributivism

Beside good and evil, or in other words, pain and pleasure, the direct
passions frequently arise from a natural impulse or instinct, which is
perfectly unaccountable. Of this kind is the desire of punishment to
our enemies, and of happiness to our friends; hunger, lust, and a few
other bodily appetites.

(Hume, *Treatise* 2.3.9)

Our norms of retributive justice are notoriously difficult to justify. This
leads many philosophers to reject the prescriptive legitimacy of those
norms. Other philosophers attempt to justify retributivism by relying on
moral realism, arguing that retributivism is one of the moral truths. In this
chapter, I will assume that moral realism is false and proceed to argue that
the retributive norm is part of a set of norms that do not need justification.
That is, it is appropriate to retain the norm even if we cannot provide
further reasons in favor of the norm. Of course, this does not mean that
retributivism should stand, all things considered. To determine whether we
should ultimately preserve our retributive norms will depend on a number
of other factors, including both the expected utilities of punishment and our
other core values. Here the aim is simply to keep retributivism on the table.

6.1 A bare retributivist norm

Perhaps the most famous proclamation on retributivism comes from
Kant's remarks on the last murderer:

Even if a civil society were to be dissolved by the consent of all its members (e.g., if a
people inhabiting an island decided to separate and disperse throughout the world),
the last murderer remaining in prison would first have to be executed, so that each
has done to him what his deeds deserve and blood guilt does not cling to the people
for not having insisted upon this punishment; for otherwise the people can be
regarded as collaborators in his public violation of justice. (*Metaphysics of Morals*)

This passage succeeds in illustrating a crucial feature of retributivism—it is a backward-looking, non-consequentialist view. But Kant's example also includes several elements that are not essential to retributivism. Most obviously, Kant demands *capital* punishment. Retributivists need not accept this. It further suggests that failing to exact retribution renders one complicit (sharing "blood guilt") in the villainy, but this isn't essential to retributivism either. Kant's passage also presumes that the *state* has the authority to deliver punishment, but this assumption is not built into retributivism (Murphy 1985; Husak 1992; Shafer-Landau 1996).

Even setting aside the additional elements in Kant's exhortation, retributivism has been developed and defined in a number of different ways.[1] The kind of retributivism to be defended here is a basic form. Michael Moore offers a representative statement: "Retributivism is a very straightforward theory of punishment: We are justified in punishing because and only because offenders deserve it" (Moore 1987, 181). According to Anthony Duff, despite the diversity in retributive theories, all attempt to answer the question, "What is the justificatory relationship between crime and punishment that the idea of desert is supposed to capture: why do the guilty 'deserve to suffer'?" (Duff 2008). There are two distinct elements in these characterizations of retributivist theories of punishment:

  i. A norm that wrongdoers should be punished because (and only because) of their past wrongdoing.
  ii. A justification for the norm.

For reasons that are central to the aim of this chapter, I want to restrict the retributivist theory to the first factor—a retrospective norm prescribing the punishment of wrongdoers.[2] Call this the *bare retributive norm*.[3] As stated, this is a retrospective, backward-looking norm. This distinguishes the theory from other prominent approaches, all of which are

---

[1] See Cottingham (1979) for a cranky paper on the diversity of uses of the term "retributivism" in retributive theories of punishment.

[2] This is still, of course, quite vague. For instance, it leaves open what makes one a "wrongdoer" in the relevant sense.

[3] Etymologically, "retribution" is tied to the notion of repayment. This accords with many prominent accounts of retributive punishment, including Kant's. But the notion of payback is itself morally thick. For it loads into the norm a *reason* for punishment ("the guilty should be punished because it's payback"). As a result, I want to avoid identifying retributivism with a payback theory of punishment.

prospective. Most obviously, a consequentialist ethics of punishment looks to future benefits of punishment (e.g., Bentham 1830; Rawls 1955). But humanitarian approaches (e.g., Menninger 1968) and moral education approaches (e.g., Hampton 1984) are equally forward looking. So too are restorative accounts of punishment, which aim to repair relationships (e.g., Braithwaite 1999). By contrast, the bare retributive norm simply says that wrongdoers should be punished for their past actions.[4]

6.2 The bare retributive norm and the folk

It is widely assumed that ordinary people are retributivists. Indeed, it's often taken for granted that retributivism has its roots in ordinary thought (e.g., Hume 1739/1964 section 2.3.9; Smith 1790/1982, 77–8, 87–91; Mackie 1982). But it is an empirical claim, so it's worth looking to some data. Is there, in folk ethics, a bare retributive norm?

Perhaps the most celebrated empirical work on punishment in recent years comes from experimental economics. There is a complementary line of research in social psychology on people's judgments about sentencing of criminals. This work indicates that people are largely retributivists about sentencing (see esp. Carlsmith et al. 2002 and Carlsmith 2008). For the purposes of this chapter, I want to focus primarily on how people think about punishment in interpersonal interactions rather than how they think about institutionalized forms of criminal punishment. The work in experimental economics is especially apt for this. These experiments involve interactions between individuals in novel scenarios. As a result, there is less chance that subjects are relying on social scripts about criminal punishment. In the economic experiments there is no suggestion of criminal behavior, and both the (apparent) wrongdoing

---

[4] Desert is often invoked in characterizing retributive theories of punishment (e.g., Moore 1987, 181; Duff 2008). The retributivist typically maintains that wrongdoers *deserve* to be punished for their past wrongs. In some cases, saying "wrongdoers deserve to be punished" might just be a restatement of the bare retributive norm. But often the appeal to desert seems to aspire to provide a substantive *justification* for retributivism—the (alleged) fact that wrongdoers deserve to be punished is supposed to be a value-adding reason for endorsing the bare retributive norm. Again, I want to focus narrowly on the bare retributive norm, not on the justifications for it. As a result, insofar as the appeal to desert is supposed to provide a deeper justification for retributive punishment, I want to set aside the notion of desert.

and the punishment are fairly minimal. The experiments even avoid explicit mention of "wrongful" action or "punishment."

Using several different economic games, researchers have shown that participants will punish—deduct money from—those who are perceived to have acted unfairly.[5] In one study, groups of four participants play public goods games anonymously on computers. Each participant gets an allotment of money and is allowed to use the money to invest in a common fund. For each 1 monetary unit an individual invests, each of the four players (including the investor) gets 0.4 units. This provides a net benefit for the group, but the investor himself loses on the transaction. Participants play a series of such games, never with any of the same players. After each game, participants are informed about the contributions of each player and are given a chance to pay to have money deducted from any of the other players in the game. For every 1 monetary unit the punisher pays, 3 monetary units are deducted from the punishee's fund. The participants know that they will not play another game with any of these particular players, so punishing apparently has no future benefit for the punisher. Nonetheless, participants often paid to punish those who contributed less than average (Fehr and Gächter 2002, 137).

In a striking extension of this work, Fehr and Fischbacher (2004b) explored whether third-party observers would punish players in an economic game. The third-party observed two participants engage in a prisoner's dilemma game.[6] The third-party was then given money and asked whether he would use some of this money to pay to deduct funds from either player. Almost half opted to punish a defector in a scenario in which the other player had cooperated (2004, 73).

In both of these studies, the motivation for punishment does not seem to be anything like explicit considerations about utilities—the punisher and punishee both lose money, and the punishers have little reason to

---

[5] I follow experimental economists in categorizing these actions as punishment. This categorization is perfectly appropriate on various philosophical definitions of punishment that aren't narrowly focused on state-sponsored punishment (see, e.g., Baier 1955; Benn 1967; Gaus 2011).

[6] In the Prisoner's Dilemma game, the two players are each given 10 monetary units. The players can either transfer this money to the other person or not. If a player transfers the money, it's tripled, so the other player gets 30 monetary units. Transferring the money counts as *cooperating*, and not transferring counts as *defecting*. So if player A cooperates and B defects, then A will end up with nothing and B will have 40 monetary units.

think the punishment will materially improve the financial situation of any of the players. As a result, Fehr and Gächter dub it "altruistic" punishment.

De Quervain et al. used brain-imaging techniques to explore neural mechanisms involved in altruistic punishment (de Quervain et al. 2004). Participants played the "trust" game, which is explained to all players before the game begins. The game is played anonymously by two people. One player, A, is given a sum of money and given the option to send the money to B. If A does send the money, the amount will be quadrupled. Then B is given the opportunity to send A half of the money or none of it. In the de Quervain experiment, after playing the trust game, A is given the option to deduct money from B. As expected, when B did not send back any money, A often opted to deduct money from B. And when A did engage in such punishment, there was increased activity in brain regions known to be associated with reward (namely, caudate nucleus and dorsal striatum). Thus, it seems that punishing, at least in these games, is rewarding.

These are beautiful and justly famous results, but they don't show that people have a retributive norm. There are many things that I expect myself to do and that no doubt stimulate my reward center but that I don't think that I *should* do. For instance, I expect that I will eat bacon in the future, and the reward structures in my brain will likely respond enthusiastically. But do I think I *should* eat bacon? Do I think that it is a good thing to eat bacon? Of course not. On neither the moral nor the prudential level do I think I should eat bacon. But that will not prevent my reward structures from firing when I eat bacon. Indeed, as de Quervain and colleagues are happy to note, the structures activated by punishment are also activated by consumption of cocaine and nicotine (Breiter et al. 1997; Stein et al. 1998). So, while the imaging results indicate that punishment is *yummy*, they don't show that punishment is guided by a retributive norm. The results don't speak to whether people normatively endorse the behavior that they find rewarding.

Fortunately, it's pretty easy to investigate whether or not people endorse this kind of punitive behavior. We can just *ask* them.[7]

---

[7] Experimental economists have tended to be uninterested in people's explanations for their actions. This might be part of the reason that the topic isn't explored in the original studies.

I conducted a small study to investigate the matter. Participants were presented with one of three versions of the trust game. In all cases, participants were told about an instance of the trust game in which A sends his money to B, and B sends no money back. And in all cases, participants were asked whether an agent *should* deduct money from B. In version 1, A has to pay to deduct money from B. In that case, roughly half of the participants said that A should pay to deduct money. This is similar to the proportions found in many of the one-shot pay-to-punish experiments (e.g. Fehr and Fischbacher 2004b). In version 2, everything was the same, but A can deduct money from B without A himself having to pay anything.[8] In that case, nearly all of the participants said that A should deduct money from B. In the final version, a third party, C, observes the entire set of transactions between A and B. Then C has an opportunity to deduct money from B without C having to pay anything. Nearly all of the participants said that C should deduct money from B.[9]

These results indicate that people do indeed endorse the punitive behavior that we see in the experimental economics games, particularly when it isn't costly. So, the case of punishment is importantly different from my bacon eating. While I don't normatively endorse my bacon consumption, people do normatively endorse punishment. There is a further question however. Just because there is normative endorsement of the punishment behavior doesn't yet mean that the norm is retributive. To begin to investigate this, we can look at the explanations people gave for their answers. Recall that a critical feature of the bare retributive norm is that it is distinctly backward looking. When we examine the explanations participants gave for saying that money should be deducted from B, some of the explanations were, in fact, forward looking. Here are a couple of examples:

---

[8] De Quervain and colleagues call this version "intentional and free" (1256).

[9] The responses were significantly greater than what would be expected by chance alone in both condition 2 and condition 3. To provide a contrast, a fourth condition was run in which a different economic game was described, modeled on an egalitarian-motive game (cf. Dawes et al. 2007). In this game, a computer randomly assigned money to two players. Sometimes the assignments were equal and sometimes they were disproportionate. Participants were asked to judge whether A should deduct money from B if the computer randomly gave B all of the money and A none of it. In this scenario, most people (12 out of 15) said that A *shouldn't* deduct money from B. This was significantly different from chance and much different from the parallel trust game (condition 2).

B was being selfish and should have some money deducted from him so he will learn not to be so self-centered.

I think that A should subtract the money because B should realize that with reward comes responsibility.

Although a few of the explanations included forward-looking considerations, the vast bulk of explanations make no reference at all to the future, focusing instead on *what B did*. Participants were much more likely to invoke only backward-looking factors in their explanations. Here are some representative examples:

It was a selfish act for B not to send any money back to A.
B made money off of A's contribution but A did not get anything in return. B should be punished.
It is unfair that A gave B $12 and B didn't send anything back to A.
B is a jerk and didn't give anything back.

These explanations share the idea that money should be deducted from B *because of what B did*.

The fact that most subjects don't mention forward-looking factors suggests that people are being genuinely retributive. But there is an important limitation to the work that attempts to demonstrate that people's allocation of punishment is retributivist. The claim that people allocate punishment based on a retributive principle is a claim about what people think is *right*. However, the work fails to be sufficiently sensitive to the distinction between a decision procedure and a criterion of rightness. The problem can be illustrated by a tradition of research in social psychology aimed at showing that people are retributivists. Several experiments show that when people make sentencing judgments, familiar consequentialist factors like deterrence and incapacitation play a much smaller role than factors associated with retributivism like severity of the offense, guilt, and extenuating circumstances (see, e.g., Darley et al. 2000; Carlsmith et al. 2002; Carlsmith 2008). For instance, people punish more when the offense is more severe, even when the prospect of re-offense is minimal. Although severity is typically an important factor in retributivist theories, it's not hard to find a reason why severity might play a role in a decision procedure for punishment, even if one thinks that the right criterion is consequentialist. Indeed, one natural possibility is that people punish other players because of the communicative effects of such punishment (e.g., for moral education or norm reinforcement). After all, in the sentencing experiments, the players expect the criminals to be aware of their punishment. Similarly, in the economic experiments, the players expect the punishees to be aware of having their welfare reduced. To address this limitation of extant work, we recently explored punishment in an economic game in which it was quite explicit that the punishee would be unaware of any welfare reduction. Even in this case, people still preferred to punish players who behave in ostensibly unfair ways (Nadelhoffer et al. 2013). Given that the punishees would not even be aware of the punishment, it is more difficult to explain how their preferences are really driven by consequentialist considerations. Rather, such punishment is plausibly driven by a retributive norm that operates without consulting consequentialist considerations.[10]

This non-consequentialism is not a unique feature of the retributive norm. Many of our ethical norms operate independently of consequentialist reasoning (Gill and Nichols 2008). Consider the norm prohibiting incest. If subjects are presented with a vignette in which a brother and sister have consensual sex, with all the prophylactic caution in the world, many subjects persist in thinking that the action was wrong, even though they can't justify their judgment (Haidt et al. 2000). Presumably what is going on here is that subjects have a norm prohibiting incest, and the behavior is categorized as an instance of the prohibited kind. Critically, however, people embrace this norm without having a deeper justification for it. The incest norm is *inferentially basic*—it is not the product of consciously available inferences from other norms or facts. Inferentially basic norms like the incest norm are not the product of another portion of the normative system—they are at the bottom of it all. The retributive norm is a member of this special class of norms. If the bare retributive norm and its downstream consequences were extirpated from our psychology, the norm would not just regenerate from our other consciously available forward-looking norms and values. The bare retributive norm is a basic, independent part of our moral worldview.

---

[10] Indeed, people tend to agree with a quite explicitly non-consequentialist justification of punishment: "People who commit crimes deserve to be punished even if punishing them won't produce any positive benefits to either the offender or society—e.g., rehabilitation, deterring other would-be offenders, etc." (Nadelhoffer et al. 2013).

6.3 Retributivism and the emotions

It's widely assumed that retributivism itself is a product of rather base emotional reactions like anger or resentment. Anger *is* important to retributivism, but the relation between anger and the retributive norm is indirect. Let's start by looking at evidence on anger and retribution in our comfortable domain of economic games.

In the *ultimatum* game—the most intensively studied economic game—one of two anonymous players is randomly assigned to be the *proposer*. The proposer is given a sum of money and told to offer a division of the money to the other player, the *responder*. If the responder accepts the offer, both players get the money, but if the responder rejects the offer, neither gets any of the money. A large body of evidence indicates that when the proposer makes a highly inequitable offer (80/20 or 90/10), responders often refuse the offer, turning down free money.[11] What precipitates this behavior? Anger, apparently. In an early study on the matter, Pillutla and Murnighan (1996) asked participants in an ultimatum game two open-ended questions: "How did you react when you received your offer?" and "How did you feel?" (215). The responses were coded for reports of anger and perceived unfairness. Subsequent analyses showed that when subjects mentioned anger in their responses, this was an excellent predictor of whether they had rejected the offer, even better than perceived unfairness. The researchers offer a simple explanation: when participants regard the offer as unfair, this often triggers anger, and anger increases the tendency to reject the offer (220; see also Bosman and van Winden 2002, 159; Hopfensitz and Reuben 2009).

Fehr and Gächter offer a similar explanation for why people pay to punish in public goods games. They asked their participants to imagine accidently encountering a fellow player who had invested much less than everyone else in the group. Participants were asked to indicate their feelings toward this person (Fehr and Gächter 2002, 139). As expected, participants indicated that they would feel high levels of anger towards this person. Fehr and Gächter draw on this finding, in conjunction with the

---

[11] It's unclear whether we should count these behaviors as instances of punishment (see Gaus 2011). Experimental economists often do presume that rejecting an offer amounts to punishment (e.g., Bolton and Zwick 1995; Sanfey et al. 2003). We don't need to take a stand on this here.

pattern of punishment behavior, to argue that anger (and perhaps related emotions) plays a critical role in generating punishment in these games.

Anger plausibly plays an online role in motivating punishment in economic games. This fits well with a standard picture of the *function* of anger, which dates back at least to Darwin. According to Darwin, anger serves to motivate retaliation. He writes:

animals of all kinds, and their progenitors before them, when attacked or threatened by an enemy, have exerted their utmost powers in fighting and in defending themselves. Unless an animal does thus act, or has the intention, or at least the desire, to attack its enemy, it cannot properly be said to be enraged (1872, 74).

Although punishment behavior is plausibly driven by anger, it would be a serious error to conclude that retributive judgment is identical to feeling anger. I can judge that a given wrongdoer should be punished even if I don't feel any anger, perhaps because the description of the incident is too vague to induce emotion. Similarly, I can think that a class of individuals (say, shoplifters) should be punished while on a perfectly even emotional keel. In addition to the emotion, we also have the retributive *norm*. And the retributive norm can be activated even in the absence of emotional reaction. The reverse is also possible. Anger is sometimes triggered when there is no sensible target of punishment, as when a turn in weather destroys your grand plans for a hike. In this case, the emotion is present, but the norm fails to be activated in any familiar way.

There are thus two elements that are important to retributive punishment—anger and a retributive norm. I've stressed their independence, but there is also, I suspect, an important causal connection between the two. The retributive norm would have inherited cultural strength from its natural links to anger. The idea here draws on epidemiological approaches to cultural evolution (Sperber 1996; Boyer 2000; Nichols 2002). By identifying characteristic features of human psychology, we can get some idea about which kinds of cultural items will be attractive to creatures like us. Many different kinds of emotions—e.g., anger, fear, jealousy, disgust, and sympathy—are characteristic features of human psychology. These emotions make some things naturally attractive and others aversive. As a result, emotions plausibly play an important role in influencing which cultural items are likely to persist. Norms and other cultural items would have increased attractiveness when they resonate with common emotional endowments. For example, etiquette norms prohibiting the display of bodily fluids seem to be preserved once they are introduced into the culture, and a plausible explanation for this is that these prohibitions resonate with our natural proclivity to feel disgust at bodily fluids (Nichols 2004c). In the present context, the relation between emotion, motivation, and norms is rather different, because the retributive norm is prescriptive rather than proscriptive. But there is obviously a closely related story to tell about the cultural evolution of prescriptive norms:

Ceteris paribus, prescriptive norms that encourage behavior that we are independently motivated to perform will enjoy an advantage over prescriptive norms that lack any such connection to motivation.[12]

This principle would apply to the case of retributive norms. For the norm that *wrongdoers should be punished* resonates with our natural anger-driven motivation to retaliate against (perceived) wrongdoers. We *want* to retaliate against wrongdoers. This anger-driven motivation would plausibly contribute to the cultural heft of a norm that prescribes inflicting harm on wrongdoers.

Although anger undergirds the retributive norm, anger itself is unruly. In many cultures, including our own recent past, anger-driven retaliation manifested in the practice of blood feuds, which are not characterized by carefully measured responses. In retaliating against an affront, the aim is often to demonstrate one's power, not to carefully measure the harm and meet it in proportional kind. Thus, retaliation in blood feud often involves harming uninvolved family members of the enemy (e.g., Miller 1990, 180, 197–8; Sommers 2012).[13] This is *not* the narrow retributive norm that we

[12] In previous work (Nichols 2002, 2004c) I formulate an "affective resonance hypothesis" that is limited to proscriptive norms. Here I am extending the idea to prescriptive norms. Of course, insofar as the behavior is motivationally attractive and there are no countervailing considerations, it's not clear that norms play any significant role. You don't need a norm to tell you to remove thorns from your feet. Norms become more obviously significant when there are considerations *against* performing the prescribed action. In the interesting cases, there will likely be such considerations. For instance, we have a prescriptive norm of benevolence, and this competes straightforwardly with self-interest. Similarly, the prescriptive norm of punishment often competes with material self-interest in the short term (though perhaps not in the long term [see Frank 1988]).

[13] Killing the relatives of wrongdoers is even prescribed in an item in the code of Hammurabi. The son of a carpenter might be executed for his father's shoddy work:

If a builder build a house for some one, and does not construct it properly, and the house which he built fall in and kill ... the son of the owner the son of that builder shall be put to death (229 and 230).

embrace today. Unlike blood feud, the bare retributive norm directly targets the wrongdoer.

Somehow the unruly retaliatory practices associated with blood feud get displaced by the narrow norm of retribution, tied to the wrongdoer and proportionality. As biblical scholars have observed for decades (see, e.g., Berlin and Brettler 2004), the injunction to take an *eye for an eye* (Ex. 21:23, 24; Lev. 24:19, 20; and Deut. 19:21) was introduced as a more *moderate* approach to retaliation than the dangerously escalating blood feuds (Gen. 4: 23–4). We get a similar phenomenon in the history of early English law. As feudalism replaces tribalism in England, compensation takes the place of the feud (Jeffery 1957, 665; Harding 1966, 21). To pacify the victim or victim's family, the law indicated that the victim needed to be paid. The laws themselves are graphically specific:

If an ear be struck off, let bot [monetary restitution] be made with 12 shillings.
If the other ear hear not, let bot be made with 25 shillings.
If an ear be pierced, let bot be made with 3 shillings.
If an ear be mutilated, let bot be made with 6 shillings. (Laws of Ethelbert)

Eventually, of course, this system of victim compensation gives way to the idea that striking off an ear is a crime against the state, requiring something more from the wrongdoer than payment of damages (cf. Maine 1861, chap. 10). This development in the history of law is a further departure from the anger-driven retaliatory practices of our ancestors.

All of this suggests that our (narrow) retributive norm was not fashioned *ex nihilo*, spewing forth from rationality. Instead, our retributive norm is a product of cultural pruning. The unfocused retaliatory norms and practices of our ancestors were reshaped and refined, leaving us with the vestige we have today. But *anger* was likely a sustaining factor throughout this cultural evolution of punishment norms. Had our ancestors lacked the propensity for anger at wrongdoers, we would likely not have the retributive norm we do today.

6.4 Justification

Thus far, I've argued that (i) judgments about punishment are guided by a bare retributive norm that is inferentially basic and (ii) anger contributed to the cultural success of this norm. If this psychological–historical account of the bare retributive norm is right, it should not be surprising if we can't justify the retributive norm. We inherited our retributive norm from emotion-driven cultural evolution and not through rational discovery.

Retributivism is, as a matter of fact, notoriously difficult to justify. The temptation is to defend retributivism by pointing to its future benefits: If we are retributive, then this will provide a deterrent. Or, if we are retributive, then this will enhance cooperation. Or, if we are retributive, this will forestall the pursuit of vengeance by the victim. These kinds of proposals are philosophically appealing. But they are intuitively unsatisfying; for they invoke *prospective* reasons for punishing, while the norm is expressly backward looking (cf. Bedau 1978, 616; Mackie 1982, 4). Insofar as the retributive norm is inferentially basic, it is natural that these "deeper" justifications are unsatisfying. Consider the inferentially basic norm that parents have special obligations to their children. Attempts to give a "deeper" justification for this norm, e.g., in terms of societal benefits, are bound to seem wrong-headed. So too, the appeal to future benefits is bound to seem intuitively inadequate as a complete justification for the backward-looking retributive norm.

In the face of this, a typical response is to renounce retributivism. Many intellectuals find bare retributivism offensive—it counsels harming someone without getting any offsetting benefit. In this light, people seem to prefer *anything else*—humanitarianism, restorative justice, utilitarianism. Duff makes this point nicely:

Many people, including those who do not take a consequentialist view of other matters, think that any adequate justification of punishment must be basically consequentialist. For we have here a practice which inflicts, indeed seeks to inflict significant hardship or pain: how else could we hope to justify it than by showing that it brings consequential benefits sufficiently large to outweigh, and thus justify, that hardship and pain (2008).

There is one prominent metaethical view that offers a haven for philosophers trying to defend an uncompromising retributivism: moral realism. According to moral realism, the basic moral truths are "stance-independent"; they are not made true because of our (or anyone else's) attitudes, norms, emotions, etc. (see, e.g., Shafer-Landau 2003, 15).[14] A retributivist can draw on this metaethical view to maintain that the

---

[14] The notion of realism here is, of course, very similar to the notion of objectivism in Chapter 5. I use the term "realism" here because I will use Michael Moore as the key figure, and he explicitly identifies as a moral *realist* (e.g., Moore 1982, 1987).

retributive norm reflects a moral truth about the rightness of punishment, a truth that is independent of what our norms or emotions or evaluative reactions happen to be. Michael Moore is perhaps the most prominent advocate of this view in the recent literature. He maintains that retributivism captures a moral truth, and he argues that the emotions play an important role in getting us to appreciate this truth: "The emotions are . . . heuristic guides for us, an extra source of insight into moral truths beyond the knowledge we can gain from sensory and inferential capacities alone" (Moore 1987, 201; also 189). The moral truth of retributivism is independent of the emotions, but the emotions help us tap into moral truths (186–7). They are "important but not essential in our reaching moral truths" (202). In the case of retributivism, Moore suggests that the emotions of guilt and fellow feeling lead us to appreciate the truth of retributivism (209ff.).

There are reasons to be skeptical of Moore's appeal to emotions as indicators of moral truth, but I want to focus on a broader point. The retributivist realist is true to the cause—no consequentialism in retributivist clothing here. But the attempted defense of retributivism is precarious. For should moral realism be false, retributivist realism leaves us with no basis for preserving the bare retributive norm. And moral realism is disputed by a great number of philosophers, starting perhaps with Hutcheson and Hume but continuing in a frenzy of late (e.g., Mackie 1977; Gibbard 1990; Harman 1996, 19; Blackburn 1998; Timmons 1999; Joyce 2002; Nichols 2004c; Sinnott-Armstrong 2006; Street 2006; Prinz 2007; Greene 2008). Should this wave of dissent from realism be right, the retributivist seems to be left without a hope of sustaining the view.

6.5 Ethical conservatism

The tempting defenses of retributivism seem to either fail to be intuitively retributive or they rely on highly contentious metaethical assumptions. I am going to assume that moral realism is false—that there is no moral truth that stands independent of our attitudes and feelings. With that (major) assumption in place, I suggest that we don't *need* to have a justification for the retributive norm in order for it to retain its legitimacy for us.[15]

---

[15] At least on some readings, similar views are suggested in Strawson (1962) and Mackie (1982).

As I argued in the previous chapter, in the case of metaphysical beliefs, if we show that a belief in the domain is formed by a process that is neither reliable nor rational, this undercuts any basis for sustaining the belief. We also saw that Greene applies a debunking argument to normative ethics, and in particular, to retributivism (Greene 2008; see also Singer 2005). First, Greene notes that our retributive inclinations are grounded in arational emotions. Attempts at justifying retribution are, Greene suggests, "just rationalizations for our retributivist feelings . . . the natural history of our retributivist dispositions makes it unlikely that they reflect any sort of deep moral truth" (2008, 71). Greene uses these considerations about the emotional origins as the basis for debunking retributivism and other deontological principles (Greene 2008; see also Singer 2005, 350).

Discovering that arational emotions generate beliefs in metaphysics, metaethics, or religion might be reason to suspend those beliefs. But in domains in which realism is rejected, it is far from clear that the normal justificatory demands on belief formation apply. The vast bulk of our ordinary ethical worldview likely derives from fundamentally arational emotional processes (Blair 1995; Prinz 2007; Gill and Nichols 2008). For instance, were it not for the fact that we find human suffering aversive, we would likely not have the moral revulsion we do at killing. Nor would we feel the moral obligation for helping strangers. I am assuming here, with irrealism, that there is no ultimate rational justification for these norms. They are the norms we happen to have, given the kinds of emotional propensities we happen to have. But notice how dramatic it would be to cast these norms out of morality. To limit our ethics to norms that have some ultimate rational justification would leave us with an ethics more barren than almost anyone would be willing to accept.[16]

---

[16] As noted in 5.5.2, Peter Singer presents a Greene-style argument that deontological intuitions are based in arational emotions and hence lack any rational justification (2005, 347ff.). However, he holds out optimism that moral skepticism can be avoided, suggesting that there are some *rational intuitions*, like "it is a bad thing if a person is killed" (Singer 2005, 350–1). Singer doesn't actually provide an argument that this intuition is somehow rationally grounded, and, for my part, I find it hard to see why we should think that this intuition has such an exceptional epistemic status. But in the present context, the more important point is that even if (as moral irrealists would maintain) this intuitive norm lacks a rational ground, that would not be enough to persuade us to abandon the norm. Indeed, presumably Singer himself, if convinced that there is no rational ground for any of our ethical commitments, would not abandon all of those commitments.

Instead of reverting to such an emaciated ethics, we might adopt an *ethical conservatism*, according to which certain ethical norms do not lose their normative legitimacy even if the norms do not derive from the kinds of processes that confer justification for beliefs about metaphysics (Nichols et al. 2014). If *none* of our ethical beliefs has an ultimate justification, then, barring a complete upheaval of commonsense ethics, we are bound to grant normative clout to *some* moral norms that lack any ultimate justification.

A full defense of this ethically conservative position is clearly beyond the scope of this chapter, but it is important to note that not *all* norms have this privileged status. It accrues to norms that run deep in our psychology—norms that are *entrenched*. Entrenched norms in this sense have three features. First, they are widespread in the community. Second, entrenched norms are inferentially basic, i.e., not inferentially dependent on other norms or facts (see section 6.2).[17] Finally, entrenched norms are rooted in human emotion—they resonate with our natural emotional endowment. The norm "help suffering children" provides a compelling example of an entrenched norm. The norm is widespread in our culture. And it is plausibly a result of our emotional reactions to suffering and not from a process of rational inference from more basic principles.[18]

Ethical conservatism maintains that the fact that our ethical norms are not ultimately justified does not eradicate their normative legitimacy.

None of this is to say that the presence of a rational ground is epistemically irrelevant. If there is a rational ground for some ethical norm, then *that's* the best reason for sustaining the norm. But if the irrealist is right that none of our ethical norms has any ultimate rational ground, that doesn't mean that we are obliged to abandon our norms.

[17] Norms that are *not* inferentially basic are undercut if they depend on factual or inferential errors. To take an obvious example, many people who oppose abortion do so on the basis of factual beliefs (e.g., about whether the fetus has a soul). If we come to know that the factual beliefs that underpin a normative conviction are false, this undermines the warrant for the conviction.

[18] We have a large body of entrenched norms, including norms against theft, incest, and harming innocents, as well as norms promoting retribution, reparations, and special obligations to family. Some normative ethicists might presume that one of our entrenched norms can be the foundation for all of ethics. These are large issues in philosophical ethics, and I can't do justice to them here. But I see no reason to expect that one of our entrenched norms will serve to fund all of the rest of our cherished ethical commitments. Nor do I see any overwhelming normative reason to impose such a monistic assumption on our ethical theorizing. As a result, I propose to proceed with an ethical conservatism that grants an initial legitimacy to each entrenched norm.

This accords with the classical sentimentalist tradition, which draws a deep analogy between aesthetics and ethics. In both cases, our normative judgments are a function of human nature—it's because of the emotional nature we happen to have that we make the aesthetic and ethical judgments that we do. In addition, classical sentimentalism maintains that the fact that emotions are at the bottom of our ethical and aesthetic lives doesn't undermine the legitimacy of either ethical or aesthetic norms (see Gill 2007).[19]

In sum, ethical conservatism accords a special status for normative commitments that are rooted in human emotion and are not inferentially dependent on other norms or facts. These norms can retain their normative legitimacy even though they might result from patently arational processes. The primary reason for accepting ethical conservatism is that it provides a natural way to preserve commonsense morality in the face of its emotional, arational origins.[20] And the analogy with aesthetics provides a kind of existence argument for how emotion-based norms can retain their normative legitimacy.

---

[19] I have been maintaining that these entrenched norms don't need justification. Others might prefer to say that such norms are "*self*-justifying." For present purposes, it's not important whether there is a real distinction here. What matters is that the entrenched norms retain their authority.

[20] One might maintain that the category of entrenched norms is too broad, and that some classes of entrenched norms should not be granted special status of initial normative legitimacy. For example, one might maintain that entrenched norms based on disgust don't merit this status. That is an interesting view, but it would require an argument to motivate it. (Dan Kelly argues that some disgust-based norms should be uprooted, but he doesn't argue for a sweeping rejection of all disgust-based norms [Kelly 2011].) In the absence of such an argument, I'll proceed with the broad category that grants the special status to all entrenched norms.

A more specific worry here is that some entrenched norms will in fact be norms that we think should be rejected. Take the norm that it is morally wrong to be homosexual. In our own community 50 years ago, this was likely an entrenched norm—widely held, rooted in the emotions, and inferentially basic. Yet I certainly don't want to say that we should have sustained this entrenched norm. The fact that conservatism seems to suggest otherwise is obviously an important objection to the view. But we can make some distance towards addressing the objection by noting that the norm that vilifies homosexuals conflicts with other important entrenched values concerning fairness, rights, and welfare. The history of dislodging the vilification of homosexuality is replete with the invocation of norms about unfair treatment, harm, and privacy. Furthermore, it is well within the available resources of the non-realist framework that I am assuming to say that we were *right* to privilege our norms of fairness, privacy, and welfare over the anti-homosexuality norm.

6.6   Competing considerations

The retributive norm is entrenched—it is widespread, inferentially basic (section 6.2), and rooted in a basic human emotion (section 6.3). Since the retributive norm is entrenched, the ethical conservatism sketched earlier entails that the retributive norm is not undermined by the absence of rational justification. The bare retributive norm thus retains an initial normative legitimacy, even in the face of its arational, emotional basis. But of course the standing of entrenched norms is not unassailable. The view is *conservative*, not *reactionary*. Being an ethical conservative does not entail rigid deference to all entrenched norms. There can be competing moral considerations that lead us to think it right to reject an entrenched norm.

Some entrenched commitments do not face obvious competing moral considerations. For example, "help suffering strangers" seems broadly consistent with the remainder of our moral concerns. Other entrenched norms do face competing moral considerations. Consider first an example quite apart from punishment—organ donation. There continues to be significant resistance to organ donation, with cultural variations in the extent of resistance (see, e.g., Braun and Nichols 1997). There *is* something repellant about the practice of having one's child disemboweled after death. It's likely that there is (or was) an entrenched norm against defiling the body of one's deceased child by extracting her organs. The majority of Westerners now accept the propriety of organ donation.[21] And we've done so because of a competing ethical consideration—an enormous benefit to another person. In light of the fact that a deceased child's organs can save another person's life, we have overcome our entrenched norm against allowing someone to root around in our dead children's bodies.

Are there competing moral factors when we look to our retributive norm? Of course. *Ceteris paribus* it's wrong to harm others. Retributivism involves *intentionally harming* others. This is the core of the familiar complaint against retributivism—retributivism promotes intentionally harming someone without getting any (other) benefit out of it (Duff 2008). This is obviously an important challenge to retributivism. To begin to meet it, I first want to suggest that in Western philosophical

---

[21]   The Gallup Organization, Inc. 2005 National Public Opinion Survey on Organ Donation.

ethics, we have come to fetishize harm, as if it trumps any other ethical considerations. But there are plausibly cases in which it can be appropriate to cause harm to someone in the service of other non-harm-based concerns. Say that I promised my grandmother that I would visit her grave every Memorial Day, but that when the time comes, I need to wake my sleeping wife to get the car keys. Waking someone from sleep sets back their welfare, probably more so than a punch on the arm. But we regard waking someone under those circumstances as permissible. Or, to take a pervasive case, most readers will agree that it is okay to tax the successful bachelor farmer even if the government services he gets are not commensurate with the amount of taxes he pays. Many programs that our tax dollars support do not provide any benefit for the successful bachelor farmer: public broadcasting, NEH, NEA, humanitarian aid. The bachelor farmer might well not want to relinquish a penny for any of these programs. At best, they are of no use to him; at worst, he might find them despicable. In any case, taking his money for these services is an unequivocal harm to him. But that doesn't make us think it wrong to tax him. For, at least in some cases, like humanitarian aid, we think that moral considerations outweigh the harm to him.

Of course, the fact that it can be acceptable to cause a harm in the service of some competing ethical norms doesn't show that this holds in the case of retributive punishment. It might be that harming really does globally override the retributive norm. But the nature of the issue is obscured by focusing on the severity of the punishment. Thus Duff speaks of the worry that our practice of punishment "seeks to inflict significant hardship or pain" (2008). The issue is further obscured by the fact that discussions of retributivism typically revolve around punishing criminals in a large-scale society. But the bare-retributive norm doesn't say anything directly about technique or state-sponsored punishment. It just says that wrongdoers should be punished.

I want to argue that there are cases of punishment in which the fact that we are producing a harm isn't, by itself, enough to override the legitimacy of the retributive norm. The fact that we're harming someone isn't enough to undermine the judgment that the wrongdoer should be punished. To soften the ground, though, I want to return to the case of organ donation. In "The Wisdom of Repugnance," Leon Kass maintains that our natural revulsion at various medical procedures is ethically revelatory: "Repugnance . . . revolts against the excesses of human willfulness, warning us not to transgress what is unspeakably profound" (Kass 1997, 20). This repugnance suggests to us, according to Kass, that there is something wrong with, *inter alia*, in vitro fertilization, cloning, and organ donation. Kass has been rightly criticized for his faith in repugnance as an ethical indicator (e.g., Harris 1998). While "wisdom" no doubt inflates the epistemic value of repugnance, there is something to the idea that repugnance is not to be ignored. As noted earlier, there is a natural resistance to the idea that it's okay to have one's child disemboweled after death. In our culture, we have come to accept the propriety of organ donation. But note that the benefits of organ donation are tremendous. Imagine that the benefits were smaller, say, that by organ transplantation, the net gain would be a reduction in the number of sniffles. In that case, it would scarcely be worth suspending the norm against disemboweling dead children. I would not sanction harvesting the organs of my dead child to help relieve someone's runny nose. Kass might be wrong to view repugnance as wise. But it's not like our felt resistance to organ donation counts for *nothing*.

Recall where we are—the claim is that we have an entrenched commitment to the retributive norm and this endows the norm with a legitimacy that isn't eradicated by the fact that the norm has an arational source. Does the fact that retribution involves intentional harm count as sufficient reason to overturn the retributive norm? The point of the organ donation example is that the stakes can make a big difference to how we think about competing ethical considerations. To evaluate the competing considerations in the case of punishment, it will be important to avoid vexed issues about criminality and incarceration. Instead, let's return to our economic games. In these games, people think that those who behave unfairly should have money deducted from their fund. For instance, many people say that one should pay $.25 to have $.75 deducted from the unfair player. And virtually everyone says that if it doesn't cost the punisher any money, he should deduct money from the unfair player. Here we have a sharp case of competing factors. The retributive norm says *punish* B (by $.75), and this competes with the fact that we would be setting back B by $.75 (with no benefit). In this competition, does the loss of $.75 to B suffice to overturn the norm that wrongdoers should be punished? Does our commitment to retributivism count for so little—75 cents? It is an affront to commonsense ethics that our commitment to retribution is so cheaply bought off. Of course, as the harms increase in scale, the competition can become more challenging. At some point, no doubt, the retributive norm does get overridden in virtue of the competing considerations. However, if it's right that $.75 doesn't buy off the retributive norm, then there is no general rejection of retributivism issued by the fact that it involves intentionally harming someone.

Competing considerations about intentional harm might tip the balance against harsh punishments, but that doesn't justify *globally* overturning our entrenched commitment to retribution. When we consider institutionalized forms of punishment, like incarceration or the death penalty, it might be appropriate to oppose those techniques on a variety of grounds. These practices might be excessively severe; the practices might unfairly skew to certain racial groups; the practices might demand a higher standard of evidence of guilt than is typically obtained. There are numerous reasons one might oppose capital punishment or incarceration. But, if the line of argument here is right, the fact that the punishment is retributive is not itself a reason to oppose it.[22]

6.7 Conclusion

Despite its ubiquity in ordinary life, the retributive norm has resisted rational justification. This leads many to reject the legitimacy of retributivism. But unless we take on controversial metaethical assumptions like moral realism, we are bound to accept some basic moral norms without justification. For the vast bulk of ordinary moral thought likely emanates from arational, emotional sources. Rather than conclude that this invalidates ordinary moral thought, we can reject the assumption that, in order to carry normative legitimacy, a norm must be justified (or capable of justification). Some norms retain normative legitimacy even if they have no independent justification. I've suggested that the norms that have this

---

[22] In my defense of brute retributivism, I have avoided appealing to any benefits of retributivism. For to appeal to benefits of retributivism leaves one open to that charge that retributivism is being justified by nonretributive, consequentialist considerations (Bedau 1978, 616; Mackie 1982, 208). However, when we turn to the broader question about whether to sustain the retributive norm in light of other ethical considerations, we must consider the costs and benefits of the retributive norm. And the benefits appear to be quite significant. In particular, the retributive norm likely plays a crucial role in facilitating cooperation (see Gaus 2011).

special status are those that are widespread, rooted in emotions, and inferentially basic. The bare retributive norm falls in this class. As a result, the fact that we can't justify the norm doesn't defeat the norm. This leaves open a number of issues about punishment—how to punish, what to punish, who should punish. Indeed, as we will explore in the next chapter, the hard incompatibilist has a global argument against moral responsibility and retributivism. So it remains an open question whether, all things considered, we should sustain retributivism. But we shouldn't take the lack of independent justification as a sufficient reason to abandon our brute retributivism.

7

After Incompatibilism

> Some philosophers have...written as if moral concepts were a
> timeless, limited, unchanging, determinate species of concept,
> necessarily having the same features throughout their history...In
> fact, of course, moral concepts change as social life changes.
>
> (MacIntyre 1966)

From the first time I encountered the problem of free will in college, it
struck me that a clear-eyed view of free will and moral responsibility
demanded some form of eliminativism. Libertarianism seemed delusional,
and compatibilism seemed in bad faith. Hence I threw my lot in with
philosophers like Paul Holbach, Galen Strawson, and Derk Pereboom who
conclude that no one is truly morally responsible. But after two decades of
self-identifying as an eliminativist, it occurred to me that I had continued
to treat my friends, colleagues, and acquaintances as morally responsible.
Hardly ever did I call on my philosophical views to excuse people's actions.
I'm increasingly inclined to think that my practice was often appropriate
and that it was my philosophical view that was defective. In this chapter,
I defend the practice. The guiding vision is provided in the epigraph from
MacIntyre. Even though we are committed to incompatibilism about
responsibility, we needn't be completely hostage to this commitment. In
many contexts, we might relinquish or ignore the commitment rather than
give up our practices that depend on moral responsibility.

In this chapter, I will assume that incompatibilism is intuitive. More
precisely, I will assume that the folk find it intuitive that if determinism is
true, moral responsibility is undermined (see Chapter 4). Further, I will
assume that determinism is true.[1] The questions of interest will be

---

[1] The broader assumption is really that we lack libertarian free will, and various
indeterminist theses are also incompatible with free will. I focus on determinism merely
to ease exposition.

subsequent to this. If people came to believe in determinism, would this lead to major changes in our everyday lives? *Should* it lead to major changes? Eliminativists tend to answer *yes* to both questions. Determinism would and should lead to major changes in our everyday interactions.[2] I'll maintain that the answer to both questions is likely *no*. In the case of the descriptive question, the evidence is fragmentary, but it suggests that people will pretty much stick with the status quo. I'll then turn to the prescriptive question, and for the bulk of the chapter, I will draw on work in emotion theory to argue that there are good reasons to resist the cries for a revolution in our everyday lives. At the end of the chapter, I will return to the pluralistic themes from Chapter 3 and argue that there are also contexts where it is appropriate to affirm eliminativism.

7.1 The descriptive question

If people come to accept determinism, what will happen? Opinions on this question differ radically. Some maintain that this would usher in a glorious revolution in our practices. Others worry that the recognition of determinism would lead to catastrophe. I have a more humdrum guess— if people come to accept determinism, things will remain pretty much the same.

It's natural for incompatibilists to assume that a broad-scale recognition that we lack free will would have dramatic implications. For incompatibilists think that our everyday practices of praise and blame, as well as related emotions like pride, guilt, and resentment, presuppose that we have libertarian free will. As a result, if we come to reject such free will, this would rip out the undergirding of the practices. These kinds of considerations lead Joshua Greene and Jonathan Cohen to predict a major shift:

> As more and more scientific facts come in, providing increasingly vivid illustrations of what the human mind is really like, more and more people will develop moral intuitions that are at odds with our current moral practices (Greene and Cohen 2004, 28).

---

[2] The focus in this chapter concerns our private lives and personal interactions, not the penal system or other matters of public policy. Those issues merit a separate discussion.

In particular, they say, we will stop thinking that people are responsible and that the guilty deserve punishment. "The law will continue to punish misdeeds, as it must for practical reasons, but the idea of distinguishing the truly, deeply guilty from those who are merely victims of neuronal circumstances will . . . seem pointless" (30). In this bright new future, we will dispense with our barbaric views that depend on libertarianism.

Other philosophers have worried that if people give up on libertarian free will, this might have dire effects on everyday life, and as a result, some have suggested that we ought to keep the truth hidden from the hoi polloi. This fits with a venerable strand of paternalism in ethics. A number of philosophers who embrace a utilitarian ethics maintain that there would be bad consequences if the man on the street actually knew that utilitarianism captured the truth about ethics. Hence, they counsel concealment. In his influential utilitarian treatise, Henry Sidgwick writes:

a Utilitarian may reasonably desire, on Utilitarian principles, that some of his conclusions should be rejected by mankind generally; or even that the vulgar should keep aloof from his system as a whole, in so far as the inevitable indefiniteness and complexity of its calculations render it likely to lead to bad results in their hands (1907, 490).

More colorfully, William Lycan writes, "I believe . . . firmly in some form of act-utilitarianism in ethics, but the sacred principle of utility itself forbids me even telling you this" (1987, 136n1). The worry is that people will behave badly if they come to believe utilitarianism. Hence, the utilitarian maintains that we should keep the truth secret.

Similarly, if we thought that anarchy and despair would ensue if people knew that there is no libertarian free will, this might count as a reason to resist informing the public of the truth. Such is the view of Saul Smilansky. He maintains that if people come to realize the absence of libertarian free will, this will very likely harm "our fundamental values, practices, and attitudes, such as abhorrence about the 'punishment' of the innocent, the inherent value we put on 'equality of opportunity', belief in our potential for blameworthiness" (Smilansky 2000, 189). The guilt-response will also come under threat, according to Smilansky: "compunction seems conceptually problematic and psychologically dubious when it concerns matters that, it is understood, ultimately one could not in fact help doing. But such genuine feelings of responsibility . . . are crucial to being responsible selves!" (2002, 500). More generally, Smilansky fears that if people recognize that they lack free will, they "might succumb to . . . an unprincipled nihilism" (2000, 189). As a result of this, Smilansky counsels that we not disabuse people of their mistaken belief in free will. Better to let them live in the illusion of free will than to risk catastrophe.

To evaluate the descriptive question, we should be explicit about the playing field. If people come to accept determinism, this will generate a kind of competition between theoretical incompatibilist considerations and standing practices that impute responsibility. There are two primary possibilities of interest for how this competition plays out:

(i) people will recognize that no one is really responsible and hence grant blanket exemptions;

(ii) people will persist pretty much as before in their responsibility attributions and practices.

The latter option might come about in different ways—people might renounce their commitment to incompatibilism, or they might simply neglect this aspect of their thought. For present purposes, we can remain neutral about this.

General considerations about cultural evolution provide some reason to favor (ii). For we know that emotions and motivation are powerful factors in cultural evolution. Of special relevance for our purposes, norms that resonate with our emotions are more likely to persist than norms that don't resonate (Nichols 2004c). And our practices of attributing responsibility come with strong emotional backing. Consider, for instance, the retributive norm that the guilty deserve to be punished. This plausibly gets support from the fact that anger is a powerful and pervasive response to wrongdoing (see section 7.2.1).

There is a modicum of historical evidence that suggests that anger does play a sustaining role in punishment norms. In the history of ancient law, one central theme is that early law arose by institutionalizing vengeance. Oliver Wendell Holmes writes, "It is commonly known that the early forms of legal procedure were grounded in vengeance. Modern writers have thought that the Roman law started from the blood feud, and all the authorities agree that the German law begun in that way" (Holmes 1881). If we look at the history of criminal law in England, we find that laws against actions likely to provoke anger (e.g., assault, rape, murder, theft) all get preserved once they are entered. Most statutes do not get revoked, but the ones that did get revoked were not closely tied to actions intrinsically likely to provoke anger. Rather, here are central examples of the kinds of actions for which statutes were repealed (Stephen 1883):

Denying the trinity
Skipping church
Convincing others to skip church
Exportation of wool
Taking more than 10 percent interest
Buying up goods to raise prices
Buying goods wholesale and then selling them wholesale
Vagrancy
Non-elite hunting game on own land

These laws lacked the kind of intrinsic emotional support that attends actions like assault, murder, theft, and rape.[3]

Given the emotional support that underpins our retributivist norms and responsibility practices, the general considerations about cultural evolution predict that those norms and practices will persist. Still, that's a weak prediction base, and there might be emotional factors that push in the other direction. So we would do well to consult some evidence on the matter.

There are, as it happens, some major cultural groups that have embraced a kind of determinism—religious predestination. Such groups are found in Jewish, Islamic, and Christian traditions. The Essenes were a Jewish sect that existed around the time of Jesus, and are presumed to be responsible for the Dead Sea Scrolls. Josephus characterizes their view as follows: "the sect of the Essenes affirm, that fate governs all things, and that nothing befalls men but what is according to its determination" (Josephus, *Antiquities* 13, 172). In early Islam, the Jabarites believed that God determines everything (Thompson 1950, 215; Khadduri 1984, 41). And, most familiarly, Calvinists maintain that our fates are all predestined. Calvin puts it thus: "By predestination we mean the eternal decree

---

[3] People can be led to feel anger over anything, including violations of norms about church and commerce. But the point is that our emotion systems are independently primed to be activated by rape, murder, and theft.

of God, by which he determined with himself whatever he wished to happen with regard to every man. All are not created on equal terms, but some are preordained to eternal life, others to eternal damnation" (Calvin, *Institutes*, vol. 3, chapter 21, section 5).

So, what are the attitudes about responsibility and justice among these groups that embrace religious determinism? Let's start with the Essenes. Josephus says that the Essenes "allot to bad souls a dark and tempestuous den, full of never-ceasing punishments" (Josephus, *War* 2, 157). And in the Dead Sea Scrolls, we find a description of an initiation rite that includes the following curse on evildoers: "Be cursed because of all your guilty wickedness! May He deliver you up for torture at the hands of the vengeful Avengers! May He visit you with destruction by the hand of all the Wreakers of Revenge! Be cursed without mercy because of the darkness of your deeds! Be damned in the shadowy place of everlasting fire!" (1 Qumram Scroll, II, 5–9). In Islam, although there is variation on whether predestination is true, all parties agreed that "Divine Justice is perfect, eternal, and ideal" (Khadduri 1984, 41). Finally, we have Calvin, who espouses an explicitly compatibilist view. He writes, "none perish without deserving it" and "the reprobate suffer nothing which is not accordant with the most perfect justice." Indeed, Calvin scolds, "there is not the least occasion for our caviling" (Calvin, *Institutes*, vol. 3, chapter 24, sections 12 and 14).

Thus, in these examples of major cultural groups who embrace a kind of determinism, we find that the groups do not renounce responsibility. To be sure, the Essenes, Jabarites, and Calvinists have not endured so well to this day. But the key point for our purposes is that their de facto compatibilist views were not displaced by a rejection of moral responsibility. Rather, their views were displaced by *libertarian* views (see, e.g., Slone 2004, 93–6). Perhaps, then, Libertarianism culturally trumps the kind of compatibilist views we find in Calvin, but Hard Determinism apparently trumps neither.

Now, one might well complain that these cases are compromised by the fact that they derive from religious views. So let's consult the history of philosophy. Again, our question is what will happen if people come to embrace determinism. What we find in the early modern period is that philosophers who accept determinism are *at least* as likely to be compatibilists as they are to be hard determinists. Of the major philosophers in the period, we traditionally count Locke, Leibniz, Hobbes, Hume, Pascal,

Wolff, and Condillac as compatibilists, and Spinoza, Holbach, Diderot, Lessing, and Voltaire as hard determinists (see Nichols 2007 for citations). So even among those we take to be most reflective and philosophically sensitive, we find at least as many embrace compatibilism as hard determinism.

Finally, there is a modicum of recent experimental evidence that bears on this issue. In a large cross-cultural study, we found that people who responded as determinists were more likely to respond as compatibilists about responsibility (Sarkissian et al. 2010). Using a different strategy, Adina Roskies and I conducted an experiment in which determinism was presented either as something true in an alternate universe or as something true in our own world.[4] In the experiment, subjects read nontechnical descriptions of determinism. In one condition, subjects were told to imagine another universe that was deterministic, and in the other condition, subjects were told to imagine that *our* universe was deterministic. In the "other universe" condition, subjects tended to say that it's impossible for agents to be fully morally responsible in that universe; however, in the "our universe" condition, subjects tended to say that it would still be possible for agents to be fully morally responsible if our universe is deterministic (Roskies and Nichols 2008). This suggests that people's views about responsibility and determinism become more compatibilist when they are forced to consider determinism about their own world.

The foregoing evidence is obviously fragmentary. But every bit of it— from cultural and intellectual history to experimental evidence—points in the same direction. What *would* happen if people embraced determinism is apparently neither revolution nor catastrophe. Rather, what would happen seems to be largely *status quo*. Of course, we might exert effort to dislodge the status quo if we came to think that morality demanded it. So we need to ask whether we should start a revolution.

---

[4] I reviewed this experiment in section 4.1.1, but I only told part of the story—the alternate universe part, which suggests intuitive incompatibilism. Here we see the rest of the story—people become more inclined to embrace compatibilism when they are faced with the prospect that determinism is true of our own world. Chris Weigel got related results in a subtle study using different kinds of construal (Weigel 2011).

7.2 The prescriptive question

Even if a belief in determinism is unlikely to change people's behavior, many incompatibilists maintain that it *should* do so. That's part of what makes hard determinism so bracing. It typically counsels revolution. Some incompatibilists who deny free will do not promote revolution (e.g., Smilansky 2000). But the main line of free will eliminativists are *revolutionaries* who maintain that since we lack libertarian free will, we need to radically revise our everyday practices (e.g., Waller 1990; Strawson 1994; Pereboom 2001, 2007; Sommers 2005, 2007).[5] In this section, I will offer broadly Strawsonian considerations that weigh against revolution.[6]

In the wake of P. F. Strawson's "Freedom and Resentment," perhaps the major battle between revolutionaries and counter-revolutionaries has been fought over the "reactive attitudes"—moral sentiments like resentment, indignation, guilt, and gratitude which are tied up with blaming and praising others. These sentiments directly impact our day-to-day lives; by contrast, theoretical reflections occupy us only fleetingly and with sustained effort.[7] Revolutionaries want to extirpate the practices and attitudes that depend on the mistaken belief in moral responsibility, and they are rightly sensitive to the importance of the reactive attitudes in our everyday lives (Strawson 1986; Waller 1990; Pereboom 2001, 2007; Sommers 2005, 2007).

I want to explore two Strawsonian considerations against a revolution. The first consideration is an appeal to insulationism about our normal reactive attitudes. This move might not suffice to beat back the revolutionary, but it is instructive nonetheless. The second consideration, the appeal to "gains and losses to human life," does, I argue, provide a powerful reason to oppose the revolution.

---

[5] On Vargas' taxonomy of revisionism, revolutionaries would count as strongly revisionist. Vargas characterizes strong revisionists as follows: "strong revisionism maintains that our concept, practices, or attitudes themselves are in need of elimination . . . Strong revisionism argues that we must dispose of some or all of the main elements addressed by a theory of responsibility" (2005, 408).

[6] Strawson concedes less to the revolutionary than I do, for he doesn't seem to acknowledge the incompatibilist intuition at all (see Vargas 2004).

[7] While Strawson brought this issue to prominence, important elements of the view are anticipated by Hume (*Enquiry*, section VII), as noted by Russell (1995, 71–84) and Pereboom (2001, 90–2).

7.2.1 Insulationism

Strawson maintains that it would be preposterous to revise our reactive attitudes in response to considerations about determinism because the thesis of determinism is entirely external to the reactive attitudes: "our natural human commitment to ordinary inter-personal attitudes ... is part of the general framework of human life, not something that can come up for review as particular cases can come up for review within this general framework" (1962, 83). This basic insulationist move would overturn the entire revolutionary cause because it would show that our actual commitments as revealed in our reactive attitudes are not threatened by determinism. The argument suggests both that learning about determinism won't change our reactive attitudes and that it *shouldn't*. Determinism is simply irrelevant to the appropriateness of resentment, indignation, and guilt. Such attitudes are no more hostage to determinism than they are to special relativity.

7.2.1.1 ENSHRINEMENT

Perhaps the most famous rejection of this insulationism comes from Galen Strawson. He writes, "the roots of the incompatibilist intuition lie deep in the very reactive attitudes that are invoked in order to undercut it. The reactive attitudes enshrine the incompatibilist intuition ... [It] seems very difficult for us not to acknowledge that the truth of determinism ... brings the propriety of the reactive attitudes seriously into doubt" (Strawson 1986, 89). The incompatibilist intuition is part of the reactive attitudes.

Pereboom also maintains that the reactive attitudes are sensitive to incompatibilist concerns. To illustrate, Pereboom draws on Gary Watson's discussion of the ruthless murderer Robert Harris. We first hear how Harris abducted two 16-year-old boys from a fast-food restaurant, drove them to a remote area, and killed them. Then he ate one of their hamburgers. This provokes a strong sense of moral outrage. But we subsequently learn that Harris had an appalling upbringing. His father frequently beat him. His mother apparently hated the boy. His sister reported that Robert craved some physical contact from his mother: "He'd come up to my mother and just try to rub his little hands on her leg or her arm. He just never got touched at all. She'd just push him away or kick him" (Watson 1987, 273). Pereboom notes that after you hear about Harris' terrible childhood, your retributive attitude diminishes, and perhaps disappears ... Arguably the best explanation for this change is that your retributive attitude presupposed the belief that the killer deserved, in the basic sense, to be the object of this attitude, and because you no longer have this belief, the attitude is deprived of the presupposition that sustained it (Pereboom 2007, 202).

Robert Kane reports a similar case from his own experience, triggered by a trial of a man who raped and murdered a teenage girl:

> My initial thoughts of the young man were filled with anger and resentment. But as I listened daily to the testimony of how he came to have the mean character and perverse motives he did have—a sordid story of parental neglect, child abuse, bad role models, and so on—some of my resentment toward him decreased and was directed toward other persons who abused and influenced him.... In such manner, the changes in reactive attitudes ... are related to beliefs about ultimate responsibility (Kane 1996, 84).

Thus, Pereboom and Kane suggest, the reactive attitudes are not so isolated as Strawson had suggested (see also Nagel 1986, 125; Pereboom 2001, 95, 99; Sommers 2005).

There are various ways to challenge this claim. We might deny that the attenuation of anger is connected with incompatibilist intuitions. But I won't press this, for I'm interested in what follows if we grant the incompatibilist the case. Alternatively, we might challenge the claim that people's reactive attitudes about murderers are affected at all by considering their histories. But I am not inclined to make this charge either, since I share the reactions that Pereboom and Kane report—my retributive emotions become less pronounced when I learn about the sad history of these murderers. Even if we grant all this, there remains an important question about how the diminishment transpires. Does the fact that our reactions are diminished vindicate the claim that "the roots of the incompatibilist intuition lie deep in the very reactive attitudes that are invoked in order to undercut it" (Strawson 1986)? How deep does it really go?

7.2.1.2 NARROW VS. WIDE PSYCHOLOGICAL PROFILES

To proceed, we need a distinction between two ways of construing the profile of an emotion, what I'll call "narrow" and "wide" psychological profiles. I'll begin with the narrow profile. In contemporary emotion theory, specific emotions are typically characterized in terms of *local judgments/appraisals* and *local tendencies for action*. Despite important

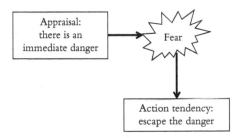

Figure 7.1 Narrow psychological profile of fear

differences, most emotion theorists (e.g., Lazarus 1991; Ekman 1992; Griffiths 1997; Haidt 2003; Prinz 2004; Prinz and Nichols 2010) focus on such relatively proximal inputs and outputs of the emotion system. The local appraisals are the characteristic triggers for the emotion, and the local action tendencies are the immediate behavioral inclinations generated by the emotion.[8] To take an example that is relatively well understood, fear is caused by an appraisal that amounts to a recognition that there is an immediate danger (e.g., Lazarus 1991, 235–8; Griffiths 1997, 92, 98). This appraisal itself can be triggered fairly automatically upon learning that there is a bear in the camp or by the perceptual representation of a barn spider. The local action tendency generated by fear is to avoid or escape the danger (e.g., Lazarus 1991, 238; Griffiths 1997, 80). (See Figure 7.1.)

When we're engaged in the project of characterizing a given emotion, we often want to identify the narrow psychological profile. But we might instead be interested in the *wide* psychological profile of an emotion, i.e., how a given emotion presents in the overall context of the psychological system. This will include, for instance, our conscious attitudes about the emotion, our associations with the emotion, and our inclinations to amplify or suppress the emotion in different contexts. This kind of wide psychological profile can accommodate more intelligent responses. As noted, the percept of a barn spider triggers fear, but once a person realizes that the barn spider is harmless to humans, this can affect the wide response. If we want to characterize the emotion of fear in the overall psychological environment, we must include this kind of information.

---

[8] On some theories (e.g., Prinz 2004), the emotions can also be triggered directly by perceptions. For instance, the perception of a snarling dog can cause fear without any appraisal.

We get a more informative picture of the wide psychological profile of an emotion if we think of the wide profile as embedding the narrow profile. On the narrow psychological profile of fear, fear is a normal, appropriate response to the perception of a barn spider. But this can be regulated at two junctures—upstream and downstream of the narrow system.[9] One way to modify the response is by altering what the fear-system gets as input. So, for instance, if a person is distracted (perhaps intentionally) from the spider-representation, then it might not end up activating the fear response. This phenomenon is familiar enough. One way to cope with unpleasant emotions is to avoid thinking about the things that trigger the emotion. This kind of modulation occurs upstream of the appraisal. Emotional reaction can also be modified by affecting what happens downstream of the narrow response. So, for instance, on recognizing that in fact the barn spider poses no threat, one might still have an unpleasant sensation, but resist the natural inclination to avoid the stimulus. When we try to characterize the wide profile of an emotion, we want to accommodate these kinds of coping responses.

7.2.1.3 MORAL ANGER

With this distinction between narrow and wide psychological profiles, we can now turn to the reactive attitudes themselves. I will focus on the reactive attitude *moral anger* (Keltner and Haidt 2001; see also Fessler and Haley 2003; Haidt 2003), which includes resentment and indignation (Pereboom 2007, 123). I focus on moral anger partly because there is a good deal of research on this emotion, but also because this is one of the key reactive attitudes targeted by revolutionaries.

We begin with the narrow psychological profile of moral anger. Moral anger is triggered by perceived injustices. In a large cross-cultural work, *unjust* is the highest-rated factor subjects use in characterizing the trigger of an angry episode (Scherer 1997, 905). Such judgments of injustices do not require anything philosophically fancy—no Rawlsian procedure or Kantian reasoning is involved. Rather, anger is triggered by judgments of disloyalty or failure to reciprocate. Lazarus puts it in a nutshell—the

---

[9] The phenomenon of emotion regulation is considerably more complicated than my sketch (see, e.g., Ochsner and Gross 2005; Gross 2006), but the additional complexities don't change the point here.

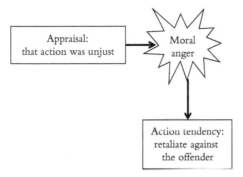

Figure 7.2 Narrow psychological profile of moral anger

appraisal for anger is the recognition of "a demeaning offense against me and mine" (Lazarus 1991, 222). The action tendency generated by moral anger is retaliation against the offender (Izard, 1977; Shaver et al., 1987; Keltner et al. 1993). Jonathan Haidt writes that the behavioral inclination is "to attack, humiliate, or otherwise get back at the person who is perceived as acting unfairly or immorally" (2003, 856). This gives us the narrow psychological profile of anger depicted in Figure 7.2. It's worth noting that, at least in our culture, the motivation that accompanies moral anger is not to rehabilitate the offender or to improve society. Rather, the motivation seems retributive in nature. In a neat study, Haidt et al. (2000) showed subjects film clips of injustices and then asked them to rate which endings they liked best. Subjects tended to be unsatisfied by endings in which the offender was forgiven and grew as a result. Rather, subjects preferred the ending in which the offender was made to suffer, and suffer in a way that fit the original offense (see also section 6.2).

Part of the evidence for this general profile for moral anger comes from the kinds of economic games discussed in Chapter 6 (sections 6.2 and 6.3). As we saw, in the ultimatum game, subjects who receive low offers often report perceiving the action as unfair and feeling angry, and the subjects who report perceived unfairness and anger are more likely to reject the offer than other subjects (Pillutla and Murnighan 1996). Using different sorts of economic games, other researchers have confirmed that inequitable offers generate anger, which in turn generates retaliation (e.g., Bosman and van Winden 2002, 159; Hopfensitz and Reuben 2009).

7.2.1.4 MORAL ANGER AND ENSHRINED INCOMPATIBILISM

Now let's return to the issue at hand. We have conceded that the incompatibilist intuition is in some way enshrined in reactive attitudes like moral anger. Drawing on the distinction between narrow and wide profiles, we can note that at a minimum, our concession requires that we allow that the incompatibilist intuition plays a role in the *wide psychological profile* of moral anger. For when we consider the upbringing of Robert Harris, our moral anger abates. But now, to see how deeply enshrined this is, we need to ask whether the incompatibilist intuition is enshrined in the *narrow* psychological profile of moral anger.

On the narrow profile, an appraisal of injustice or a demeaning offense will trigger the emotion of moral anger. If an agent comes to believe that determinism is true, is moral anger still the appropriate response to a demeaning offense? By the narrow lights of the moral-anger system, the answer is presumably *yes*. It is implausible that the moral-anger system is sensitive to high-level theoretical concepts like *determinism*.[10] The incompatibilist intuition doesn't go *that* deep. Just as it's narrowly appropriate for a perception of a barn spider to trigger fear, it's narrowly appropriate for a demeaning offense to trigger moral anger. It's important to keep in mind that narrow emotional systems tend not to be sensitive to a very wide range of inputs. Griffiths likens emotion systems to Fodorean modules (1997, 93–6). In the case of moral anger, the system almost certainly co-opts the phylogenetically ancient system for anger generally, and there is evidence that the response is based in phylogenetically old neural mechanisms (Sanfey et al. 2003).

Although it's likely that the narrow profile of moral anger does not enshrine the incompatibilist intuition, we do have the resources to explain why our moral anger at Robert Harris is attenuated. As noted, sometimes our natural emotional response is regulated by processes that occur "outside" the narrow system. In the case of the barn spider, we can distract ourselves from the image, we can remind ourselves that the spider poses no threat. We can reappraise the situation by recognizing

---

[10] Something similar likely holds for *guilt*. As we will see, a familiar model of the narrow profile of guilt is that the guilt mechanism is triggered by the appraisal that *I intentionally harmed someone important to me* and produced the action tendency to *make amends*. It's unlikely that this narrow mechanism is sensitive to determinism. Thus, *pace* Smilansky, we might not need the illusion of libertarian free will in order to preserve the natural tendency for feeling guilt.

that the spider is catching flies and mosquitoes. This kind of emotion regulation is common. It is plausibly implicated in the Harris case as well. When Watson recounts Harris' childhood, he distracts the moral-anger system—he leads us to attend to *something else*. Distraction alone is enough to attenuate affective responses (cf. Tracey et al. 2002). In addition, we are encouraged to *reappraise* the situation—instead of thinking about Harris' victims, we now think about Harris *as* victim. Again, reappraisal serves to attenuate or alter emotional response. We might direct some of our anger at Harris' parents. Moreover, in the case at hand, thinking of Harris as victim likely generates a new emotional response—sympathy. This new emotional response would presumably compete with moral anger, thus further suppressing the moral-anger response.[11]

Let's return to the barn spider. When I perceive a barn spider, if the narrow fear system generates fear, it is responding normally. This is an appropriate narrow response to the perception of a barn spider. Similarly, when I judge that someone treated me badly, if the narrow moral-anger system generates anger, it is responding normally. That is a perfectly appropriate narrow response to the judgment of an offense against me. In both cases, the wide emotional profile is much more complicated. Knowing that the spider isn't dangerous can affect my wide fear response, and knowing that the agent was determined can affect my wide moral-anger response. But there is a further question about what the *right* response is. So far we've been considering the emotion systems, both narrow and wide, from a purely descriptive standpoint. We have tried to characterize how the emotion systems actually work, at narrow and wide levels of analysis. But we can also ask a properly evaluative question—what is the right response? In the case of the barn spider, presumably the right response is to try to override the fear reaction whenever there is the slightest reason to do so. The spider poses no danger, so on reflection, it makes sense to regulate the fear response. In the case of determinism and moral anger, we have allowed that determinism does, as a matter of fact, modify the wide moral-anger response via emotion regulation and emotion

---

[11] The competition between anger and sympathy plays out in public debate on punishment. One group trots out the victims, in an attempt to trigger anger at the offender; the other group tries to generate sympathy for the offender by personalizing him and his plight.

competition. But again, it's a further question whether we *should* respond this way. Even in the case of the barn spider, it takes effort to regulate the emotion. We have to change our focus, remind ourselves it's harmless, attempt to reappraise the situation, and so forth. Similarly, it would take significant effort to engage in the systematic regulatory override of our moral-anger system. Dislodging these reactive attitudes will not be easy.[12] The question now is, should we make the effort?

7.2.2 Gains and losses to human life

After promoting the insulationist point, Strawson (1962) offers a second argument. He says that if we want to decide whether it's rational to retain the reactive attitudes if determinism is true, "we could choose rationally only in the light of an assessment of the gains and losses to human life, its enrichment or impoverishment" (1962, 83). On one interpretation, Strawson is arguing that the gains and losses are the *only* thing we need consult, and since determinism is in principle irrelevant to the gains and losses to human life, determinism poses no threat whatsoever (see, e.g., Wallace 1994, 99ff.). We don't need to take such a strong stance here. For our purposes, it will suffice to treat the gains and losses as important considerations, but not as unassailable in principle. The practical considerations might get overturned by an overwhelming moral reason. For present purposes, I will be satisfied to argue that a revolution in the reactive attitudes would generate significant losses to human life.

There are a couple of important preliminary observations before we get to the main affair of gains and losses. First, one might claim that gains and losses are beside the point. The question is whether people really are morally responsible. It might be that, given our current conception of morally responsibility, people aren't responsible. In Chapter 3, I went to considerable lengths to explore whether we should be eliminativists

---

[12] This is entirely consonant with the views of at least some of the revolutionaries (see, e.g., Waller 1990, 161; Sommers 2007, 20).

Although it would be difficult to repress completely moral anger, it may not be beyond human capacity either. According to Briggs (1970), the Utku, an Eskimo group, largely repress anger behavior. Briggs suggests that the Utku suppress anger behavior because any serious social disruption could be devastating given the perils of their arctic life and the tiny size of their society. Perhaps, then, we could, with sustained effort, suppress our problematic reactive attitudes.

about free will. I argued for a pluralist, discretionary view on which we should grant that, in certain contexts, it's true to say "Free will exists" despite deep misconceptions in folk views about the nature of free will. The same pluralism plausibly applies to the notion of moral responsibility (section 7.3). But even if the right view is eliminativism about free will and responsibility, that by itself does not mean that we should instigate a revolution in our *practices*, which is what the revolutionary is urging. Moreover, as the epigraph from MacIntyre suggests, even if our current notion of moral responsibility is incompatibilist, our moral notions are not immutable. In the future, our notion of moral responsibility (or a nearby replacement for the notion) might have different features than our current notion of moral responsibility.

The second preliminary point is that all the considerations about gains and losses raised here might be construed in consequentialist terms. That doesn't mean that gains and losses *must* be interpreted in consequentialist terms. It might be that some of the losses that we would suffer would be *non-consequentialist* losses. Nonetheless, it is convenient to focus on consequences, since virtually everyone agrees that consequences do matter ethically, even if they aren't all that matters.

The Strawsonian claim of interest is that our lives would be greatly diminished if we uprooted our reactive attitudes. Hard incompatibilists, who maintain that we lack free will even if determinism is false, have recently labored to assuage these worries (e.g., Waller 1990; Pereboom 2001, 2007; Sommers 2007). Part of the response maintains that many of the reactive attitudes, e.g., love, are largely unscathed by hard incompatibilism (Pereboom 2007, 121–2; Sommers 2007, 11–13). There are, however, reactive attitudes that are seriously threatened by hard incompatibilism. Pereboom writes, "Moral resentment, indignation, and guilt would likely be irrational for a hard incompatibilist, since these attitudes would have presuppositions believed to be false" (Pereboom 2007, 122; also Sommers 2007, 15). These are the attitudes targeted by the revolution. Pereboom has a two-pronged strategy for making the revolution palatable. He claims that either the targeted attitudes aren't necessary for good interpersonal lives or there are analogues that can serve in their stead (Pereboom 2007, 122). Since we've already considered in some detail the character of moral anger, we'll continue to explore the role of this reactive attitude.

7.2.2.1 BENEFITS OF MORAL ANGER

Moral anger seems, from a rational choice perspective, completely irrational. It generates a motivation for retribution even when there is no immediate benefit for *anyone*. People who are motivated to retaliate often foresee no tangible benefit at all. They just want the offender to pay. Although people often can't see any benefits for their anger and retaliation, recent work suggests that there are indeed tangible benefits.

Let's first consider the benefits for self. In Robert Frank's excellent *Passions within Reason*, he argues that emotions like guilt, empathy, and anger generally serve to counteract immediate gratification. We tend to go for the quick pleasure, and emotions play the role of giving you short-term motivation for actions that are only in your long-term best interests. So, from the short-term perspective, emotions like anger look irrational because they generate costly behaviors. But when we take a longer view, it becomes clear that anger is good for us. In particular, it signals intolerance for abuse (Tavris 1989, 285; Haidt 2003, 856), and this plausibly discourages mistreatment. It's an important feature of Frank's account that the individual is generally unaware that anger is in his long-term best interests. It does good that we don't even recognize.

Moral anger also has broader benefits. The most impressive recent empirical work comes from experimental economics. In Chapter 6 (6.2) I recounted the punishment behavior in classic experiments, but I did not review the *effects* of punishment. In public goods games, again, participants are given an allotment of funds and in each round of the game, players are allowed to contribute to the common fund. For every 1 monetary unit an individual contributes, 1.6 units go into the common fund, which is a net benefit for the group, but a net loss for the individual (since he only gets 40 percent of his investment back). Obviously it's optimal for the group if everyone invests in the common fund, but for each individual, it's selfishly better not to invest. A number of studies have shown that in these games, people will pay to punish players who do not contribute to the common fund (for a review, see Fehr and Fischbacher 2004a).

Why would subjects spend their money to punish even when it's obviously not in their material self-interest? As we saw earlier (6.3), *anger* is the prevailing explanation. Fehr and Gächter asked their subjects to report how they would feel under the following circumstances: "You decide to invest 16 francs to the project. The second group member invests 14 and the third 18 francs. Suppose the fourth member invests 2 francs to the project. You now accidentally meet this member. Please indicate your feeling towards this person" (Fehr and Gächter 2002, 139). Subjects reported that they would be quite angry with this person. This of course fits with the results on the ultimatum game, in which subjects who receive low offers report high anger (Pillutla and Murnighan 1996). Anger seems to provide the critical motivation to punish defectors.

Now, what are the consequences of this anger-driven punishment? As it happens, punishment dramatically changes behavior in these games. Fehr and colleagues have consistently found increased cooperation when punishment is an available option. Perhaps the most impressive illustration comes from experiments in which players first engage in several games in which punishment is not available. Fehr and Gächter (2000) conducted such an experiment in which subjects played 10 rounds of a public goods game with no option of punishment; by the tenth round the level of contribution was quite low (below 20 percent). Then participants are told that they will play 10 more rounds of public goods games, but now they will be allowed to punish other players after each round. On the very first round of the new series, the contributions leapt to over 60 percent and within a few more rounds with punishment, the level of contributions was at 90 percent! Fehr and Gächter maintain that such punishment is driven by anger, and if they're right, then anger is a potent force for motivating cooperation (2002, 139).

There are three important facts about the relationship between punishment and cooperation in these studies. First, cooperation deteriorates without punishment. Many people start out contributing a significant amount of their endowment, but in the absence of punishment, this drops off precipitously. Second, mere knowledge that punishment is available increases cooperation. Fehr and Gächter maintain that this is because people anticipate that if they defect, the others will be angry and punish them. (A supplementary explanation is that people might be more willing to contribute if they know that they have some recourse to punish those who are taking advantage of them.) The final point is the most obvious—punishment pushes cooperation near ceiling.[13]

---

[13] By contrast, reward is much less effective than punishment at securing cooperation (e.g., Andreoni et al. 2003).

It's worth emphasizing that people *expect* retributive punishment if they treat others unfairly. We find this in the Fehr and Gächter study in which they anticipate that others will be angry if they fail to contribute. In their third-party punishment studies, Fehr and Fischbacher found that participants playing the game predict fairly well the conditions under which third parties will punish (2004b, 70 [fig. 2]). It's likely that retributive punishment is effective partly because we are so receptive to it.[14]

So, what does moral anger do for us? It's plausible that moral anger historically played a critical role in securing social norms, including conventions of cooperation. The norms were probably partly fixed through a regime of punishment for defectors (see Richerson and Boyd 2005, 199–201). The experimental results suggest that moral anger *still* plays an important role in securing cooperative behavior.

There's an irony here for the moral anti-retributivist. Punishment secures cooperation, but punishment is costly. This leads researchers to worry that the system itself is fragile (e.g., Henrich and Boyd 2001), for the best overall strategy for an individual is to always cooperate and never punish. Such an individual gets all the benefits of cooperation and bears none of the costs of punishing. But he is a second-order free rider. He's taking a free ride on the costly punishments of others. As it happens, second-order free riding might not be much of a problem, for it might be that our anger system provides a sufficiently powerful motivation that the additional cash pales in comparison. But notice that the person who renounces retributive punishment falls in with the second-order free riders. He gets the benefits of our retributivism without paying the costs.

---

[14] Subsequent cross-cultural work produced the disturbing result that in many cultures, people engage in a considerable amount of *anti-social* punishment. That is, they punish *cooperators* (Herrmann et al. 2008; see also Gächter et al. 2010). In the U.S., Australia, and other Western countries, participants rarely punished cooperators. But in other countries, including Oman, Greece, and Saudi Arabia, there was a great deal of anti-social punishment. Not surprisingly, this had a dramatic effect on cooperation. The greater the amount of anti-social punishment, the lower the average contributions in the group (Herrmann et al. 2008, 1364).

These findings on anti-social punishment don't change the point in the chapter. For the key result—that punishment of defectors leads to greater cooperation—is upheld even in this data set (Gächter et al. 2010, 2656).

There remain open questions about the extent to which the results in experimental economics are representative of real life. But the studies certainly suggest that moral anger and its punitive expressions work to discourage cheating, defection, and violations of reciprocity (Keltner and Haidt 2001). In Keltner and Haidt's taxonomy of social emotions, they make the plausible suggestion that social emotions like moral anger function to solve problems in the social domain. In the case of moral anger, they maintain that the function is to "motivate other to repair transgression" (2001, Table 1).[15] Insofar as anger has that function, it presumably has beneficial effects for social welfare.

7.2.2.2 ANALOGUE FOR MORAL ANGER

The reactive attitude of moral anger apparently does make quite significant contributions to human life. Moral anger has benefits both at the individual level and the group level. Of course, moral anger sometimes has bad consequences—feuds, seething resentment—and much more work needs to be done to understand the costs of moral anger.[16] But at a minimum, it seems that we would want to be very cautious about fomenting a revolution if it means we lose the benefits of moral anger charted earlier. The revolutionary still has an important response, though. Recall that the claim was that for the reactive attitudes that are inconsistent with determinism, either we are better off without them *or* there are analogues that will do the needed work. We now need to consider the proposed analogues.

Once again, Derk Pereboom has provided the most extensive and illuminating discussion of the matter. Returning to the case of Robert

---

[15] Note that this function—motivate the other person to make amends—can be implemented by a mechanism for which incompatibilism is entirely irrelevant. What matters for moral anger is exhibiting your willingness to punish for no apparent material benefit (Frank 1988).

[16] Pereboom (2009) points out that moral anger is likely implicated in ethnic conflict, and that beliefs about desert probably play a role as well. Obviously eliminating ethnic conflict would be a great gain, so stemming moral anger would be a good thing in this case. However, anger is likely not the only factor involved in ethnic conflict—many of the victims of ethnic conflict are not themselves the target of moral anger (cf. Sommers 2012). Ethnic conflict might also be driven by manifestly false beliefs about the inferiority (moral and otherwise) of the rival ethnic group. Furthermore, even though moral anger does likely exacerbate the situation, one might reasonably think that this is a case in which a system that is normally beneficial has spun out of control (cf. Frank 1988 on the Hatfields and McCoys).

Harris, Pereboom has us recall how one's attitude changes upon learning of Harris' past:

> Indignation gradually gives way to a kind of moral sadness—a sadness not only about his past but also for his character and his horrible actions. This kind of moral sadness is a type of attitude that would not be undermined by a belief in determinism. Furthermore, I suspect that it can play much of the role that resentment and indignation more typically have in human relationships (2001, 97–8; see also 2007, 120, 203).[17]

Thus, on Pereboom's view, while moral anger is theoretically irrational, moral sadness can largely serve in its stead.

Can sadness do the requisite work for moral anger, then? Well, to answer this we need to know more about sadness itself. The most important question concerns how sadness affects our behavior. For we know that moral anger produces behavior that discourages cheating, defecting, and mistreatment. What kind of behavior does sadness tend to produce? *None*, according to emotion theorists. Lazarus writes, "In sadness there seems to be no clear action tendency—except *inaction*, or withdrawal into oneself" (Lazarus 1991, 251). This is illustrated in infancy research. Infants show individual differences in their propensities to feel sad or angry when blocked from attaining a desired end— some babies are more likely to feel sad, others to feel angry. Researchers have found that when infants show sadness as their predominant emotion, this is associated with giving up (Lewis and Ramsey 2005, 518), and it seems to be akin to learned helplessness (Abramson et al. 1978). By contrast, infants who respond with anger are more likely to try to overcome an obstacle (Lewis and Ramsey 2005, 518). As a result, sadness seems too behaviorally weak to do the work of anger.[18]

I've focused here on Pereboom, because he has offered the most explicit story about analogue emotions. But I think that the case

---

[17] Relatedly, Tamler Sommers says that moral anger at, say, the murder of a family member is irrational, but it can be "succeeded by a lasting grief. And grief, no matter how passionate or intense, is perfectly consistent with the objective attitude" (Sommers 2007, 9).

[18] In a reply to this line of thought, Pereboom (2009) has suggested that sadness can serve important communicative functions that moral anger has served. This might be so, but there remains an important shortcoming even here. The general worry I've been pressing is that sadness won't play the *motivational* role that anger does. And this will apply to communication as well. So, for instance, if sadness typically leads to withdrawal, it's not clear that John's sadness would motivate him to communicate to Mary that she has wronged him. It might just lead him to withdraw and wallow.

illustrates a more general worry for revolutionaries. We cannot lightly assume that emotions are sufficiently fungible that we can co-opt emotions that are consistent with hard incompatibilism to do the work of the reactive attitudes that are under threat.

Similar considerations might apply to revolutionary treatments of guilt, though the situation is more complicated because the discussion by revolutionaries has been less clear about replacements. Emotion theorists have been fairly clear, though. The basic appraisal that triggers guilt for an agent is roughly the recognition that *I have harmed someone that matters to me* (Baumcister et al. 1994; Haidt 2003, 861; Prinz and Nichols 2010). The action tendency for guilt is to repair the relationship, for example, by apologizing or making amends (Lazarus 1991, 243; Baumeister et al. 1994; Haidt 2003, 861).[19] As a result, guilt is an important emotion for guiding the reparation of damaged relationships. It is probably also an important motivator for *not* mistreating people you care about, because you anticipate the guilt (Prinz and Nichols 2010). All of this suggests that guilt is *good*. Suffice to say that when you're looking for a mate, you probably want to avoid the ones who don't feel guilt.

What does the revolution have in store for guilt? Pereboom and Waller propose that regret can do substitute service for guilt. Pereboom writes, "suppose that you behave immorally, but because you endorse hard incompatibilism, you deny that you are blameworthy. Instead, you acknowledge that you have done wrong, you feel sad that you were the agent of wrongdoing, and you deeply regret what you have done" (Pereboom 2007, 120; see also Waller 1990, 165–7). Unfortunately, regret is not well defined. Indeed, some theorists assimilate it to guilt (e.g. Storm and Storm 1987). Lazarus claims that the term is simply too ambiguous to be usefully compared to other emotions (1991, 244–5). Without a more detailed description of the emotion, it's hard to say whether it is likely to do the good services that guilt provides.

Pereboom brings in a further element that might be thought to address the shortcomings of the analogue emotions: resolve. In addition to moral sadness, we might be committed to opposing wrongdoing, and this "would allow for a resolve to resist abuse, discrimination, and oppression"

---

[19] This is not to say that guilt *always* has this effect. Rather, the point is that guilt is a beneficial emotion because it serves this interpersonally beneficial function in paradigmatic cases.

(Pereboom 2007, 124). In his discussion of guilt, he says something similar: "because you have a commitment to doing what is right, and to personal moral progress, you might resolve not to perform an immoral action of this kind again, and seek out therapeutic procedures to help treat one's character problems" (Pereboom 2001, 205). People no doubt differ in the strength of their resolve. But it strikes me as unlikely that resolve will provide sufficient motivation for the bulk of the population. After all, many teenagers think that they risk going to hell if they have sex, yet this often provides insufficient motivation for abstinence. Or consider the Marxist belief that working hard will generate benefits for the state which will in turn benefit everyone. This turns out to be motivationally feeble. Marxism seems incredibly rational, which is why it is so attractive to us intellectuals. But it turns out to be naively optimistic about the plasticity of human motivation. I suspect the same is true of the revolutionary's hope for replacing problematic reactive attitudes.

7.2.2.3 MORAL CONSIDERATIONS

I've argued that there would be significant losses to human life if we made a concerted effort to eradicate moral anger from our lives. This is a prima facie argument in favor of retaining moral anger. However, we sometimes think it appropriate to accept significant losses because of an overwhelming moral concern. Before bringing this chapter to a close, I want to consider—too briefly—two such concerns.

Hard incompatibilists maintain that treating people as if they were morally responsible is morally objectionable because it's unfair. The fairness argument is a common theme among hard incompatibilists, though it's never articulated very fully. Thus, Waller writes, "It is unfair to ... praise Rachel and blame Sarah ... when their character and behavioral differences are products of earlier environments for which neither is morally responsible" (Waller 1990, 129; also Pereboom 2001, 156; Smilansky 2002, 493). I resonate with this reaction—it does seem unfair to give differential treatment to people if their behavior is the product of the past (for which they are clearly not responsible). The moral reaction here is obviously closely related to the core incompatibilist intuition that people aren't morally responsible under determinism. But again to hark back to McIntyre, our moral concerns change as social life changes. And if social life leads us to deterministic views about human decision making, the sense that it is unfair to blame the determined might shift.

Furthermore, such a shift might be precipitated by a process of moral reflection. Our moral interests in punishing defectors and securing cooperation might be so central to our lives that these concerns suffice to offset our incompatibilist compunctions about unfairness. It's worth noting that among these moral interests might well be non-consequentialist commitments. For instance, our allegiance to the retributive norm might be among the reasons that lead us, in a process of moral reflection, to suppress our acknowledged incompatibilist concern about fairness.

A different concern is that extirpating incompatibilism would uproot the foundations of our attitudes about moral responsibility. In Chapter 4, I argued that our commitment to incompatibilism is actually disconnected from the rest of our responsibility imputing and excusing practices. It is an implicit commitment, not one that gave birth to our other commitments. If incompatibilism is merely an implicit commitment, then the broader effects of simply giving up the incompatibilist commitment will be, to a first approximation, nothing. The idea that it's wrong to punish the innocent, the ignorant, and the deranged will naturally be sustained even if we give up the idea that it's wrong to punish the determined.

7.3 Discretion redux

This chapter has promoted a counter-revolutionary agenda. Although incompatibilism might somehow be enshrined in reactive attitudes, it is probably not implicated in the narrow psychological profile—the local inputs and outputs—of the reactive attitudes. As a result, it's not surprising that the available evidence suggests that even if people come to believe in determinism, they will continue to hold each other responsible. This leaves us with the difficult question whether we should undertake a concerted effort to alter these responses. I have argued in favor of retaining moral anger and other targeted reactive attitudes. My goal has been to emphasize some powerful and largely unnoticed social benefits of moral anger. Instead of trying to globally subdue moral anger in deference to the incompatibilist intuition, we are right to ignore or relinquish the commitment to incompatibilism.

I have defended sustaining the reactive attitudes and the social institutions they support. But there is also a more conciliatory note to strike with the hard incompatibilist. In Chapter 3, I argued that, because different reference conventions are available, it's plausible to maintain that when Galen Strawson says, "There is no free will," he is saying something true, and when Manuel Vargas says, "Free will exists, it just isn't what we thought," he is saying something true as well. The same point applies to the notion of moral responsibility. Strawson says, "Moral responsibility doesn't exist"; Vargas says, "Moral responsibility does exist." Each can be saying something true, given the flexibility of reference. More importantly for the present context, I argued that this might afford us the luxury of being discretionary about when to affirm free will and moral responsibility and when to deny them (section 3.4).

Giving up the reactive attitudes entirely would do considerable damage to social life, and this is why I have stressed here the reasons to set aside our incompatibilist intuitions. For social institutions like punishment, the costs of an unqualified eliminativist revolution are very high. But there are other occasions where moral anger and self-blame are really counterproductive and damaging. When dealing with someone with depression or very low self-regard, it might be best to remind ourselves of our intuitive incompatibilism. When a loved one is wracked by guilt or shame, in ways that seriously threaten their psychic health, eliminativism offers a therapeutic strategy. The discretionary approach also applies to one's own outlook towards life. It might be prudent for me to be a compatibilist in the morning, as I look forward to a productive day of work; but then I can be an eliminativist at night, when I try to sleep after another day of failure.

References

Abramson, L., Seligman, M., and Teasdale, J. (1978). Learned helplessness in humans: critique and reformulation. *Journal of Abnormal Psychology*, 87, pp. 49–74.

Ady, T. (1656). *A Candle in the Dark*. London: Robert Ibbitson.

Andreasen, R. O. (2000). Race: Biological reality or social construct? *Philosophy of Science*, 67, pp. S653–S666.

Andreoni, J., Harbaugh, W., and Vesterlund, L. (2003). The Carrot or the Stick: Rewards, Punishments, and Cooperation. *The American Economic Review*, 93, pp. 893–902.

Appiah, K. A. (1995). The Uncompleted Argument: Du Bois and the Illusion of Race. In L. A. Bell and D. Blumenfeld (eds), *Overcoming Racism and Sexism*. Lanham, MD: Rowman and Littlefield, pp. 59–78.

Arico, A., Fiala, B., Goldberg, R. F., and Nichols, S. (2011). The Folk Psychology of Consciousness. *Mind & Language*, 26(3), pp. 327–52.

Ariely, D., Loewenstein, G., and Prelec, D. (2003). Coherent Arbitrariness. *Quarterly Journal of Economics*, 118, pp. 73–105.

Baier, K. (1955). Is Punishment Retributive? *Analysis*, 16, pp. 25–32.

Balaguer, M. (2010). *Free Will as an Open Scientific Problem*. Cambridge, MA: MIT Press.

Bargh, J., Chen, M., and Burrows, L. (1996). Automaticity of Social Behavior. *Journal of Personality and Social Psychology*, 71, pp. 230–44.

Baumeister, R., Masicampo, E., and DeWall, C. (2009). Prosocial Benefits of Feeling Free: Disbelief in Free Will Increases Aggression and Reduces Helpfulness. *Pers Soc Psychol Bull*, 35, pp. 260–8.

Baumeister, R. F., Stillwell, A. M., and Heatherton, T. F. (1994). Guilt: An interpersonal approach. *Psychological Bulletin*, 115, pp. 243–67.

Bedau, H. (1978). Retribution and the Theory of Punishment. *Journal of Philosophy*, 75, pp. 601–20.

Benn, S. (1967). Punishment. In P. Edwards (ed.), *The Encyclopedia of Philosophy*, vol. 7. New York: Macmillan and the Free Press, pp. 29–36.

Bentham, J. (1830). *The Rationale of Punishment*. London: Robert Heward.

Berlin, A., and Brettler, M. (2004). *The Jewish Study Bible*. Oxford: Oxford University Press.

Berlyne, D. (1950). Novelty and curiosity as determinants of exploratory behaviour. *British Journal of Psychology*, General Section, 41(1–2), pp. 68–80.

Bishop, M. (1999). Semantic flexibility in scientific practice: A study of Newton's optics. *Philosophy & Rhetoric* 32.3, pp. 210–32.

Bishop, M., and Stich, S. (1998). The flight to reference, or how not to make progress in the philosophy of science. *Philosophy of Science*, pp. 33–49.

Björnsson, G. (forthcoming). Incompatibilism and "Bypassed" Agency. In Al Mele (ed.), *Surrounding Free Will*. New York: Oxford University Press.

Blackburn, S. (1985). Errors and the Phenomenology of Value. In Ted Honderich (ed.), *Morality and Objectivity*. Routledge & Kegan Paul, pp. 1–22.

Blackburn, S. (1998). *Ruling Passions*. Oxford: Oxford University Press.

Blair, R. (1995). A Cognitive-Developmental Approach to Psychopathy. *Cognition*, 57, pp. 1–29.

Blakemore, S., and Frith, C. D. (2003). Self-Awareness and Action. *Current Opinion in Neurobiology*, 13, pp. 219–24.

Bolton, G., and Zwick, R. (1995). Anonymity versus punishment in ultimatum bargaining. *Games and Economic Behavior*, 10, pp. 95–121.

Bosman, R. A. J., and van Winden, F. A. A. M. (2002). Emotional Hazard in a Power-to-Take Experiment. *Economic Journal*, 112, pp. 147–69.

Boulton, R. (1715). *Compleat History of Magick, Sorcery, and Witchcraft*. London, Great Britain: E. Curll, J. Pemberton, and W. Taylor.

Boyd, R. (1983). On the current status of the issue of scientific realism. *Erkenntnis*, 19, pp. 45–90.

Boyd, R. (2002). Scientific Realism. *The Stanford Encyclopedia of Philosophy (Summer 2002 Edition)*, Edward N. Zalta (ed.), URL = <http://plato.stanford.edu/archives/sum2002/entries/scientific-realism/>.

Boyer, P. (2000). Evolution of the Modern Mind and the Origins of Culture. In P. Carruthers and A. Chamberlain (eds), *Evolution and the Human Mind*. Cambridge, UK: Cambridge University Press, pp. 93–113.

Braithwaite, J. (1999). Restorative Justice: Assessing Optimistic and Pessimistic Accounts. In M. Tonry (ed.), *Crime and Justice: A Review of Research*, vol. 23. Chicago: University of Chicago Press, pp. 241–367.

Braun, K., and Nichols, R. (1997). Death and dying in four Asian American cultures: A descriptive study. *Death Studies*, 21, pp. 327–59.

Breiter, H., Gollub, R., Weisskoff, R., Kennedy, D., Makris, N., Berke, J., Goodman, J., Kantor, H., Gastfriend, D., Riorden, J., Mathew, R., Rosen, B., and Hyman, S. (1997). Acute Effects of Cocaine on Human Brain Activity and Emotion. *Neuron*, 19, pp. 591–611.

Briggs, J. (1970). *Never in Anger*. Cambridge, MA: Harvard University Press.

Brower-Toland, S. (forthcoming). Ockham on the Nature and Scope of Consciousness *Vivarium*.

Bruner, J. S. (1966). *Toward a theory of instruction*. Cambridge, Mass.: Harvard University Press.

Callanan, M. A., and Oakes, L. M. (1992). Preschoolers' questions and parents' explanations: Causal thinking in everyday activity. *Cognitive Development*, 7(2), pp. 213–33.

Cameron, C. D., Payne, B. K., and Doris, J. M. (2013). Morality in high definition: Emotion differentiation calibrates the influence of incidental disgust on moral judgments. *Journal of Experimental Social Psychology*. 49, pp. 719–25.

Campbell, C. (1957). *On Selfhood and Godhood*. London: George Allen & Unwin.

Campbell, C. (1967). *In Defence of Free Will*. London: Allen & Unwin.

Carlsmith, K. (2008). On justifying punishment: The discrepancy between words and actions. *Social Justice Research*, 21, pp. 119–37.

Carlsmith, K., Darley, J., and Robinson, P. (2002). Why Do We Punish? Deterrence and Just Deserts as Motives for Punishment. *Journal of Personality and Social Psychology*, 83, pp. 284–99.

Carruthers, P. (2008). Cartesian Epistemology. *Journal of Consciousness Studies*, 15, pp. 28–53.

Casaubon, M. (1670). *Of credulity and incredulity in things divine and spiritual*. London: S. Lownds.

Chan, H., Deutsch, M., and Nichols, S. (forthcoming). Free Will and Experimental Philosophy. In W. Buckwalter and J. Sytsma (eds), *Blackwell Companion to Experimental Philosophy*. Malden, MA: Blackwell.

Chernyak, N., Kushnir, T., Sullivan, K., and Wang, Q. (2013). A Comparison of American and Nepalese Children's Concepts of Freedom of Choice and Social Constraint. *Cognitive Science*, 37, pp. 1343–55.

Clark, C., Luguri, J., Ditto, P., Knobe, J., Shariff, A., and Baumeister, R. (forthcoming) Free to Punish: A Motivated Account of Free Will Belief.

Clarke, R. (1993). Toward a credible agent-causal account of free will. *Noûs*, 27, pp. 191–203.

Clarke, R. (2003). *Libertarian Accounts of Free Will*. New York: Oxford University Press.

Clarke, R., and Capes, J. (2013). Incompatibilist (Nondeterministic) Theories of Free Will, *The Stanford Encyclopedia of Philosophy* (Spring 2013 edition), Edward N. Zalta (ed.), URL = <http://plato.stanford.edu/archives/spr2013/entries/incompatibilism-theories/>.

Cohen, S. (1984). Justification and Truth. *Philosophical Studies*, 46, pp. 279–95.

Comesaña, J. (2005). We Are (Almost) All Externalists Now. *Philosophical Perspectives*, 19, pp. 59–76.

Cooper, J. (2007). *Cognitive Dissonance*. London: Sage Publications.

Cottingham, J. (1979). Varieties of Retributivism. *The Philosophical Quarterly*, 29.

Craig, E. (1998). *Routledge Encyclopedia of Philosophy*. London: Routledge.

Cross, H., Halcomb, C., and Matter, W. (1967). Imprinting or Exposure Learning in Rats Given Early Auditory Stimulation. *Psychonomic Science*, 7, pp. 233–4.

D'Andrade, R. (1987). A Folk Model of the Mind. In D. Holland and N. Quinn (eds), *Cultural Models in Language and Thought*. Cambridge: Cambridge University Press, pp. 112–48.

Darley, J., Carlsmith, K., and Robinson, P. (2000). Incapacitation and just deserts as motives for punishment. *Law and Human Behavior*, 24, pp. 659–83.

Dawes, C., Fowler, J., Johnson, T., McElreath, R., and Smirnov, O. (2007). Egalitarian Motives in Humans. *Nature*, 446, pp. 794–6.

Dawson, C., and Gerken, L. A. (2011). When global structure "explains away" evidence for local grammar: A Bayesian account of rule induction in tone sequences. *Cognition*, 120(3), pp. 350–9.

De Brigard, F., Mandelbaum, E., and Ripley, D. (2009). Responsibility and the brain sciences. *Ethical Theory and Moral Practice*, 12(5), pp. 511–24.

Deery, O., Bedke, M., and Nichols, S. (2013). Phenomenal Abilities: Incompatibilism and the Experience of Agency. In D. Shoemaker (ed.), *Oxford Studies in Agency and Responsibility*, pp. 126–50.

De Quervain, D., Fischbacher, U., Treyer, V., Schellhammer, M., Schnyder, U., Buck, A., and Fehr, E. (2004). The Neural Basis of Altruistic Punishment. *Science*, 305, no. 5688, 1254–8.

Devitt, M., and Sterelny, K. (1999). *Language and reality: an introduction to the philosophy of language*. Cambridge, MA: MIT Press.

Doris, J. (forthcoming). *Talking to Our Selves*. Oxford, UK: Oxford University Press.

Doris, J., and Plakias, A. (2008). How to Argue about Moral Disagreement: Evaluative Diversity and Moral Realism. In *Moral Psychology*, vol. 2, ed. W. Sinnott-Armstrong. Cambridge, Mass.: MIT Press.

Duff, A. (2008). Legal Punishment. *The Stanford Encyclopedia of Philosophy* (Fall 2008 edition), E. Zalta (ed.), URL = <http://plato.stanford.edu/archives/fall2008/entries/legal-punishment/>.

Earman, J. (1986). *A Primer on Determinism*. Dordrecht, Holland: Reidel.

Ekman, P. (1992). An argument for basic emotions. *Cognition and Emotion*, 6, pp. 169–200.

Fehr, E., and Fischbacher, U. (2004a). Social norms and human cooperation. *Trends in Cognitive Sciences*, 8, pp. 187–90.

Fehr, E., and Fischbacher, U. (2004b). Third party punishment and social norms. *Evolution and Human Behavior*, 25, pp. 63–87.

Fehr, E., and Gächter, S. (2000). Cooperation and punishment in public goods experiments. *American Economic Review*, 90, pp. 980–94.

Fehr, E., and Gächter, S. (2002). Altruistic punishment in humans. *Nature*, 415, pp. 137–40.

Feldman, R. (2003). *Epistemology*. Englewood Cliffs, NJ: Prentice Hall.

Feltz, A., and Cokely, E. T. (2008). The fragmented folk: More evidence of stable individual differences in moral judgments and folk intuitions. In *Proceedings of the 30th annual conference of the cognitive science society* (pp. 1771-6). Austin, Tex.: Cognitive Science Society.

Feltz, A., Cokely, E., and Nadelhoffer, T. (2009). Natural Compatibilism versus Natural Incompatibilism: Back to the Drawing Board. *Mind & Language*, 24(1), pp. 1-23.

Feltz, A., and Cova, F. (forthcoming). Moral responsibility and free will: A Meta-analysis.

Fessler, D., and Haley, K. (2003). The strategy of affect: Emotions in human cooperation. In P. Hammerstein (ed.), *The Genetic and Cultural Evolution of Cooperation*. Cambridge, Mass.: MIT Press, pp. 7-36.

Feyerabend, P. K. (1962). Explanation, reduction and empiricism. In H. Feigl and G. Maxwell (eds), *Minnesota Studies in the Philosophy of Science, vol. 3: Scientific Explanation, Space, and Time*. Minneapolis: University of Minnesota Press, pp. 28-97.

Fiala, B., Arico, A., and Nichols, S. (2012). On the Psychological Origins of Dualism: Dual-process Cognition and the Explanatory Gap. In E. Slingerland and M. Collard (eds), *Creating Consilience: Issues and Case Studies in the Integration of the Sciences and Humanities*. New York: Oxford University Press, pp. 88-109.

Fischer, J. (1999). Recent work on Moral Responsibility. *Ethics*, 110, pp. 93-139.

Fischer, J. (2004). Responsibility and Manipulation. *Journal of Ethics*, 8, pp. 145-77.

Fischer, J., Kane, R., Pereboom, D., and Vargas, M. (2007). *Four Views on Free Will*. Malden, MA: Blackwell.

Fodor, J. (1987). *Psychosemantics*. Cambridge, MA: MIT Press.

Fodor, J. (1998). *Concepts*. Oxford: Oxford University Press.

Frank, R. (1988). *Passions Within Reason*. New York: W. H. Norton.

Frankfurt, H. (2002). Reply to John Martin Fischer. In S. Buss and L. Overton (eds), *Contours of Agency: Essays on Themes from Harry Frankfurt*. Cambridge, Mass.: MIT Press.

Freud, S. (1961 [1927]). *The Future of an Illusion*. Translated by J. Strachey. New York: Norton & Co.

Gächter, S., Herrmann, B., and Thöni, C. (2010). Culture and cooperation. *Philosophical Transactions of the Royal Society B: Biological Sciences*, 365 (1553), pp. 2651-61.

Gaus, J. (2011). Retributive Justice and Social Cooperation. In M. White (ed.), *Retributivism: Essays on Theory and Practice*. Oxford: Oxford University Press.

Gelman, S. (2003). *The Essential Child*. Oxford: Oxford University Press.

Gerken, L. (2010). Infants use rational decision criteria for choosing among models of their input. *Cognition*, 115(2), pp. 362–6.

Gibbard, A. (1990). *Wise Choices, Apt Feelings*. Cambridge, Mass.: Harvard University Press.

Gill, M. (2007). Moral Rationalism vs. Moral Sentimentalism: Is Morality more like Math or Beauty? *Philosophy Compass*, 2, pp. 16–30.

Gill, M., and Nichols, S. (2008). Sentimentalist Pluralism. *Philosophical Perspectives*, 18, p. 143–63.

Gilovich, T. (1991). *How We Know What Isn't So*. New York: The Free Press.

Glimcher, P. (2005). Indeterminacy in Brain and Behavior. *Annual Review of Psychology*, 56, pp. 25–56.

Goldman, A. (1967). A Causal Theory of Knowing, *Journal of Philosophy*, 22, pp. 357–72.

Goldman, A. (1979). What is Justified Belief? In G. Pappas (ed.), *Justification and Knowledge*. Dordrecht: Reidel.

Goodwin, G., and Darley, J. (2008). The Psychology of Meta-ethics: Exploring Objectivism. *Cognition*, 106, pp. 1339–66.

Gopnik, A. (2000). Explanation as orgasm and the drive for causal understanding: The function, evolution, and phenomenology of the theory-formation system. In F. C. Keil and R. A. Wilson (eds), *Explanation and Cognition*. Cambridge, MA: MIT Press, pp. 299–324.

Gopnik, A., Sobel, D. M., Schulz, L. E., and Glymour, C. (2001). Causal learning mechanisms in very young children: two-, three-, and four-year-olds infer causal relations from patterns of variation and covariation. *Developmental Psychology*, 37(5), 620–9.

Greene, J. (2008). The Secret Joke of Kant's Soul. In *Moral Psychology*, vol. 3, ed. W. Sinnott-Armstrong. Cambridge, Mass.: MIT Press.

Greene, J., and Cohen, J. (2004). For the law, neuroscience changes nothing and everything. *Philosophical Transactions of the Royal Society of London* B, 359, pp. 1775–85.

Griffiths, P. (1997). *What Emotions Really Are*. Chicago and NY: Chicago University Press.

Gross, J. (ed.) (2006). *Handbook of Emotion Regulation*. New York: Guilford Press.

Haidt, J. (2003). The moral emotions. In R. J. Davidson, K. R. Scherer, and H. H. Goldsmith (eds), *Handbook of Affective Sciences*. Oxford: Oxford University Press, pp. 852–70.

Haidt, J., Bjorklund, F., and Murphy, S. (2000). Moral Dumbfounding: When Intuition Finds No Reason. Unpublished manuscript. University of Virginia.

Haidt, J., Sabini, J., and Worthington, E. (2000). What exactly makes revenge sweet? Unpublished manuscript.

Hampton, J. (1984). The Moral Education Theory of Punishment. *Philosophy and Public Affairs*, 13, pp. 208–38.

Harding, A. (1966). *A Social History of English Law*. Baltimore, Md.: Penguin Books.

Harman, G. (1977). *The Nature of Morality*. New York: Oxford University Press.

Harman, G. (1996). Moral relativism, part 1 of Harman, G. and Thomson, J., *Moral Relativism and Moral Objectivity*. Cambridge, Mass.: Blackwell.

Harris, J. (1998). *Clones, Genes, and Immortality*. Oxford: Oxford University Press.

Hearst, E. (1991). Psychology and Nothing. *American Scientist*, 79, pp. 432–43.

Henrich, J., and Boyd, R. (2001). Why people punish defectors—Weak conformist transmission can stabilize costly enforcement of norms in cooperative dilemmas. *Journal of Theoretical Biology*, 208, pp. 79–89.

Herrmann, B., Thöni, C., and Gächter, S. (2008). Antisocial punishment across societies. *Science*, 319(5868), pp. 1362–7.

Hickling, A. K., and Wellman, H. M. (2001). The emergence of children's causal explanations and theories: Evidence from everyday conversation. *Developmental Psychology*, 37(5), p. 668.

Holbach, P. (1889 [1770]). *The System of Nature: Or, Laws of the Moral and Physical World*. Translated by H. D. Robinson. New York, B. Franklin.

Holland, R., Hendriks, M., and Aarts, H. (2005). Smells Like Clean Spirit. *Psychological Science*, 16, pp. 689–93.

Holmes, O. (1881). *The Common Law*. Boston: Little, Brown.

Holton, R. (2006). The Act of Choice. *Philosophers' Imprint*, 6, pp. 1–15.

Hood, L., Bloom, L., and Brainerd, C. J. (1979). What, when, and how about why: A longitudinal study of early expressions of causality. *Monographs of the Society for Research in Child Development*, pp. 1–47.

Hopfensitz, A., and Reuben, E. (2009). The Importance of Emotions for the Effectiveness of Social Punishment. *Economic Journal*, 119, pp. 1534–59.

Horgan, T. (2011). The Phenomenology of Agency and Freedom. *Humana. Mente*, 15.

Hume, D. (1955 [1743]). *An Enquiry concerning Human Understanding*. L. Selby-Bigge (ed.). Oxford: Clarendon Press.

Hume, D. (1964 [1739]). *A Treatise of Human Nature*. Oxford: Clarendon Press.

Hurley, S. (2000). Is Responsibility Essentially Impossible? *Philosophical Studies*, 99, pp. 229–68.

Husak, D. (1992). Why Punish the Deserving? *Noûs*, 26, pp. 447–64.

Hutchinson, F. (1718). *An Historical Essay concerning Witchcraft*. London: Knaplock and Midwinter.

Irwin, T. (1999). *Classical Philosophy*. Oxford, UK: Oxford University Press.

Izard, C. E. (1977). *Human Emotions*. New York: Plenum Press.

Jackson, F. (1998). *From Metaphysics to Ethics: a Defence of Conceptual Analysis.* Oxford: Oxford University Press.

Jackson, F. (2001a). Précis of From Metaphysics to Ethics. *Philosophy and Phenomenological Research,* 62(3), pp. 617–24.

Jackson, F. (2001b). Responses. *Philosophy and Phenomenological Research,* 62(3), pp. 653–64.

James I, King of England. (1597). *Daemonology.* Edinburgh: Printed by Robert Walde-graue. Printer to the Kings Majestie. Cum Privilegio Regio.

Jeffery, C. R. (1957). The development of crime in early English society. *The Journal of Criminal Law, Criminology, and Police Science,* pp. 647–66.

Joyce, R. (2002). *The Myth of Morality.* Cambridge: Cambridge University Press.

Joyce, R. (2006). *The Evolution of Morality.* Cambridge, Mass.: MIT Press.

Kahane, G. (2011). Evolutionary Debunking Arguments. *Noûs,* 45, pp. 103–25.

Kane, R. (1996). *The Significance of Free Will.* New York: Oxford University Press.

Kane, R. (ed.) (2002). *The Oxford Handbook of Free Will.* New York: Oxford University Press.

Kant, I. (1956 [1788]). *The Critique of Practical Reason.* Trans. L. Beck. Indianapolis: Bobbs-Merrill.

Kass, L. (1997). The Wisdom of Repugnance. *New Republic,* June 2, pp. 17–26.

Kaye, S. (2004). Why the Liberty of Indifference is Worth Wanting. *History of Philosophy Quarterly,* 21, pp. 21–42.

Kelly, D. (2011). *Yuck! The Nature and Moral Significance of Disgust.* Cambridge, MA: MIT Press.

Keltner, D., Ellsworth, P. C., and Edwards, K. (1993). Beyond simple pessimism: Effects of sadness and anger on social perception. *Journal of Personality and Social Psychology,* 64, pp. 740–52.

Keltner, D., and Haidt, J. (2001). Social functions of emotions. In T. Mayne and G. A. Bonanno (eds), *Emotions: Current issues and future directions.* New York: Guilford Press, 192–213.

Khadduri, M. (1984). *The Islamic Conception of Justice.* Baltimore, MD: Johns Hopkins University Press.

Kitcher, P. (1993). *The Advancement of Science: Science without Legend, Objectivity without Illusions.* New York: Oxford University Press.

Knobe, J. (forthcoming). Free Will and the Scientific Vision.

Koenigs, M., Young, L., Adolphs, R., Tranel, D., Cushman, F., Hauser, M., and Damasio, A. (2007). Damage to the Prefrontal Cortex Increases Utilitarian Moral Judgments. *Nature,* 446, pp. 908–11.

Kozuch, B., and Nichols, S. (2011). Awareness of Unawareness: Folk Psychology and Introspective Transparency. *Journal of Consciousness Studies,* 18, pp. 135–60.

Kuczaj, S., and Maratsos, M. (1975). What children can say before they will. *Merrill-Palmer Quarterly*, 21, pp. 87–111.

Kuhlmeier, V. A., Wynn, K., and Bloom, P. (2003). Attribution of Dispositional States by 12-month-olds. *Psychological Science*, 14, pp. 402–8.

Kunda, Z. (1999). *Social cognition: making sense of people*. Cambridge, Mass.: MIT Press, Bradford Books.

Kushnir, T., Wellman, H., and Chernyak, N. (2009). Preschoolers' understanding of freedom of choice. *Proc 31st Cognitive Science Society*.

Laudan, L. (1984). *Science and values*. Vol. 66. Berkeley: University of California Press.

Lazarus, R. (1991). *Emotion and Adaptation*. New York: Oxford University Press.

Leibniz, G. (1714/1898). *The Monadology and other philosophical writings*. Trans. R. Latta. Oxford, UK: Oxford University Press.

Leibniz, G. (1765/1981). *New Essays on Human Understanding*. Trans. P. Remnant and J. Bennett. Cambridge: Cambridge University Press.

Leibniz, G. (1976). Philosophical papers and letters (vol. 2). Trans. L. Loemker. Dordrecht: Springer.

Lerner, J., Goldberg, J., and Tetlock, P. (1998). Sober Second Thought: The Effects of Accountability, Anger, and Authoritarianism on Attributions of Responsibility. *Personality and Social Psychology Bulletin*, 24, pp. 563–74.

Lerner, J., and Tiedens, L. (2006). Portrait of The Angry Decision Maker. *Journal of Behavioral Decision Making*, 19, pp. 115–37.

Levin, D. T., Momen, N., Drivdahl IV, S. B., and Simons, D. J. (2000). Change blindness blindness: The metacognitive error of overestimating change-detection ability. *Visual Cognition*, 7(1–3), pp. 397–412.

Lewis, D. (1972). Psychophysical and Theoretical Identifications. *Australasian Journal of Philosophy*, 50, pp. 249–58.

Lewis, D. (1973). *Counterfactuals*. Oxford, UK: Blackwell.

Lewis, D. (1973). Causation. *The Journal of Philosophy*, vol. 70, no. 17, pp. 556–67.

Lewis, M., and Ramsey, D. (2005). Infant Emotional and Cortisol Responses to Goal Blockage. *Child Development*, 76, pp. 518–30.

Luhrmann, T. M. (1991). *Persuasions of the witch's craft: ritual magic in contemporary England*. Cambridge, MA: Harvard University Press.

Lycan, W. (1987). *Consciousness*. Cambridge, Mass.: MIT Press.

Lycan, W. (1988). *Judgement and Justification*. Cambridge: Cambridge University Press.

Machery, E., Olivola, C., Cheon, H., Kurniawan, I., Mauro, I., Struchiner, N., and Susianto, H. (forthcoming). Is Folk Essentialism a Fundamental Feature of Human Cognition? A Cross-Cultural Study.

MacIntyre, A. (1966). *A Short History of Ethics*. New York: Macmillan.

McKenna, M. (2008). A Hard-line Reply to Pereboom's Four-Case Manipulation Argument. *Philosophy and Phenomenological Research*, 77(1), pp. 142–59.

McKenna, M. (2009). Compatibilism. *The Stanford Encyclopedia of Philosophy* (Winter 2009 edition), Edward N. Zalta (ed.), URL = <http://plato.stanford.edu/archives/win2009/entries/compatibilism/>.

Mackie, J. (1977). *Ethics: Inventing Right and Wrong.* New York: Penguin.

Mackie, J. (1982). Morality and the Retributive Emotions. *Criminal Justice Research*, 1, pp. 3–10.

Maine, H. (1861). *Ancient Law.* London: John Murray.

Mallon, R. (2006). Race: Normative, not metaphysical or semantic. *Ethics*, 116(3), pp. 525–51.

Mallon, R., and Nichols, S. (2010). Rules. In J. Doris (ed.), *The Moral Psychology Handbook.* Oxford: Oxford University Press.

Mele, A. (1995). *Autonomous Agents.* New York: Oxford University Press.

Mele, A. (2005). A critique of Pereboom's "four-case argument" for incompatibilism. *Analysis*, 65(285), pp. 75–80.

Mele, A. (2006). *Free Will and Luck.* New York: Oxford University Press.

Menninger, K. (1968). *The Crime of Punishment.* New York: Viking Press.

Miller, W. (1990). *Bloodtaking and Peacemaking.* Chicago: University of Chicago Press.

Millstein, R. L. (2006). Discussion of "Four Case Studies on Chance in Evolution": Philosophical Themes and Questions. *Philosophy of Science*, 73(5), 678–87.

Misenheimer, L. (2008). Predictability, causation, and free will. Unpublished manuscript. University of California, Berkeley.

Mittman, L. R., and Terrell, G. (1964). An experimental study of curiosity in children. *Child Development*, 35(3), pp. 851–5.

Monroe, A. E., and Malle, B. F. (2010). From uncaused will to conscious choice: The need to study, not speculate about people's folk concept of free will. *Review of Philosophy and Psychology*, 1(2), pp. 211–24.

Moore, M. (1982). Moral reality. *Wisconsin Law Review*, p. 1061.

Moore, M. (1987). The Moral Worth of Retribution. In F. Schoeman (ed.), *Responsibility, Character, and the Emotions.* Cambridge, UK: Cambridge University Press.

Murphy, J. (1985). Retributivism, Moral Education and the Liberal State. *Criminal Justice Ethics*, 4, pp. 3–11.

Murray, D., and Nahmias, E. (2014). Explaining Away Incompatibilist Intuitions. *Philosophy and Phenomenological Research*, 88(2), pp. 434–67.

Nadelhoffer, T., Heshmati, S., Kaplan, D., and Nichols, S. (2013). Folk Retributivism and the Communication Confound. *Economics and Philosophy*, 29(02), pp. 235–61.

Nagel, T. (1986). *The View from Nowhere.* Oxford: Oxford University Press.

Nahmias, E., Coates, D. J., and Kvaran, T. (2007). Free will, moral responsibility, and mechanism: Experiments on folk intuitions. *Midwest Studies in Philosophy*, 31, pp. 214–42.

Nahmias, E., Morris, S. G., Nadelhoffer, T., and Turner, J. (2006). Is incompatibilism intuitive? *Philosophy and Phenomenological Research*, 73, pp. 28–53.

Nahmias, E., and Murray, D. (2010). Experimental philosophy on free will: An error theory for incompatibilist intuitions. *New Waves in Philosophy of Action*, pp. 189–215.

Nahmias, E., and Thompson, M. (forthcoming). A Naturalistic Vision of Free Will. In E. O'Neill and F. Machery (eds), *Current Controversies in Experimental Philosophy*. London: Routledge.

Nichols, S. (2002). On the Genealogy of Norms. *Philosophy of Science*, 69, pp. 234–55.

Nichols, S. (2004a). After Objectivity: An Empirical Study of Moral Judgment. *Philosophical Psychology*, 17, pp. 3–26.

Nichols, S. (2004b). The folk psychology of free will: Fits and starts. *Mind & Language*, 19, pp. 473–502.

Nichols, S. (2004c). *Sentimental Rules: On the Natural Foundations of Moral Judgment*. New York: Oxford University Press.

Nichols, S. (2006). Folk intuitions about free will and responsibility. *Journal of Cognition and Culture*, 6, pp. 57–86.

Nichols, S. (2007). The rise of compatibilism: A case study in the quantitative history of philosophy. *Midwest Studies in Philosophy*, 31(1), pp. 260–70.

Nichols, S. (2008). How Can Psychology Contribute to the Free Will Debate? In J. Baer, J. Kaufman, and R. Baumeister (eds), *Are We Free?* New York: Oxford University Press, pp. 10–31.

Nichols, S. (2012). The Indeterminist Intuition: Source and Status. *The Monist*, 95, pp. 290–307.

Nichols, S. (2014). Process Debunking and Ethics. *Ethics.*, 124, pp. 727–49.

Nichols, S., and Folds-Bennett, T. (2003). Are Children Moral Objectivists? *Cognition*, 90, B2332.

Nichols, S., and Knobe, J. (2007). Moral Responsibility and Determinism: The Cognitive Science of Folk Intuitions. *Noûs*, 41, pp. 663–85.

Nichols, S., Pinillos, A., and Mallon, R. (forthcoming). Ambiguous reference. *Mind.*

Nichols, S., Timmons, M., and Lopez, T. (2014). Ethical Conservatism and the Psychology of Moral Luck. In M. Christen et al. (eds), *Empirically Informed Ethics*. Dordrecht: Springer.

Nichols, S., and Ulatowski, J. (2007). Intuitions and Individual Differences: The Knobe Effect Revisited. *Mind & Language*, 22, pp. 346–65.

Nisbett, R., and Schachter, S. (1966). Cognitive Manipulation of Pain. *Journal of Experimental Social Psychology*, 2, pp. 227–36.

Nisbett, R., and Wilson, T. (1977). Telling more than we can know. *Psychological Review*, 84, pp. 231–59.

Norton, J. D. (2003). Causation as Folk Science. *Philosopher's Imprint*, 3(4).

Notestein, W. (1911). *A History of Witchcraft in England from 1558 to 1718.* Washington: The American Historical Association.

O'Connor, T. (1995). Agent causation. In T. O'Connor (ed.), *Agents, Causes, and Events: Essays on Indeterminism and Free Will.* New York: Oxford University Press, pp. 173–200.

Ochsner, K., and Gross, J. (2005). The cognitive control of emotion. *Trends in Cognitive Sciences*, 9, pp. 242–9.

Ockham, W. (1980). *Opera Theologica* IX, J. Wey (ed.). St. Bonaventure N.Y.: Franciscan Institute.

Pacer, M. (2010). Mentalistic Mechanism: Undermining Free Will through Scientific Language. Unpublished manuscript. Yale University.

Pearl, J. (2000). *Causality: Models, Reasoning, and Inference.* Cambridge, UK: Cambridge University Press.

Pereboom, D. (2001). *Living without Free Will.* Cambridge: Cambridge University Press.

Pereboom, D. (2007). Hard Incompatibilism and Response to Fischer, Kane, and Vargas. In J. Fischer, R. Kane, D. Pereboom, and M. Vargas (eds), *Four Views on Free Will.* Malden, MA: Blackwell.

Pereboom, D. (2009). Hard Incompatibilism and Its Rivals. *Philosophical Studies*, 144, pp. 21–33.

Pereboom, D. (2009). Free will, love, and anger. *Ideas y Valores*, 141, pp. 5–25.

Perfors, A., Tenenbaum, J., Griffiths, T., and Xu, F. (2011). A tutorial introduction to Bayesian models of cognitive development. *Cognition*, 120, pp. 302–21.

Petty, R., and Cacioppo, J. (1979). Issue involvement can increase or decrease persuasion by enhancing message-relevant cognitive responses. *Journal of Personality and Social Psychology*, XXXVII, pp. 1915–26.

Phillips, J., and Shaw, A. (forthcoming). Manipulating Morality. *Cognitive Science.*

Pillutla, M., and Murnighan, J. (1996). Unfairness, anger and spite. *Organizational Behavior and Human Decision Processes*, 68, pp. 208–24.

Plantinga, A. (2000). *Warranted Christian Belief.* Oxford: Oxford University Press.

Priestley, J. (1775). *Experiments and Observations on Different Kinds of Air*, vol. 2. London: J. Johnson.

Prinz, J. (2004). *Gut Reactions.* New York: Oxford University Press.

Prinz, J. (2007). *The Emotional Construction of Morals.* Oxford, UK: Oxford University Press.

Prinz, J. (2011). Wittgenstein and the Neuroscience of Self. *American Philosophical Quarterly,* 48, pp. 147–60.

Prinz, J., and Nichols, S. (2010). Moral Emotions. In J. Doris et al. (eds), *Oxford Handbook of Moral Psychology.* Oxford, UK: Oxford University Press.

Railton, P. (1986). Moral Realism. *Philosophical Review,* 95, pp. 163–207.

Rawls, J. (1955). Two Concepts of Rules. *The Philosophical Review,* 64, pp. 3–32.

Reid, T. (1969 [1788]). *Essays on the Active Powers of the Human Mind.* Cambridge, Mass.: MIT Press.

Rescher, N. (2005). *Scholastic Meditations.* Washington, DC: Catholic University of America Press.

Richerson, P., and Boyd, R. (2005). *Not by Genes Alone.* Chicago: University of Chicago Press.

Robertson, D. (2010). *The Philosophy of Cognitive Behavioural Therapy: Stoic Philosophy as Rational and Cognitive Psychotherapy.* London: Karnac Books.

Roelandts, R. (2007). History of human photobiology. In H. Lim and H. Honigsman (eds), *Photodermatology.* New York: Informa Healthcare.

Rose, D., and Nichols, S. (2013). The Lesson of Bypassing. *Review of Philosophy and Psychology,* 4(4), pp. 1–21.

Rose, D., and Nichols, S. (forthcoming). From Punishment to Objectivity. In T. Cuneo and D. Loeb (eds), *The Empirical Dimensions of Metaethics.* Oxford: Oxford University Press.

Roskies, A. (forthcoming). Can Neuroscience Resolve Issues about Free Will?

Roskies, A., and Nichols, S. (2008). Bringing Moral Responsibility Down to Earth. *Journal of Philosophy,* 105(7), pp. 371–88.

Rozenblit, L., and Keil, F. (2002). The Misunderstood Limits of Folk Science: An illusion of explanatory depth. *Cognitive Science,* 26, pp. 521–62.

Rozin, P. (1999). The Process of Moralization. *Psychological Science,* 10, p. 218.

Ruse, M. (1986). *Taking Darwin seriously: A naturalistic approach to philosophy.* Oxford: Blackwell.

Russell, P. (1995). *Freedom and Moral Sentiment: Hume's Way of Naturalizing Responsibility.* Oxford, UK: Oxford University Press.

Sanfey, A. G., Rilling, J. K., Aronson, J. A., Nystrom, L. E., and Cohen, J. D. (2003). The neural basis of economic decision making in the Ultimatum Game. *Science,* 300, pp. 1755–8.

Sarkissian, H., Chatterjee, A., De Brigard, F., Knobe, J., Nichols, S., and Sirker, S. (2010). Is Belief in Free Will a Cultural Universal? *Mind & Language,* 25, pp. 346–58.

Sarkissian, H., Park, J., Tien, D., Wright, J., and Knobe, J. (2011). Folk Moral Relativism. *Mind & Language,* 26(4).

Scherer, K. (1997). The Role of Culture in Emotion-Antecedent Appraisal. *Journal of Personality and Social Psychology*, 73, pp. 902–22.

Scholl, B., Simons, D., and Levin, D. (2004). "Change blindness" blindness. In D. Levin (ed.), *Thinking and Seeing*. Cambridge, Mass.: MIT Press.

Schulz, L. E., and Sommerville, J. (2006). God does not play dice: Causal determinism and preschoolers' causal inferences. *Child Development*, 77(2), 427–42.

Scot, R. (1584). *The Discoverie of Witchcraft*. London: William Brome.

Shafer-Landau, R. (1996). The Failure of Retributivism. *Philosophical Studies*, 82, pp. 289–316.

Shafer-Landau, R. (2003). *Moral Realism*. Oxford: Oxford University Press.

Shaver, K. (1985). *The attribution of blame*. New York: Springer-Verlag.

Shaver, P., Schwartz, J., Kirson, D., and O'Connor, C. (1987). Emotion knowledge: Further exploration of a prototype approach. *Journal of Personality and Social Psychology*, 52, pp. 1061–86.

Sias, J. (unpublished). Decisions, decisions: A study of folk intuitions.

Sidgwick, H. (1907). *The Methods of Ethics*. London: Macmillan.

Sigmund, F. (1927/1961). *The Future of an Illusion*. Trans. J. Strachey. New York: Norton & Co.

Singer, P. (2005). Ethics and Intuitions. *Journal of Ethics*, 9, pp. 331–52.

Sinnott-Armstrong, W. (2006). *Moral Skepticisms*. Oxford: Oxford University Press.

Slone, D. (2004). *Theological Incorrectness*. New York: Oxford University Press.

Smilansky, S. (2000). *Free will and illusion*. Oxford, UK: Oxford University Press.

Smilansky, S. (2002). Free Will, Fundamental Dualism, and the Centrality of Illusion. In R. Kane (ed.), *The Oxford Handbook of Free Will*. New York: Oxford University Press.

Smith, A. (1790/1982). *The Theory of Moral Sentiments*. Indianapolis: Liberty Classics.

Smith, C., and Ellsworth, P. (1985). Patterns of Cognitive Appraisal in Emotion. *Journal of Personality and Social Psychology*, 48, pp. 813–38.

Sobel, D. M., Tenenbaum, J. B., and Gopnik, A. (2004). Children's causal inferences from indirect evidence: Backwards blocking and Bayesian reasoning in preschoolers. *Cognitive Science*, 28(3), 303–33.

Sommers, T. (2005). *Beyond Freedom and Resentment: an Error Theory of Free Will and Moral Responsibility*. PhD Dissertation, Duke University.

Sommers, T. (2007). The Objective Attitude. *Philosophical Quarterly*, 57(228), pp. 1–21.

Sommers, T. (2012). *Relative Justice*. Princeton, NJ: Princeton University Press.

Sperber, D. (1996). *Explaining Culture*. Cambridge, Mass.: Blackwell.

Spinoza, B. (1887 [1677]). *The Chief Works of Benedict de Spinoza*, vol. II, trans. R. Elwes. London: Bell & Sons.

Spirtes, P., Glymour, C., and Scheines, R. (2000). *Causation, Prediction, and Search.* Second edition. Cambridge, MA: MIT Press.

Stein, E., Pankiewicz, J., Harsch, H., Cho, J., Fuller, S., Hoffmann, R., Hawkins, M., Rao, S., Bandettini, P., and Bloom, A. (1998). Nicotine-Induced Limbic Cortical Activation in the Human Brain: A Functional MRI Study. *American Journal of Psychiatry,* 155, pp. 1009–15.

Stephen, J. (1883). *History of the Criminal Law of England.* London: Macmillan.

Stich, S. (1983). *From folk psychology to cognitive science: The case against belief.* Cambridge, MA: MIT Press.

Stich, S. (1996). *Deconstructing the Mind.* USA: Oxford University Press.

Storm, C., and Storm, T. (1987). A taxonomic study of the vocabulary of emotions. *Journal of Personality and Social Psychology,* 53, pp. 805–16.

Strawson, G. (1986). *Freedom and Belief.* Oxford: Oxford University Press.

Strawson, G. (1994). The Impossibility of Moral Responsibility. *Philosophical Studies,* 75, pp. 5–24.

Strawson, G. (2005). Free Will. In E. Craig (ed.), *Shorter Routledge Encyclopedia of Philosophy.* London: Routledge, pp. 286–94.

Strawson, P. F. (1950). On referring. *Mind,* 59(235), 320–44.

Strawson, P. F. (1962). Freedom and Resentment. *Proceedings of the British Academy,* 48, pp. 1–25. Reprinted in G. Watson (ed.), *Free Will.* Second edition. Oxford University Press, 2003, pp. 72–93. (Page references are to the reprinted version.)

Street, S. (2006). A Darwinian Dilemma for Realist Theories of Value. *Philosophical Studies,* 127, pp. 109–66.

Swain, S., Alexander, J., and Weinberg, J. M. (2008). The instability of philosophical intuitions: Running hot and cold on Truetemp. *Philosophy and Phenomenological Research,* 76(1), pp. 138–55.

Tavris, C. (1989). *Anger: The misunderstood emotion.* New York: Simon & Schuster.

Taylor, R. (1983). *Metaphysics.* Fourth edition. Englewood Cliffs: Prentice Hall.

Tersman, F. (2008). The Reliability of Moral Intuitions: A Challenge from Neuroscience. *Australasian Journal of Philosophy,* 86, pp. 389–405.

Thomas, K. (1971). *Religion and the Decline of Magic.* New York: Macmillan.

Thompson, W. (1950). Free Will and Predestination in Early Islam: A Critique and Appreciation. *Muslim World,* 40, pp. 207–16.

Tierney, H. (2013). A Maneuver Around the Modified Manipulation Argument. *Philosophical Studies,* 165, pp. 753–63.

Timmons, M. (1999). *Morality Without Foundations: A Defence of Ethical Contextualism.* New York: Oxford University Press.

Timmons, M. (2008). Towards a Sentimentalist Deontology. In W. Sinnott-Armstrong (ed.), *Moral Psychology,* vol. 3. Cambridge, Mass.: MIT Press.

Timmons, M. (2013). *Moral theory: An introduction*. Second edition. Lanham, MD: Rowman & Littlefield Publishers.

Tracey, I., Ploghaus, A., Gati, J. S., Clare, S., Smith, S., Menon, R. S., and Matthews, P. M. (2002). Imaging attentional modulation of pain in the periaqueductal gray in humans. *The Journal of Neuroscience*, 22(7), pp. 2748–52.

Tversky, A., and Kahneman, D. (1973). Availability: A heuristic for judging frequency and probability. *Cognitive Psychology*, 5, pp. 207–32.

Tversky, A., and Kahneman, D. (1983). Extensional versus Intuitive Reasoning: The Conjunction Fallacy in Probability Judgment. *Psychological Review*, 90(4), pp. 293–315.

Valdesolo, P., and DeSteno, D. (2006). Manipulations of Emotional Context Shape Moral Judgment. *Psychological Science*, 17, pp. 476–7.

Valdesolo, P., and DeSteno, D. (2007). Moral hypocrisy: Social groups and the flexibility of virtue. *Psychological Science*, 18, pp. 689–90.

Van Inwagen, P. (1983). *An Essay on Free Will*. New York: Oxford University Press.

Van Inwagen, P. (1989). When is the will free? *Philosophical Perspectives*, 3, pp. 399–422.

Vargas, M. (2004). Responsibility and the Aims of Theory: Strawson and Revisionism. *Pacific Philosophical Quarterly*, 85(2), pp. 218–41.

Vargas, M. (2005). The revisionist's guide to moral responsibility. *Philosophical Studies*, 125, pp. 399–429.

Vargas, M. (2007). Revisionism. In J. Fischer, R. Kane, D. Pereboom, and M. Vargas, *Four Views on Free Will*. Malden, MA: Blackwell.

Vargas, M. (2011). Revisionist Accounts of Free Will: Origins, Varieties, and Challenges. In *The Oxford Handbook of Free Will*, 2nd edn, edited by Robert Kane. New York: Oxford University Press, pp. 457–84.

Vargas, M. (2013). *Building Better Beings: A Theory of Moral Responsibility*. Oxford, U.K.: Oxford University Press.

Vohs, K. D., and Schooler, J. W. (2008). The Value of Believing in Free Will Encouraging a Belief in Determinism Increases Cheating. *Psychological Science*, 19(1), pp. 49–54.

Wagstaffe, J. (1671). *The Question of Witchcraft Debated*, second edition. London: Edw. Millington, at the Pelican in Duck-Lane.

Wainryb, C., Shaw, L., Langley, M., Cottam, K., and Lewis, R. (2004). Children's Thinking about Diversity of Belief in the Early School Years: Judgments of Relativism, Tolerance, and Disagreeing Persons. *Child Development*, 75, pp. 687–703.

Wallace, J. (1994). *Responsibility and the Moral Sentiments*. Cambridge, MA: Harvard University Press.

Waller, B. (1990). *Freedom without Responsibility*. Philadelphia, PA: Temple University Press.

Watson, G. (1987). Responsibility and the Limits of Evil. In F. Schoeman (ed.), *Responsibility, Character, and the Emotions*. Cambridge: Cambridge University Press, pp. 256–86.

Watson, G. (1999). Soft libertarianism and hard compatibilism. *The Journal of Ethics*, 3(4), pp. 353–68.

Webster, J. (1677). *The Displaying of Supposed Witchcraft*. London: J. M.

Weigel, C. (2011). Distance, anger, freedom: An account of the role of abstraction in compatibilist and incompatibilist intuitions. *Philosophical Psychology*, 24(6), pp. 803–23.

Wellman, H., and Liu, D. (2007). Causal reasoning as informed by the early development of explanations. In A. Gopnik and L. Schulz (eds), *Causal Learning*. New York: Oxford University Press, pp. 261–79.

Wielenberg, E. (2010). On the Evolutionary Debunking of Morality. *Ethics*, 120, pp. 441–64.

Wimmer, H., and Perner, J. (1983). Beliefs about beliefs: Representation and constraining function of wrong beliefs in young children's understanding of deception. *Cognition*, 13(1), 103–28.

Wolpe, J. (1990). *Practice of behavior therapy*, fourth edition. New York: Pergamon Press.

Wolpe, J., and Lazarus, A. A. (1966). *Behavior therapy techniques: A guide to the treatment of neuroses*. Elmsford, NY, US: Pergamon Press.

Woolfolk, R., Doris, J., and Darley, J. (2006). Identification, Situational Constraint, and Social Cognition: Studies in the Attribution of Moral Responsibility. *Cognition*, 100, pp. 283–301.

Wright, J. C. (2010). On intuitional stability: The clear, the strong, and the paradigmatic. *Cognition*, 115(3), pp. 491–503.

Wright, J., Cullum, J., and Grandjean, P. (forthcoming). The Cognitive Mechanisms of Intolerance. In J. Knobe et al. (eds), *Oxford Studies in Experimental Philosophy*. Oxford: Oxford University Press.

Wright, J., Cullum, J., and Schwab, N. (2008). The Cognitive and Affective Dimensions of Moral Conviction. *Personality and Social Psychology Bulletin*, 34, pp. 1461–76.

Xu, F., and Kushnir, T. (2013). Infants are rational constructivist learners. *Current Directions in Psychological Science*, 22(1), pp. 28–32.

Xu, F., and Tenenbaum, J. B. (2007). Word learning as Bayesian inference. *Psychological Review*, 114(2), p. 245.

Young, L., Nichols, S., and Saxe, R. (2010). Investigating the neural and cognitive basis of moral luck: It's not what you do but what you know. *Review of Philosophy and Psychology*, 1(3), pp. 333–49.

Index